Airport Management

C. Daniel Prather, Ph.D., A.A.E., CAM

Airport Management

Aviation Supplies & Academics, Inc.
Newcastle, Washington

Airport Management
by C. Daniel Prather, Ph.D., A.A.E., CAM

Aviation Supplies & Academics, Inc.
7005 132nd Place SE
Newcastle, Washington 98059-3153
asa@asa2fly.com | www.asa2fly.com

See the ASA website at **www.asa2fly.com/reader/airptmgt** for the "Reader Resources" page containing additional information and updates relating to this book.

Resources for instructors using this textbook in their courses are available at **www.asa2fly.com/instructor/airptmgt**.

ASA-AIRPT-MGT
ISBN 978-1-61954-209-9

Printed in the United States of America
2019   2018   2017   2016   2015   9   8   7   6   5   4   3   2   1

Photography © C. Daniel Prather unless otherwise noted.
Cover photos: Bottom image courtesy of Louisville Regional Airport Authority.
Top image ©iStock.com/jxfzsy.
The airport photo used as a background for the chapter beginnings is courtesy of Hillsborough County Aviation Authority.

Library of Congress Cataloging-in-Publication Data:
Prather, C. Daniel
  Airport management / by C. Daniel Prather, Ph.D., A.A.E., CAM.
     pages cm
  Includes index.
  "ASA-AIRPT-MGT."
  ISBN 978-1-61954-209-9 (trade paper) – ISBN 1-61954-209-9 (trade paper)
1. Airports–United States—Management–Textbooks. I. Title.
  TL725.3.M2P73 2015
  387.7'36068–dc23
                          2014041887

Contents

Foreword

I consider it an honor to be asked to write the foreword for *Airport Management*. This textbook's author, Dr. C. Daniel Prather, A.A.E., CAM, has been my mentor since I entered this dynamic and fast-paced community of airports. Dr. Prather has extensive airport experience from his tenure as an Assistant Director of Operations at Tampa International Airport, and is now a key player in education program development and in the training of hundreds of airport professionals nationally and internationally. He is an accredited member of the American Association of Airport Executives (AAAE), and recently developed and implemented the first aviation program at California Baptist University in Riverside, California.

Dr. Prather's objective in all of his educational development and presentations is to provide airport professionals with practical, industry-focused information. You will find this as the baseline throughout all chapters of *Airport Management*. This textbook covers the exciting areas that other airport professionals and I are involved with on a daily basis, including airport planning, design, and construction; air traffic and capacity delay; environmental issues; regulatory compliance; airport operations and maintenance; safety and security; and much more. The chapter scenarios and case studies are designed to allow readers to apply knowledge gained in the text to solving real-world airport challenges.

Some of the more specific topics on the minds of airport professionals include the integration of the National Incident Management System (NIMS), Incident Command System (ICS) into airport emergency plans, and the training and exercise of personnel for use during incidents and events; operational safety on airports during construction, as most airports are always in some phase of construction; addressing FAA Runway Safety Action Team (RSAT) action items; implementation of safety management systems (SMS); measurable metrics; and airport sustainability, just to name a few.

I personally began my aviation career in the United States Marine Corps as an avionics technician on CH-46E Sea Knight helicopters, and quickly progressed through the enlisted ranks as well as becoming a qualified Aerial Observer/Door Gunner, Quality Assurance Inspector, and working on other helicopter and fixed-wing aircraft platforms. While traveling and serving in the United States Marine Corps, I was fortunate to have the opportunity to complete my undergraduate degree from Southern Illinois University, Carbondale, where I got my first taste of aviation industry business management from an academic perspective.

At the end of my second enlistment in the United States Marine Corps, my family and I decided to take the leap from the military and I began my civilian aviation career as an Airport Operations—Communications Center Dispatcher at Tampa International Airport in Tampa, Florida. This position was ideal for someone new to an airport. I was able to experience the full spectrum of daily operations at an airport, ranging from response coordination to small incidents such as broken plumbing pipes in a terminal, to higher-level incidents such as security breaches, people jumping from parking structures to commit suicide, and aircraft alerts. Since that first position as a dispatcher, I have again been very fortunate to hold several positions within airport operations departments at Tampa International Airport (TPA), Burbank Bob Hope Airport (BUR), and now at Los Angeles International Airport (LAX). I have held positions ranging from my initial position as a dispatcher, to Airside and Landside Operations Manager, to my current position as a Chief of Operations I at LAX.

My current job responsibilities include working some shifts as the Airport Duty Manager, and serving as the LAX Department Operations Center (DOC) Director during large-scale events. In this position, I was on duty for the Asiana Airlines Flight 214 accident at San Francisco Airport in which we received multiple flight diversions; utility disruptions affecting multiple terminals and other facilities; and one of the most challenging incidents our airport has experienced in the past ten years involving an active shooter at Terminal 3 in which three of our nine terminals were evacuated, and Terminal 3 remained closed for 28 hours.

If this is your first exposure to the airport community, airports are often referred to as "cities within cities." Airports have several components, regulations, and political pressures similar to a city. Depending on the size of an airport, it may have components similar to a city, such as a municipal fire station or its own fire department; a police, security, and/or public safety department; emergency medical personnel; administrative and financial services; and a maintenance department similar to city public works. Unlike a city, however, hazards at airports can pose unique challenges since the operation of aircraft traffic, vehicle traffic, pedestrian traffic, baggage, and cargo through-put must continue to flow, or be restored promptly, to sustain commerce and e-commerce.

In addition, airports have multiple federal agencies, private entities, contractors, and airport personnel that all operate within the same few acres of airport property to provide safe and secure services to the traveling public. In addition to these departments and divisions that are similar to those of a city, airports will also have an airport operations department. The personnel in this department conduct inspections of the airside, terminals, and landside to identify and report any irregular conditions that impact operations, and coordinate the response by emergency services, maintenance personnel, and others to resolve these issues. Airport operations, along with public safety, agency, and stakeholder partners, also responds to emergencies such as aircraft accidents, security breaches, structure fires, hazmat spills, property damage incidents, utility disruptions, etc., with the primary objective of coordinating the flow of the airport's operation around the incident, and then becoming the incident commander during the recovery phase of an accident or incident.

The best phrases, words, and guidance that I have learned from fellow employees and leaders in airports include: exciting, high consequence, and political; operations revolve around local, state, and federal regulatory compliance; airports must partner, train, and build solid relationships with stakeholders and mutual aid responders to ensure efficient response plans and procedures have a common operational picture; the only thing constant at an airport is change; your customers include the traveling public, airport tenants, contractors, and your own airport employees; and the most critical asset at an airport are the employees that keep it operating, so keep them involved.

In conclusion, you will find this textbook and the aviation professionals you meet to be valuable resources as you progress through your career. Anyone who intends to work and succeed in this exciting and challenging field must master a thorough understanding of the rules, regulations, and standards that affect airports, and be able to apply critical thinking skills to continue to progress. *Airport Management* will prove to be an excellent resource for current and future airport professionals.

Richard N. Steele, C. M., MCA
Chief of Operations I
Los Angeles International Airport (LAX)
Los Angeles World Airports (LAWA)

Acknowledgments

The development of this book would not have been possible without the significant level of support provided by colleagues in the industry. My experiences have been enriched because of others. I would like to thank Mr. Robert Burr, Mr. Grant Young, and Mr. Ed Cooley for believing in me. These gentlemen provided me with ten outstanding years of experience in airport operations at Tampa International Airport (TPA). Ms. Marilyn Gauthier, a coworker at TPA, was a friend from day one and continues to be to this day. I would also like to thank collegiate aviation faculty everywhere who are members of the University Aviation Association (UAA), as well as Mrs. Carolyn Williamson, former UAA Executive Director. Collegiate aviation faculty are a small group of devoted professionals, and I have learned from and with them extensively over the years. These professionals have supported me in many ways as I transitioned from the airport industry to being a faculty member at a collegiate aviation program. I especially benefitted from the annual UAA Fall Education Conferences and the *Collegiate Aviation Review*. I would like to particularly thank Dr. Julie Speakes for providing me an opportunity to teach online as an adjunct faculty member in the Delta State University Master of Commercial Aviation degree program and being a close friend. Dr. Alexander Wells graciously provided me the first opportunity to author a book, by asking me to revise his *General Aviation Marketing and Management* textbook. Mr. Dave Boelio and Ms. Nicole Sgueglia both encouraged me to write this *Airport Management* text, while Mr. Fred Boyns and Ms. Jackie Spanitz enthusiastically asked me to write this text for ASA.

I would like to thank Dr. Paul Craig for giving me my first position as a faculty member at Middle Tennessee State University. California Baptist University (CBU) President Dr. Ronald Ellis, former Provost Dr. Jonathan Parker, and College of Arts and Sciences Dean Dr. Gayne Anacker believed in me and trusted that I was the right person to develop the nation's newest collegiate aviation program at their fine institution. I am humbled by this opportunity and would like to express my heartfelt gratitude for their tremendous support. This has been by far the greatest professional challenge and thrill of my life. Mrs. Kim Roper and Mrs. Maria LeBlanc have been instrumental in my success at CBU, as have our wonderful team of faculty and flight instructors.

I would also like to thank the staff of the American Association of Airport Executives, specifically Mr. James Johnson, A.A.E. (now retired), Ms. Starla Bryant, Mr. Kevin Miller, C.M., ACE (now with the Boca Raton Airport Authority) and Mr. Scott Boeser, C.M., ACE for trusting me to revise the Airport Certified Employee (ACE)—Operations modules and subsequently train airport professionals across the country in Part 139. I would also like to thank

Upon completion of this chapter, you should:

- Understand the historical events and important pieces of legislation affecting the development of airlines.

- Understand the historical events and important pieces of legislation affecting the development of airports.

- Understand the historical funding of airport development.

- Understand the pre- and post-deregulation periods.

- Understand the significance of the events of 9/11 on the aviation industry.

- Be able to discuss contemporary issues and future challenges confronting the airport industry.

Essential Air Service (EAS)
Federal Aid to Airports Program
Federal Airport Act of 1946
Federal Aviation Act of 1958
Federal Aviation Administration Authorization Act of 1994
Federal Aviation Agency (FAA)
Federal Aviation Reauthorization Act of 1996
Federal Emergency Relief Administration (FERA)
Federal Water Pollution Control Act
general aviation (GA) airports
Homeland Security Act of 2002
hub and spoke
Implementing Recommendations of the 9/11 Commission Act of 2007
Kelly Act
load factors
low-cost airlines
Military Airport Program (MAP)
National Airport Plan

National Civil Aviation Review Commission
National Commission on Terrorist Attacks Upon the United States
National Transportation Safety Board (NTSB)
oligopolistic
omnibus spending bill
passenger facility charge (PFC)
Planning Grant Program (PGP)
revenue passenger miles
Security Guidelines for General Aviation Airports
spending bill
State Block Grant Program
Transportation Security Administration (TSA)
Vision 100—Century of Aviation Reauthorization Act of 2003
Works Progress Administration (WPA)
World War I
World War II

In Chapter 1

FEATURES

**The Role of Federal Express
in the Air Cargo Industry** 25

Federal Express played an integral
role in establishing the air cargo
industry and the subsequent
deregulation of that industry.

**The Rise and Fall of
People's Express** 27

A low-cost airline that attained great
success, but eventually went out of
business due to competition from
other airlines during the deregulated
era.

Introduction

Airports are an integral part of the aviation industry. In this industry, billions of passengers and billions of tons of cargo have been moved from point to point since it began, which could not have occurred without airports. The industry is a little more than 100 years old and yet responsible for more than $1 trillion per year in economic activity and almost 10 million jobs. Consider the U.S. airlines (Figure 1-1). Although down from a ten-year high of 769.6 million enplaned passengers in 2007, U.S. airlines enplaned 720.5 million passengers, which equates to 798 billion **revenue passenger miles**, in 2010. Additionally, airlines generated more than 27 billion **cargo revenue ton miles** and generated more than 10 million departures during the year (Air Transport Association, 2011).

Each of these departures, passengers, and pounds of cargo were accommodated at an airport. Whether large or small, public or private, airports serve as an interface between ground and air transportation (Figure 1-2). As an industry, they directly serve the needs of pilots, passengers, and meeters and greeters, and provide employment to hundreds of thousands of employees nationwide. Indirectly, they serve the communities in which they are located by providing facilities to support emergency medical transport, law enforcement services, and the movement of goods and services. Even **general aviation** (GA) **airports** provide beneficial economic impacts to the local community. Airports in the United States have a significant impact on local, state, regional, and national economies. As part of an industry that provides 10 million jobs, $396 billion in wages, and an impact of $1.3 trillion to the economy, airports clearly play a crucial role in the aviation industry (Federal Aviation Administration, n.d.). In sum, airports serve a unique and substantial need throughout the world, and have an interesting history in the United States—the birthplace of aviation.

Figure 1-1.
Number of enplaned passengers, U.S. airlines, 2000–2010

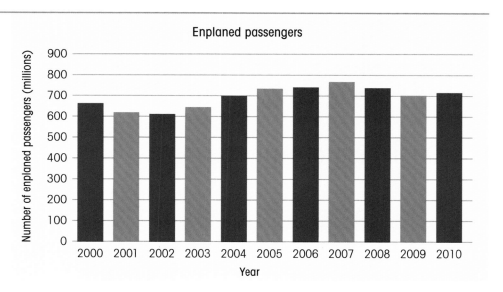

Figure 1-2.
Airports are transportation lifelines, often serving airline passengers and cargo carriers, flight training and general aviation pilots, with beneficial economic impacts felt locally, regionally, and nationally.

(jlye/Bigstock.com)

The Beginning of an Industry

The history of the aviation industry in the United States began on December 17, 1903. It was on this day that Orville Wright first flew the now-famous Wright Flyer I in a controlled flight lasting 12 seconds (see Figure 1-3). However, aviation did not immediately succeed. After these first flights at Kitty Hawk, North Carolina, the Wright brothers faced quite a challenge in promoting their aircraft to a willing buyer. In fact, five years passed before they were able to convince the U.S. government to test a much improved version.

Figure 1-3.
The first flight of Orville Wright (1871–1948) at Kill Devil Hills, Kitty Hawk, North Carolina, on December 17, 1903 (120 feet in 12 seconds). His brother Wilbur Wright (1867–1912) is standing on the right.

(Wikimedia Commons; see credit on page 623)

Although the four flights flown by the Wright brothers on that day marked the beginning of controlled, powered, and sustained heavier-than-air human flight, the first scheduled commercial airline flight using heavier-than-air aircraft did not occur until eleven years later, when on January 1, 1914, Tony Jannus piloted the Benoist XIV flying boat biplane across Tampa Bay (Florida) on an historic 23-minute flight (see Figure 1-4). This inaugural flight also carried the mayor of St. Petersburg, Florida—Mr. Abram C. Pheil. At a fare of five dollars per passenger, this was the first time in history that tickets were sold to the general public for point-to-point scheduled air travel. Known as the St. Petersburg-Tampa Airboat Line, the airline offered service six days per week with two roundtrip flights daily until ceasing service on March 31, 1914, which was five weeks after the termination of a three-month contract that had been signed with the St. Petersburg Board of Trade. This service greatly improved travel between the two cities, as travel by steamship took 2 hours, rail between 4 and 12 hours, and automobile around 20 hours (Bluffield, 2010).

Figure 1-4.
The historic departure of Jannus and Pheil.

(Wikimedia Commons; see credit on page 623)

Although the early days of aviation did not start and end at airports as we know them, these airfields did serve as the first airports. Whether in the form of a grassy field, sand dune, body of water, or other flat place, these first airfields served the unique needs of the early aviators. As more aircraft were built and the aviation industry began growing, the need for landing areas grew.

Providing dedicated airfields was seen as the best solution to this need. One way in which to do this was to develop dirt-only fields (see Figure 1-5). This option improved aircraft performance on takeoff roll, due to an elimination of the drag produced by grass. As can be imagined, however, these dirt landing sites were only usable in dry conditions. Muddy landing sites were, in fact, worse than the old grass landing sites. Often, race tracks, golf courses, or fairgrounds doubled as landing sites.

A significant boost in the quality of airfields came about with the addition of concrete landing areas. Portland cement, which had been invented in 1824 by English inventor Joseph Aspdin, was the preferred material. However, macadam or cinders were also used. Macadam was a type of road construction pioneered by Scotsman John Loudon McAdam around 1820. Single-sized aggregate layers of stone with a coating of binder as a cementing agent were mixed in an open-structured macadam. Cinder, on the other hand, is a small type of volcanic rock that has many uses, including material for road construction and decorative rock for landscaping, especially in the southwest U.S.

Possibly the first use of the term "airport" was by a Brazilian airship inventor, Mr. Alberto Santos-Dumont. According to the April 11, 1902 edition of *The New York Times*, Mr. Santos-Dumont explained his expectation that the city of New York would be "the principal 'airport' of the world in less than a score of years" (*The New York Times*, 1902). However, the nation's first municipal airport was built in 1908 in Albany, New York. Located on a former polo field, the airport was moved to Westerlo Island after one year due to the unsuitability of the former polo field. Deemed an ideal location, Westerloo Island had long, level stretches of land bordering the Hudson River. During its early years, the airport welcomed such famous aviators as Glenn Curtis, Charles Lindbergh, Amelia Earhart, and James Doolittle. The mayor of Albany at the time, Mr. John Boyd Thacher II, once said, "A city without the foresight to build an airport for the new traffic may soon be left behind in the race for

Figure 1-5.
Early landing strip.

(©iStock.com/andipantz)

AIRPORT MANAGEMENT

competition." So, in 1928, a new modern airport was built. The new airport originally consisted of 249 acres and contained two brick hangars and a brick administration building. As part of airport construction, three runways were built—the first was 2,200 feet long, the second 2,350 feet long, and the third measured 2,500 feet long. Two of the runways were paved with macadam and one with cinders. By 1930, Albany was known as the "aerial crossroads of the great Northeast." Although the airport was closed for a brief period by the Civil Aeronautics Administration (CAA), it remains in operation to this day, overseen by the Albany County Airport Authority (Hakes, n.d.).

Although Albany Airport was initially funded by the City of Albany, its operation and upkeep during the first eight years was financed through a special fund established by the Albany Chamber of Commerce. Even in those early years, airports required financial resources for maintenance and operation. Airport maintenance during this time involved grading to maintain the level runway, mowing grass, and keeping the runway free of obstructions. In January 1939, however, the newly formed **Civil Aeronautics Authority (CAA)** closed the new airport to commercial flights declaring it unsuitable for use. This action was taken by the CAA following a long dispute between the city and federal officials over who should be responsible for paying for needed improvements to the airport. Mayor Thacher believed the city should not have to pay for improvements that would benefit national defense and commerce. The CAA disagreed and as a result, eventually closed the field to all air traffic. The city then initiated a **Works Progress Administration (WPA)** project to make the necessary improvements at the airport, resulting in the CAA allowing daylight operations to begin once again in December 1940. On January 21, 1942, the CAA, recognizing the improvements to the airport, allowed the airport to reopen for nighttime use. Except for wartime restriction, the airport has had uninterrupted flight service since that time (Hakes, n.d.).

The College Park Airport in Maryland was established by Wilbur Wright in 1909, one year after the Albany Airport. It claims the distinction of being the "World's Oldest Continually Operating Airport." It is indeed an airport with a long history. In 1909, after the U.S government agreed to purchase a Wright Flyer, the aircraft was officially accepted by the U.S government. However, the contract required the Wrights to teach two army officers to fly the plane. A field in the small town of College Park, Maryland, was selected for this flight instruction and the College Park airfield was established. Operating strictly as a general aviation facility, in 1977 the airport was added to the National Register of Historic Places (College Park Aviation Museum, n.d.).

Even so, very few airports were built during these early years of aviation. Rather than focus on areas at which to land aircraft, efforts were focused on improving the design of aircraft. In fact, by 1912, only 20 landing facilities were thought to exist in the U.S. Although this seems like a small number, this network of landing facilities was sufficient to meet the needs of aviation at that time. It is interesting to note that all of these landing facilities, including Albany and College Park, grew from fields or country clubs. They had not been designed as airports, per se (Mola, n.d.).

World War I

However, the environment soon changed as **World War I** (WWI) began in 1914, triggered by the assassination on June 28 of Archduke Franz Ferdinand of Austria, the heir to the throne of Austria-Hungary. Thousands of aircraft were subsequently produced to serve in WWI, most of which were produced and utilized in France, Germany, and England (Figure 1-6). Of course, hundreds of pilots were needed to fly these aircraft and numerous landing facilities were needed to accommodate their operation. Although the U.S. Army had established three military airfields by the time WWI began, an additional 67 military airfields were established during the war to meet this need. These airfields provided facilities for fueling, maintenance, and aircraft parking. At the time, the military envisioned returning these airfields to grassland upon the war's conclusion.

By the end of WWI in 1918, the U.S. Army listed no less than 980 official landing fields. However, many of these fields were unsuitable for regular aircraft operations. For instance, pilots may have had to avoid flags, sand traps, and water hazards while landing on a golf course. Additionally, racetracks were generally sufficient for landing aircraft, but too short to allow for takeoffs. Some, however, worked quite well—including dry lakebeds in Nevada or long stretches of country roads. During this time, "aerial garages" were being built to accommodate aircraft storage and maintenance needs. These forerunners to contemporary hangars and maintenance shops were oftentimes built out of whatever materials were on hand, including the packing crates used for new aircraft delivery (Mola, n.d.).

Figure 1-6.
Aviation in use during World War I.

(©iStock.com/igs942)

Post World War I

Upon the conclusion of WWI, there were a large number of aircraft and skilled pilots that desired to utilize their talents. Conveniently, in 1918, the U.S. Congress appropriated $100,000 for the first regularly scheduled airmail service. This route, between Washington, DC, and New York, was to be flown roundtrip once daily by U.S. Army Service pilots (Figure 1-7). Major Reuben H. Fleet was picked by Army Colonel E.A. Deeds to manage the first regular airmail flights. Although Assistant Postmaster General Otto Praeger and Fleet disagreed about landing fields, pilots, and the date airmail service would begin, the inaugural airmail flight occurred on schedule on May 15, 1918.

Interestingly, the two pilots selected for these inaugural airmail flights were not chosen for their experience or abilities; rather, they were the sons of politically important men. Lt. George Boyle was to fly from the Potomac Park Polo Grounds in Washington, DC, to a relay handover point in Philadelphia. Simultaneously, Lt. James Edgerton was to fly from Hazelhurst Field on Long Island, New York, to the same relay handover point in Philadelphia. Lt. Boyle's flight was a failure. He was inexperienced, encountered low visibility due to thick fog, flew a poorly equipped airplane in the form of an open cockpit Curtiss Jenny, and followed the wrong railroad tracks to Philadelphia. He quickly became lost,

Figure 1-7.
Early days of airmail in the United States.

(Wikimedia Commons; see credit on page 623)

flying for only 24 miles before landing in a field and flipping over. Although he was not injured, the mail he was carrying (3,300 letters weighing 140 pounds) had to be offloaded and placed on a train to Philadelphia. Lt. Edgerton's flight, however, was a success, leading the newspapers to declare this inaugural airmail service a success (Mola, n.d.).

Two months later, pilot Leon Smith refused to fly his route of New York to Washington, DC, due to rain, clouds, and 200 feet visibility. Praeger ordered him to make the trip regardless of the weather. Smith and his fellow pilot, E. Hamilton "Ham" Lee refused to fly in those weather conditions. As a result, they were both fired, which then led to a strike by all pilots in the airmail system. After three days of talks, it was agreed that field managers would make a flight check in bad weather. If the field managers were not pilots, they would sit in the mail bin in front of the pilot to visually verify the weather. Flights would then continue only if the field manager gave the go-ahead (U.S. Centennial of Flight Commission, n.d.[c]).

Over the following three months, pilots flying these airmail routes were heartily challenged. With only a simple magnetic compass and maps with no elevations or landmarks, these pilots were pressured to maintain a six day per week schedule regardless of weather. In less than three months, the army had made 270 flights and carried 40,500 pounds of mail. Although several pilots had been injured, none had been killed. However, the Post Office felt that the army had not sufficiently met the schedule and had been uncooperative. As a result, the army contract was cancelled and the Post Office began carrying the mail on August 12, 1918 (Mola, n.d.).

As the airmail system grew, so did the country's airports. Indeed, many communities began constructing airports to allow them a connection to the rest of the world. Early airfields built by the Post Office typically had a 2,000-foot by 2,000-foot square to allow for takeoffs and landings in any direction. Landing surfaces were generally of gravel or cinders, as they allowed for adequate drainage. Airfields generally ranged in size from 70 to 100 acres and consisted of a hangar, storage of gasoline and oil, a wind indicator, a telephone connection, and a location marker. By the end of 1920, there were 145 airports owned and operated by municipalities. Clearly, a national network of airports was being established (Mola, n.d.).

The first permanent, hard-surfaced runway in the United States, at 1,600 feet long, is thought to have been constructed at Newark, New Jersey, in 1928. Some airports were being developed by airlines. For instance, Pan American Airways, flying a Miami–Key West–Havana route twice daily, constructed the first U.S. land-based international airport: Pan American Field.

Yet as airmail began crossing the country successfully in the mid-1920s, the owners of various railroads expressed their frustration with the government's sponsorship of the airmail system. They felt that railroad profits were being negatively impacted due to the carriage of mail by air. Congressman Clyde Kelly of Pennsylvania, chairman of the House Post Office Committee, was a friend of the railroad industry and on February 2, 1925, sponsored H.R. 7064: the Contract Air Mail Bill, which, upon enactment, became the **Contract Air Mail Act of 1925**, also known as the **Kelly Act**. The act elevated airmail to another level by allowing the postmaster general to contract for domestic airmail service with commercial air carriers. It also set airmail rates and the level of cash subsidies to be paid to companies that carried the mail. The Act was successful in expanding airmail service without undue burden on the taxpayers. Routes created as part of the Act were known as **Contract Air Mail routes** or **CAM routes** (see Figure 1-8). Initial routes were flown between cities such as New York and Boston, Detroit and Cleveland, and Atlanta and Jacksonville. Eventually, a transcontinental route was established. In essence, this Act effectively established the commercial aviation industry. Indeed, several airlines that existed well into the twentieth century (such as Trans World Airlines, Northwest Airlines, and United Airlines) were formed during this time (U.S. Centennial of Flight Commission, n.d.[a]).

To financially support the airmail service, 80 percent of the airmail stamp revenues received by the Post Office were to be paid to the airmail carriers. The number of stamps needed depended on the weight of the mail and the number of zones the mail had to cross.[1] Due to the structure of the system, air-

---

[1] The country had been divided into three air zones on July 1, 1924.

other things, $250 million annually for the "acquisition, establishment, and improvement of air navigational facilities" and security equipment for the next ten years (U.S. Centennial of Flight Commission, n.d.[b]). It also provided authority for the FAA to establish minimum standards for airports and issue operating certificates to commercial-service airports that met these standards.[5] Title I accomplished this via the **Planning Grant Program (PGP)** and the **Airport Development Aid Program (ADAP)**. The PGP provided up to $25 million annually for airport planning purposes, including master plans and system plans. ADAP provided $250 million annually for air carrier and reliever airports and $30 million annually for GA airports.

Title II of the Act created the **Airport and Airway Trust Fund,**[6] which was financed by an eight-percent tax on domestic passenger fares, a three-dollar surcharge on passenger tickets originating in the United States, a tax of seven cents per gallon on gasoline and jet fuel, a five-percent tax on airfreight waybills, and an annual registration fee and charge per pound for aircraft. The trust fund concept created a steady source of revenue for the continued development of airports and airways, which meant that the aviation system now would not have to compete with other needs for general treasury funds (U.S. Centennial of Flight Commission, n.d.[b]).

Of the $3.9 billion in development undertaken during the first eight years of ADAP, $2.7 billion were federal funds and $1.2 billion were state and local funds. This surpassed the $1.2 billion spent by the federal government during the entire twenty-four-year history of the Federal Aid to Airports Program. About half of ADAP funds were used to increase airport safety, while the other half were used to increased airport capacity (FAA, 1980).

Due to the original five-year lifespan of the two grant-in-aid programs, amendments were necessary to continue funding the programs. On July 12, 1976, President Gerald Ford signed amendments to the law that increased the taxes levied. Additionally, snow removal equipment, noise mitigation strategies, and the purchase of land to meet environmental needs were considered eligible for federal funding.[7] Additionally, federal money could now meet 90 percent of project costs for certain airport projects. This amendment, as well as subsequent ones, also raised the amount of money available to airports.

---

[5] Thus, airports being served by commercial air carriers using aircraft with 30 seats or more were required to obtain an operating certificate from the FAA. 14 CFR Part 139 eventually grew from this authority.

[6] Commonly referred to as the "aviation trust fund."

[7] Noise mitigation strategies included equipment to reduce aircraft noise, physical barriers and landscaping.

Deregulation

Although the airline industry had been economically regulated since the establishment of the CAB in 1939, that period of regulation came to an end, ironically enough, with the passage of new legislation in the form of the **Air Cargo Deregulation Act of 1976** and the **Airline Deregulation Act of 1978**. The deregulation of both cargo carriers and passenger carriers was not a decision made overnight, however. During the 1970s, the general political climate favored less involvement in private industries. When President Jimmy Carter appointed economist and former professor Alfred Kahn, a vocal supporter of deregulation, to head the CAB, the stage was set for deregulation.

Yet another force for deregulation was occurring overseas. In 1977, Freddie Laker, a British entrepreneur who owned Laker Airways, created the Skytrain service, which offered extraordinarily low fares for transatlantic flights. These low-priced flights occurred during the same time there was a boom in low-cost domestic flights in the United States as the CAB eased limitations on charter flights. The major carriers responded by proposing their own lower fares. Although they had to seek CAB approval, American Airlines was one airline able to gain that approval for their Super Saver fares. At the same time, however, deregulation of the airline industry had its opponents. Mainly, the major airlines were fiercely opposed to the bill. The airlines in opposition feared free competition, its impacts on the industry, and negative consequences to their bottom line. Additionally, labor unions were opposed because they feared nonunion employees. Many safety proponents were also opposed, as they felt that safety would be sacrificed. However, the support of the public was strong enough to enable passage of these acts. The Airline Deregulation Act appeased the major airlines by offering generous subsidies and it pleased workers by offering high unemployment benefits if they lost their jobs as a result. It also allowed for a six year phase-out of the CAB[8] (American Association of Airport Executives, 2005; Kahn, 1993).

Post-Deregulation

As a result of the deregulation of both the air cargo industry and air carriers, the industry was permanently altered. First, air cargo carriers were now free to raise or lower rates, serve any markets they chose, and own and operate trucks in support of their operation to pick up and deliver goods.[9] Additionally, airlines could now enter the market at will. Beginning in 1981, airlines also had the freedom to expand their routes. Beginning in 1982, airlines were completely free to set airfares. By 1984, the CAB had been abolished, as it was no longer necessary in an economically deregulated industry.

---

[8] The sunset of the CAB would not occur until December 31, 1984.
[9] As long as the movement of goods was related to an air cargo operation.

The Role of Federal Express in the Air Cargo Industry

Federal Express was one cargo carrier that lobbied heavily for deregulation of the air cargo industry. Having been incorporated in June 1971 and begun operations on April 17, 1973, founder Frederick W. Smith was aware of the benefits that deregulation would bring to his company and the air cargo industry. With deregulation, Federal Express was allowed to use larger aircraft (such as Boeing 727s and McDonnell-Douglas DC-10s) and grow rapidly from its humble beginning with 14 small aircraft serving 25 U.S. cities. Today, FedEx Express has the world's largest all-cargo aircraft fleet, including Boeing 777s, MD-11s, Airbus A-300s, and A-310s (Figure 1-11). The company's aircraft have a total daily lift capacity of more than 30 million pounds. In a 24-hour period, the fleet travels nearly 500,000 miles while its couriers log 2.5 million miles a day—the equivalent of 100 trips around the earth (FedEx, 2011).

Figure 1-11. FedEx Express aircraft.
(Wikimedia Commons; see credit on page 623)

In a free market, where airlines had the freedom to set airfares and enter and leave markets at will, some negative consequences were likely to occur. For instance, in this profit-driven industry, airlines began to pull out of less profitable markets. This, of course, resulted in loss of commercial airline service for many communities. Anticipating this, the Airline Deregulation Act contained a provision known as the **Essential Air Service (EAS)** program, which provided subsidies to encourage carriers to remain in less-profitable, smaller markets. The EAS program was put into place to guarantee that small communities that had been served by air carriers before deregulation would continue to be served after deregulation. Even today, approximately 100 rural communities across the country, outside of Alaska, enjoy the benefits of the EAS program via commuter airline service that they would not otherwise have. The state of Alaska has approximately 45 EAS airports (Department of Transportation, 2010).

Yet another consequence of deregulation was the formation of the **hub and spoke** route structure. Although this was mostly adopted by the larger air carriers, it had a significant impact on the aviation industry—an impact that continues to be felt today. In essence, with a hub and spoke route structure, an airline bases their operations in one or more major cities, such as Delta Airlines in Atlanta or American Airlines in Dallas/Fort Worth. From these cities, the airlines develop routes (spokes) that serve numerous destinations (see Figure 1-12). For this route structure to be most effective, the airlines schedule banks of arrivals into a hub, with time for passengers to transfer aircraft, and then a bank of departures to take these passengers to their final destination. With this, airlines utilizing the hub and spoke network could provide a large number of roundtrip flights from their hub cities, as well as maximize aircraft productivity

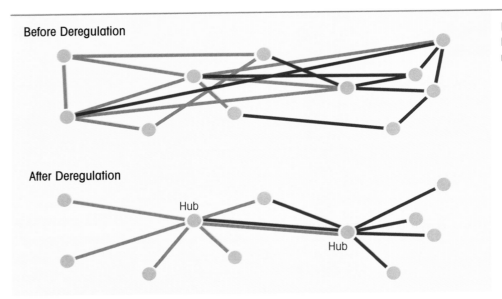

Figure 1-12.
Hub and spoke network.

and enhance **load factors**. Of course, passengers typically would have to endure at least one stop, often with a change in aircraft, to get to their final destination. The passengers greatly benefitting from the hub and spoke network are those living in hub cities. These passengers have hundreds of non-stop destinations from which to choose. Even those living in smaller outlying cities benefit by having access to numerous destinations, including international, with one stop.

Deregulation also opened up the industry and allowed the entrance of new start-up airlines. This was significant, as an **oligopolistic** industry (as the airline industry is characterized) has significant barriers to entry. While that is still true in terms of investment required (aircraft, personnel, equipment), by at least allowing airlines who could acquire the necessary capital to enter a market, the industry opened up. These new start-up airlines were not bound by the demands of the larger established airlines. They typically had much lower cost structures than the established airlines, because they were established during the period of deregulation, rather than the period of regulation (as were the established airlines). With lower wage rates and overhead, they could offer lower fares and yet still operate with a surplus due to their lower cost structures. Thus, **low-cost airlines** were born.

With freedom to expand into new markets, both regional and major airlines initiated service to new markets with gusto. Airlines began competing aggressively for passengers. This competition dramatically reduced airfares, while allowing airline operating revenues to increase to a new high in 1979. That same year was also the peak year for passengers up to that point: an unprecedented 317 million passengers flew on U.S. airlines, with system-wide load factors averaging 63 percent (ATA, 1980).

Alas, the successes of the late 1970s were not to last. Rising fuel costs, an economic recession and overcapacity began to bring about changes in the industry. Within only two years of record-breaking numbers, the airlines recorded a net operating loss of $421 million in 1981, while carrying only 286 million

in the areas of privatization of airports, innovative financing, and pavement maintenance. Lastly, the State Block Grant Program was finally made permanent, and the number of states authorized to participate was increased from seven to nine.

In an effort to ensure a stable funding source for AIP and avoid the year-to-year reauthorizations or lapses in funding that had become common, Senator Wendell H. Ford (Kentucky) led the charge that ensured the passage of the **Aviation Investment and Reform Act for the 21st Century (AIR 21)**. This Act, signed into law on April 5, 2000, authorized the AIP for fiscal years 2000 to 2003 and increased funding levels to about $3.1 billion annually. Additionally, the cap on the PFC was increased from $3.00 to $4.50. However, if a large or medium hub airport desired to implement the $4.50 PFC, they would need to demonstrate the manner by which the proposed project would make a significant contribution to improve safety or security, increase competition, reduce congestion or minimize the impact of noise. If an airport were approved to implement the $4.50 PFC, the airport would forgo 75 percent of AIP entitlements.

9/11

Just over one year later, one of the most significant events in civil aviation history occurred. On September 11, 2001, two commercial aircraft that had been hijacked by a group of terrorists were intentionally flown into the twin towers of the World Trade Center in New York City. Almost simultaneously, a third hijacked aircraft crashed into the Pentagon and a fourth slammed into a Pennsylvania field (Figure 1-15). These coordinated terrorist attacks, carried out by members of the Islamic extremist group, Al-Qaeda, resulted in extensive death and destruction. In fact, more than 3,000 people were killed in the attacks in New York City and Washington, DC, including 400 police officers and firefighters. Further, the New York City skyline was catastrophically altered (History.com, 2011).[11]

Post 9/11

In response to the terrorist attacks, and acting swiftly to address aviation security concerns in the United States, Congress drafted the **Aviation and Transportation Security Act (ATSA) of 2001**. President George W. Bush signed the Act into law on November 19, 2001, during a signing ceremony at Ronald Reagan Washington National Airport. This law created the **Transportation Security Administration (TSA)**, a new organization within the Department of Transportation. The TSA was charged with all federal security

---

[11] Chapter 9 presents a more in-depth discussion of aviation security.

Figure 1-15.
Images from the 9/11 attacks: destruction at the World Trade Center and Pentagon, and recovery efforts.

(Wikimedia Commons; see credit on page 623)

responsibilities in all modes of transportation. Specifically, all aviation security functions formerly handled by the FAA were transferred to the TSA. The ATSA also spelled out specific deadlines to enable the industry to transition to a more secure environment:

- November 19, 2001: New federal background checks required for all airport and airline employees to gain access to security sensitive areas.
- January 18, 2002: Requirement for 100 percent of checked baggage at U.S. airports to be screened using explosive detection equipment, passenger bag matching, manual searches, or canine units.
- February 17, 2002: Official transfer of all civil aviation security responsibilities from FAA to TSA.
- November 21, 2002: Requirement for TSA screeners to screen all passengers and carry-on baggage at the nation's 429 largest commercial air carrier airports.
- December 31, 2002: Requirement for TSA screeners to screen, with certified explosive detection equipment, 100 percent of checked baggage at the nation's 429 largest commercial air carrier airports.

(Aviation Transportation and Security Act, 2001; "Actions by Deadline," 2001)

Meeting these ambitious deadlines required a great deal of investment in both equipment and human resources. Specifically, the TSA invested more than $5 billion in hiring more than 50,000 screeners and administrative staff, and acquiring security screening equipment. To fund these expenses, the Act authorized a $2.50 per flight segment surcharge on air carrier passenger tickets, with a maximum $10 charge per roundtrip flight.

One year later in November 2002, President George W. Bush signed the **Homeland Security Act of 2002** into law. The Homeland Security Act consolidated 22 federal agencies into the newly established Department of Homeland Security (DHS). This was a tremendous reorganizing of the federal government and affected the Transportation Security Administration, the U.S. Customs Service, and the enforcement functions of the Immigration and Naturalization Service. Additionally, the **National Commission on Terrorist Attacks Upon the United States**, also known as the 9/11 Commission, was created. This independent, bipartisan commission was created to prepare a full and complete account of the circumstances surrounding the September 11, 2001, terrorist attacks, as well as recommendations to guard against future attacks. On July 22, 2004, the Commission released its 585-page report (Price and Forrest, 2010; National Commission on Terrorist Attacks Upon the United States, 2004).

In the latter part of 2003, and in honor of the Wright Brothers' first flight in 1903, the **Vision 100—Century of Aviation Reauthorization Act of 2003** was signed into law. This law reauthorized the Airport Improvement Program for 2004 to 2007, with funding levels between $3.4 and $3.7 billion.

By reauthorizing AIP for another multi-year period, airports were provided a more stable funding source and could plan long-term capital improvements.

Although the 9/11 Commission Report had been issued on July 22, 2004, a bill implementing the recommendations of the 9/11 Commission was not signed into law until August 3, 2007. On this day, President George W. Bush signed into law the **Implementing Recommendations of the 9/11 Commission Act of 2007**. The Act provided for a number of grants, improved communication, and enhanced security infrastructure for all areas. Regarding aviation, Title XVI had the following 18 sections:

- Section 1601—Establishes the Checkpoint Screening Security Fund, to be funded by a uniform fee on air passengers, the amounts of which shall be available for the purchase, deployment, installation, research, and development of equipment to improve the ability of security personnel at screening checkpoints to detect explosives.

- Section 1602—Requires the Secretary of the DHS to establish a system to screen 100% of cargo transported on passenger aircraft, phased in over a three-year period.

- Section 1603—Extends funding for aviation security improvements. Requires the Secretary to submit a cost-sharing study for projects to install in-line baggage screening equipment.

- Section 1604—Requires (current law authorizes) the Under Secretary for Border and Transportation Security of DHS to make grants to airport sponsors for specified airport security improvement projects, with priority to small hub and nonhub airports.

- Section 1605—Directs the Secretary to submit to Congress a plan that describes the system to be used by DHS to compare passenger information to the Automatic Selectee and No Fly Lists utilizing the consolidated and integrated Terrorist Watchlist, as well as a timeline for testing and implementing the system.

- Section 1606—Directs the Secretary to establish a timely and fair process for individuals who believe they have been delayed or prohibited from boarding a commercial aircraft because they were wrongly identified as a threat, including an Office of Appeals and Redress to oversee the process.

- Section 1607—Directs the Secretary to prepare a strategic plan, with full plan implementation within one year, to promote the optimal utilization and deployment of explosive detection equipment at airports to screen individuals and their personal property.

- Section 1608—Amends the Aviation and Transportation Security Act to extend funding for research and development of aviation security technology.

- Section 1609—Requires the TSA Administrator, before January 1, 2008, to evaluate the results of the blast-resistant cargo container pilot program; and develop and implement a program to acquire, maintain, and replace blast-resistant cargo containers, pay for the program, and make such containers available to air carriers by July 1, 2008, for use on a risk-managed basis.

- Section 1610—Directs the Secretary to expedite research and development for technology that can disrupt or prevent an explosive device from being introduced onto a passenger plane or from damaging a passenger plane while in flight or on the ground; and establish a grant program to fund pilot projects to deploy such technology and test technology to expedite the recovery, development, and analysis of information to determine the cause of aircraft accidents.

- Section 1611—Directs the Administrator to provide advanced training to transportation security officers for the development of specialized security skills, including behavior observation and analysis, explosives detection, and document examination.

- Section 1612—Provides that any statutory limitation on the number of employees in TSA, before or after its transfer to DHS from DOT, does not apply after FY2007. Directs the Secretary to recruit and hire such TSA personnel as necessary to provide appropriate levels of aviation security and to reduce the average aviation security-related delay experienced by airline passengers to less than 10 minutes.

- Section 1613—Directs the Administrator to conduct a pilot program to identify technologies to improve security at airport exit lanes.

- Section 1614—Directs the Administrator to report on the status of its efforts to institute a sterile area access system that will enhance security by properly identifying authorized airline flight deck and cabin crew members at screening checkpoints and granting them expedited access; and begin full implementation of the system no later than one year after transmitting the report.

- Section 1615—Directs the Secretary to establish a national registered armed law enforcement program for law enforcement officers needing to be armed when traveling by air.

- Section 1616—Prohibits the FAA Administrator from certifying any foreign repair station if specified conditions are not met. Reduces the period in which a security review and audit of such stations must be accomplished.

- Section 1617—Directs the TSA Administrator to develop a standardized threat and vulnerability assessment program for general aviation airports; implement a program to perform such assessments on a risk-assessment basis; complete a study of the feasibility of a program, based on a risk-managed approach, to provide grants to general aviation airport operators for projects to upgrade security; and develop a risk-based system under which foreign-registered general aviation aircraft are required to submit passenger information at the same time as advance notification requirements for Customs and Border Protection (CBP) before entering U.S. airspace and under which such information is checked against appropriate databases maintained by TSA.

- Section 1618—Extends aviation security funding through FY2011.

(Congressional Research Service, 2007)

On December 12, 2003, President Bush signed a four-year FAA reauthorization bill into law. The four-year measure contains more than $14 billion for airport construction projects, funding to help small communities retain and attract commercial air service, and funding to reimburse airports for their increased security costs (AAAE, 2004a).

On February 10, 2004, the FAA released the long-awaited final rule on **14 CFR Part 139, Certification of Airports** (Figure 1-16). The Notice of Proposed Rulemaking for this revision was issued in June 2000. There were numerous changes in the regulation, including:

- Changes the applicability of the rule from airports serving scheduled or unscheduled operations with aircraft of more than 30 passengers to airports serving scheduled passenger-carrying operations with aircraft of more than nine passengers and unscheduled of more than 30 passengers.

- Establishes four classes of airports.

- Removes the term limited certificate airport.

- Establishes that to obtain a certificate the airport must have air service.

- Changes the exemption process.

- Provides greater detail as to what needs to be in the airport certification manual for the different classes of airports.

- Includes more recordkeeping standards for training of personnel.

- Provides greater clarity for Aircraft Rescue and Firefighting (ARFF) operational requirements.

- Outlines emergency plan requirements for small airports.

- Adds new requirements to airports' wildlife hazard management plans.
  (AAAE, 2004b)

Figure 1-16.
An airport operations vehicle in use to ensure this airport's compliance with 14 CFR Part 139 and other requirements.

Figure 1-17. Airport perimeter fencing, one component contributing to security at this airport.

On May 17, 2004, the TSA released Information Publication A-001, **Security Guidelines for General Aviation Airports**. Although these guidelines are intended to provide the GA community with federally endorsed security enhancements and methods for implementing them, the document does not have any regulatory language or suggest that any recommendations or guidelines be considered a mandatory requirement. The guidelines contain the Airport Characteristics Measurement Tool that helps to define unique security needs for differing airports, as well as suggested security improvements (Figure 1-17). It is designed to be self-administered by airport operators, allowing them to assess an airport's security characteristics and determine which enhancements are most appropriate (AAAE, 2004c).

Although major pieces of legislation receive more press, funding of departments and federal agencies is often completed through the signing of spending bills. The president may sign into law fiscal year **spending bills** which continue funding for one department, such as the Department of Homeland Security or Department of Transportation. One example of this form of funding is the October 18, 2004, signing of the fiscal year 2005 spending bill for the Department of Homeland Security. This bill contained a number of provisions, one of which was $295 million for explosives detection system (EDS) installation at airports. Another form of funding is an **omnibus spending bill**. These bills, once signed into law by the president, provide funding for a number of federal departments. An example of this form of funding is the fiscal year 2005 omnibus spending bill signed into law by President Bush on December 8 to fund the federal government, which included $3.5 billion for AIP. Occasionally, the House of Representatives and Senate cannot agree on funding, and a temporary funding bill, known as a **continuing resolution**, has to be signed to allow for continued funding of the federal government. This may be a one-month or three-month extension, for example. One such continuing resolution was signed by the president in October 2008. This was necessary to ensure continued operation of the federal government as a new fiscal year began on October 1. A continuing resolution only buys some time for House and Senate negotiators to reconcile differences between the House and Senate versions of a funding bill. Multi-year FAA reauthorization bills are important for airports, especially when planning capital investment based on AIP funding levels. (AAAE, 2004d; AAAE, 2004e; AAAE, 2008).

Contemporary and Future Period

Although the aviation industry has indeed matured and experienced significant growth since the Wright Brothers' first flight in 1903, the Air Transport Association reports that the U.S. airline industry experienced net losses of $23.2 billion from 2001 through 2003. Interestingly, the low-cost carriers largely remained profitable during this period. Clearly, the effects of September 11 and the complete shutdown of the nation's air transportation system for a three-day period immediately following the attacks played a substantial role in the enormous losses experienced by U.S. airlines from 2001 to 2003. Unfortunately for the airline industry, the events of 9/11 could not have come at a worse time. The industry was already experiencing net operating losses for many reasons, including the mild recession, severe acute respiratory syndrome (SARS), and the increase in services by low-cost carriers, as well as the decline in business fares relied on by legacy carriers. Additionally, rising fuel prices, ever-present issues with labor-management relations, concerns with terrorism, and unfunded security mandates also weighed on the industry (ATA, 2011; Smith and Cox, 2008).

The effects of 9/11 and the airline industry's woes also negatively impacted the airport industry. Airports have been faced with airline bankruptcies, airline mergers, and reduced capacity, many times resulting in loss of service and reduced revenues for the airport. As a result, some airports have been faced with abandoned facilities, such as maintenance hangars, and have accordingly reduced staff and developed contingency plans to meet the dynamics of the airline industry.

Even with these challenges, today's aviation industry in the United States is strong. Approximately 590,000 active pilots, 232,000 general aviation aircraft, and 4,520 air carrier jets utilize 19,734 landing areas consisting of 5,179 public-use (open to the public) and 14,555 private use (closed to the public) facilities. This includes 13,477 airports, 5,576 heliports, 495 seaplane bases, 35 glider ports, 13 balloon ports, and 138 ultralight parks. Although student pilot starts have declined in recent years, the new Light Sport Pilot Certificate and efforts by organizations such as the Aircraft Owners and Pilots Association have had positive effects on the industry (FAA, 2010d).

Although the future is difficult to forecast, one can be fairly certain of issues of future importance for the airport industry. One such issue will involve the continued debate on proposed higher PFC amounts. Although the highest PFC amount was increased from $3 to $4.50 in the year 2000, the purchasing power

——. 2004b, February 15. "FAA Releases Final Part 139 Rule." *Airport Report*. Vol. XLIX, No. 4.

——. 2004b, February 15. "FAA Releases Final Part 139 Rule." *Airport Report*. Vol. XLIX, No. 4.

——. 2004c, June 1. "TSA Issues GA Security Guidelines." *Airport Report*. Vol. XLIX, No. 11.

——. 2004d, November 1. "President Signs DHS Spending Bill." *Airport Report*. Vol. XLIX, No. 21.

——. 2004e, December 15. "Fiscal Year 2005 Spending Bill Cleared." *Airport Report*. Vol. XLIX, No. 24.

——. 2005. "Body of Knowledge Module 1. History, the Regulation of Air Transportation, Airports, and the Federal Aviation Administration." Washington, DC: AAAE.

——. 2008, October 1. "President Signs FAA Authority Extension Bill." *Airport Report*. Vol. LIII, No. 19.

——. 2009. Press release, "AAAE's Barclay Outlines Airport Priorities Before Key Senate Committee." Retrieved from http://www.aaae.org/news_publications/aaae_press_releases/viewRelease.cfm?p=3B7F3C6E-918A-6EC6-53E975E74716A34D

——. 2010, May 5. Press release, "AAAE Questions Airline Opposition to PFCs Given Industry's Growing Embrace of Fees." Retrieved from http://www.aaae.org/news_publications/aaae_press_releases/viewRelease.cfm?p=8F8049D1-F3F1-2451-4D317FE736353EE3

Aviation Transportation and Security Act. 2001. Pub. L. No. 107-71, 115 Stat. 597. Retrieved from http://www.tsa.gov/sites/default/files/assets/pdf/aviation_and_transportation_security_act_atsa_public_law_107_1771.pdf

Bluffield, B. 2010, June. "St. Petersburg-Tampa Airboat Line: World's First Scheduled Airline." Airways. Retrieved from http://www.tonyjannusaward.com/wp-content/uploads/2010/04/Airways-article-on-Tony-Jannus-and-First-Commercial-Flight.pdf

Bureau of Transportation Statistics. 2015. "2014 Airline Financial Data." BTS Press Release No. BTS 22-15. Retrieved from http://www.rita.dot.gov/bts/press_releases/bts022_15

Bush, G. 1990. "Statement on Signing the Aviation Security Improvement Act of 1990." Retrieved from http://www.presidency.ucsb.edu/ws/index.php?pid=19048#axzz1HhzYkbNf

College Park Aviation Museum. n.d. "Founding of the College Park Airport." Retrieved from http://www.collegeparkaviationmuseum.com/About_Us/History/Founding_of_the_College_Park_Airport.htm

Commission on Aviation Security and Terrorism. "Findings and Recommendations of the Commission on Aviation Security and Terrorism." 1990. Retrieved from http://www.globalsecurity.org/security/library/congress/1990_cr/s900511-terror.htm

Congressional Research Service. 2007. "Summary—Implementing Recommendations of the 9/11 Commission Act of 2007." Retrieved from http://www.govtrack.us/congress/bill.xpd?bill=h110-1&tab=summary

Department of Transportation. n.d. "Mission and history." Retrieved from http://www.dot.gov/mission/about-us

————. 2010, January. "Subsidized EAS Report." Retrieved from http://www.dot.gov/office-policy/aviation-policy/essential-air-service-reports

Federal Aviation Administration (FAA). n.d. "NextGen 101" video. Retrieved from http://www.faa.gov/nextgen/

————. 1980. "A Review of the Airport Development Aid Program (ADAP) and Assessment of Future Program Needs." Retrieved from http://oai.dtic.mil/oai/oai?verb=getRecord&metadataPrefix=html&identifier=ADA082637

————. 2001. "Passenger Facility Charge." FAA Order 5500.1. Retrieved from http://www.faa.gov/documentLibrary/media/Order/PFC_55001.pdf

————. 2010a. "Fact Sheet—2010 Military Airport Program Selections." Retrieved from http://www.faa.gov/airports/aip/military_airport_program/

————. 2010b. "PFC Overview." Retrieved from http://www.faa.gov/airports/central/pfc/pfc_overview/

————. 2010c. "Passenger Facility Charge (PFC) Program." Retrieved from http://www.faa.gov/airports/pfc/

————. 2010d. "2011–2015 National Plan of Integrated Airport Systems."

————. 2012. "Key Passenger Facility Charge Statistics." Retrieved from http://www.faa.gov/airports/pfc/monthly_reports/media/stats.pdf

FedEx. 2011. "FedEx History." Retrieved from http://about.fedex.designcdt.com/our_company/company_information/fedex_history

Hakes, C. D. n.d. "Albany Airport History." Retrieved from http://www.albanyairport.com/alb_history.php

History.com. "9/11 attacks." 2011. Retrieved from http://www.history.com/topics/9-11-attacks

Indiana University. n.d. "More About the WPA." Retrieved from http://www.indiana.edu/~liblilly/wpa/wpa_info.html

Johnson, L. B. 1966, January 12. "Annual Message to the Congress on the State of the Union." Retrieved from http://www.lbjlib.utexas.edu/johnson/archives.hom/speeches.hom/660112.asp

Kahn, A. E. 1993. "Airline Deregulation." *The Concise Encyclopedia of Economics.* Library of Economics and Liberty. Retrieved from http://www.econlib.org/library/Enc1/AirlineDeregulation.html

Laing, K. 2015. "Airlines, airports clash over passenger fees." Retrieved from http://thehill.com/policy/transportation/239923-airlines-airports-clash-over-plane-ticket-fees

Mola, R. n.d. "The Earliest Airports." U.S. Centennial of Flight Commission. Retrieved from http://www.centennialofflight.net/essay/Government_Role/earliest_airports/POL9.htm

Morrison, S. A., and W. Clifford. 2000. "The Remaining Role for Government Policy in the Deregulated Airline Industry." In Sam Peltzman and Clifford Winston, eds., *Deregulation of Network Industries: What's Next?* Washington, D.C.: AEI Brookings Joint Center for Regulatory Studies.

Murdock, S. 1997. "The Use in 1995 of World War II Army Airfields in the United States." Retrieved from http://www.airforcebase.net/aaf/grphtml.html

National Commission on Terrorist Attacks Upon the United States. 2004. "The 9/11 Commission Report." Retrieved from http://govinfo.library.unt.edu/911/report/index.htm

Preston, E. n.d. "The Federal Aviation Administration and its Predecessor Agencies." U.S. Centennial of Flight Commission. Retrieved from http://www.centennialofflight.net/essay/Government_Role/FAA_History/POL8.htm

Price, J., and J. Forrest. 2010. Finance and Administration. Body of Knowledge modules. Washington, DC: American Association of Airport Executives.

Reagan, R. 1981, August 3. "Remarks and a Question-and-Answer Session with Reporters on the Air Traffic Controller Strike." Retrieved from http://www.reagan.utexas.edu/archives/speeches/1981/80381a.htm

Rumerman, J. n.d. "Aviation Security." U.S. Centennial of Flight Commission. Retrieved from http://www.centennialofflight.net/essay/Government_Role/security/POL18.htm

Siddiqi, A. n.d. U.S. Centennial of Flight Commission. "Deregulation and its Consequences." Retrieved from http://www.centennialofflight.net/essay/Commercial_Aviation/Dereg/Tran8.htm

Smith, F. L. and B. Cox. 2008. "Airline Deregulation." *The Concise Encyclopedia of Economics.* Library of Economics and Liberty. Retrieved from http://www.econlib.org/library/Enc/AirlineDeregulation.html

The New York Times. "Santos-Dumont Arrives." 1902. http://query.nytimes.com/mem/archive-free/pdf?_r=2&res=9807E4D91230E733A25752C1A9629C946397D6CF

U.S. Centennial of Flight Commission. n.d.(a) "Airmail. The Airmail Act of 1925 through 1929." Retrieved from http://www.centennialofflight.net/essay/Government_Role/1925-29_airmail/POL5.htm

———. n.d.(b) "Government Funding of Airports." Retrieved from http://www.centennialofflight.net/essay/Government_Role/govt_funding/POL11.htm

———. n.d.(c) "The Post Office Flies the Mail." Retrieved from http://www.centennialofflight.net/essay/Government_Role/1918-1924/POL3.htm

Chapter 2

Structure of Airports

Objectives ↘

Upon completion of this chapter, you should:

- Understand the nature of the airport industry, in terms of the number of airports and categories of airports.

- Understand the various types of airport ownership structure.

- Be able to explain the differences in organizational structure among airports of different sizes, including the typical organization chart associated with airports of various sizes.

- Understand the major departments at a large airport, and the roles and responsibilities of each department.

- Understand airport training and career opportunities, as well as methods to obtain airport employment.

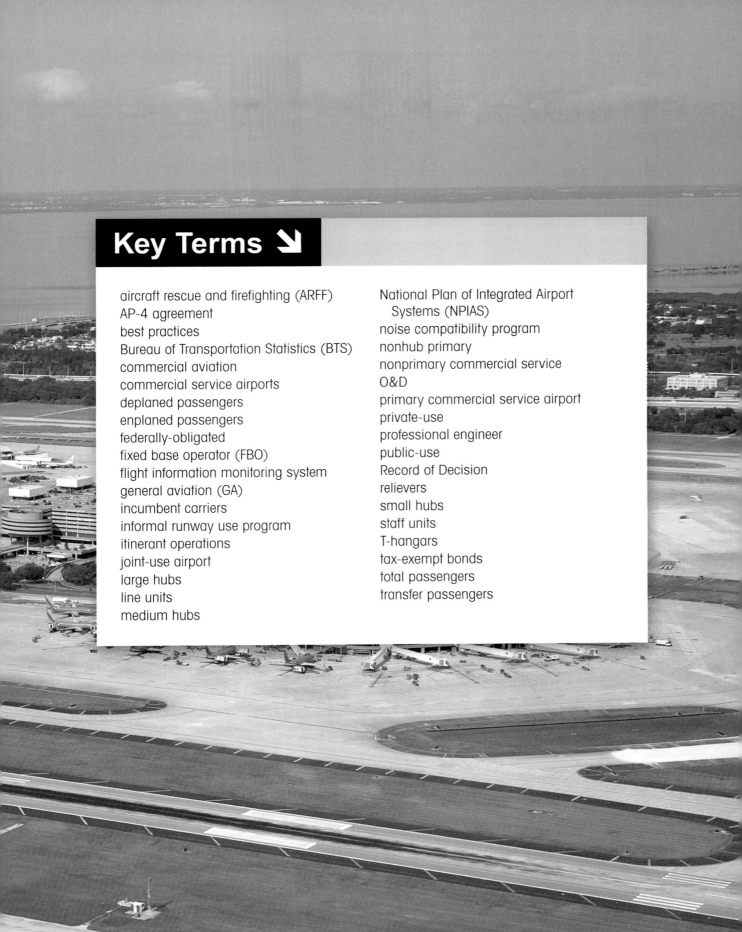

Key Terms ↘

aircraft rescue and firefighting (ARFF)
AP-4 agreement
best practices
Bureau of Transportation Statistics (BTS)
commercial aviation
commercial service airports
deplaned passengers
enplaned passengers
federally-obligated
fixed base operator (FBO)
flight information monitoring system
general aviation (GA)
incumbent carriers
informal runway use program
itinerant operations
joint-use airport
large hubs
line units
medium hubs

National Plan of Integrated Airport
   Systems (NPIAS)
noise compatibility program
nonhub primary
nonprimary commercial service
O&D
primary commercial service airport
private-use
professional engineer
public-use
Record of Decision
relievers
small hubs
staff units
T-hangars
tax-exempt bonds
total passengers
transfer passengers

In Chapter 2

FEATURES

Joint civil/military use of Marine Corps Air Station Yuma and Yuma International Airport.

A multi-use facility, Austin-Bergstrom International Airport is a commercial service airport with general aviation, the State Aircraft Pooling Board, and the Texas Army National Guard.

Branson Airport is a privately-owned, public-use commercial service airport.

The Hawaii Airports Division operates and maintains 15 airports located throughout the state.

The role and mission of the Massachusetts Port Authority

Introduction

The United States accounts for a substantial portion of the entire world's aviation activity. Specifically, **commercial aviation** in this country represents 40 percent of all commercial aviation worldwide. Additionally, the country's **general aviation (GA)** activity represents 50 percent of the worldwide GA activity. Clearly, the country needs a substantial network of airports to support this high level of activity. In fact, this need is filled by almost 20,000 airports currently in operation throughout the United States (see Figure 2-1). Of this tremendous number, however, only about 5,000 are open to the public. Therefore, almost three-quarters of the total U.S. airports are closed to the public. Additionally, approximately 1,000 of these 5,179 airports are privately owned. This differentiation is important, as these differences affect federal funding, compliance, and use by commercial air carriers (FAA, 2010b).

Figure 2-1.
U.S. airports by ownership and use.

(FAA: NPIAS)

Categories of Airports

To keep track of the huge number of airports in the United States, a system for organizing them had to be developed. U.S. airports are categorized based on their purpose and size. Commercial service airports are further categorized based on the number of **enplaned passengers**. Enplaned passengers are those passengers boarding an aircraft. This includes passengers originating, as well as those transferring to another aircraft. Each time a passenger boards an aircraft, it is counted as an enplaned passenger. These categories are important, as a large degree of funding is determined by the category of the airport. Figure 2-2 shows the breakdown of all airports included in the **National Plan of Integrated Airport Systems (NPIAS)**, which represents 65 percent of the nation's public-use airports. The NPIAS identifies nearly 3,400 existing and proposed airports that are significant to national air transportation and thus eligible to receive federal grants under the Airport Improvement Program (AIP). However, there are 1,799 airports open to the public that are not included in the NPIAS.

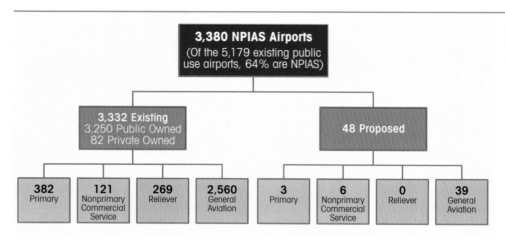

Figure 2-2.
Number of NPIAS
airports by use.

(FAA: NPIAS)

Additionally, there are 932 privately-owned, public-use airports that are not included because they are located at inadequate sites, are redundant to publicly owned airports, or have too little activity to meet NPIAS criteria. There are 867 publicly owned, public-use airports that are not included because they do not meet the minimum criteria for the NPIAS of ten based aircraft, or they are within 20 miles of a NPIAS airport, are located at inadequate sites, cannot be expanded and improved to provide safe and efficient airport facilities, or do not have adequate justification showing a significant national interest (FAA, 2010b).

COMMERCIAL SERVICE AIRPORTS

Airports with scheduled airline service are known as **commercial service airports** (see Figure 2-3). Clearly, some commercial service airports are very large, such as Hartsfield-Jackson Atlanta International Airport which has five runways and served over 96 million passengers in 2014. At the other end of the spectrum are single-runway airports such as the Gogebic-Iron County Airport in Ironwood, Michigan, which served approximately 3,500 passengers in 2014. Regardless of the size, as long as the airport is a public airport receiving scheduled passenger service and having a minimum of 2,500 annual enplaned passengers, it is categorized as commercial service. According to the 2009–2013 NPIAS and as shown in Figure 2-2, there were 503 commercial service airports in the U.S. as of 2008 (382 primary plus 121 commercial-service). Of these 503, only 382 airports had more than 10,000 annual passenger enplanements, thus meeting the threshold to be qualified as a **primary commercial service airport**.

Confusion often results when discussing total passengers and enplaned passengers. Enplaned passengers are those boarding an aircraft and **deplaned passenger**s are those leaving the aircraft. Airports typically advertise their **total passenger** numbers, which would include both enplaned and deplaned passengers. In other words, total passengers represent every passenger at an airport,

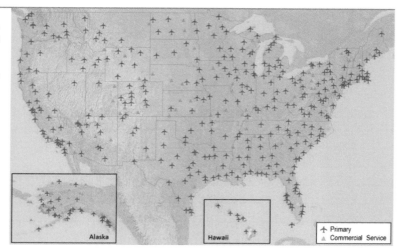

Figure 2-3.
Commercial service airports.

(FAA: NPIAS)

generally measured on a monthly and annual basis—whether this passenger was departing or arriving. However, when categorizing airports, the focus is on enplaned passengers. As a result, the number of enplaned passengers is typically half of total passengers. Or stated alternatively, one could multiply the number of enplaned passengers by two to get a rough idea of total passengers. For instance, Hartsfield-Jackson Atlanta International Airport had 41.4 million enplanements in calendar year (CY) 2006. Yet the airport's 2006 Annual Report begins by stating, "It was another record-setting year in 2006 for Hartsfield-Jackson Atlanta International Airport, which was once again named the world's busiest, with more than 85 million passengers." (Hartsfield-Jackson International Airport, 2006)

Large Hubs

The largest of the commercial service airports are known as **large hubs** (see Figure 2-4). To be categorized as a large hub airport, the airport must serve at least one percent of total U.S. passenger enplanements; based on 739 million enplanements nationwide in CY13, this would amount to 7.39 million. This number changes every year; thus, the numerical threshold for being categorized as a large hub changes each year. If all U.S. passenger enplanements are added up for the 12-month period, any airport serving at least one percent of that total would be categorized as a large hub. Keep in mind that the hub category does not refer to airline hubs.[1] In fact, an airport could be categorized as a large hub airport and yet have no airline hub located there (FAA, 2010b).

It does not matter if these passengers originate in the local community (as would be the case at a mostly **O&D** [origin and destination] airport such as Orlando International) or are **transfer passengers** connecting from one flight to another (as would be the case at a mostly hub airport such as Atlanta). Due to the sheer size of these large hub airports, there are only 30 in the United States. In sum, they account for almost 70 percent of total U.S. passenger

---

[1] As in hub and spoke route structure.

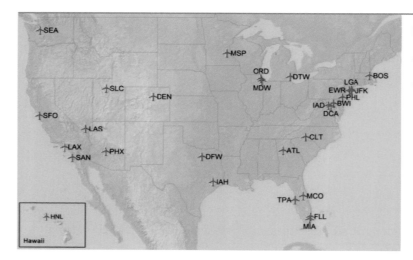

Figure 2-4.
Large hub airports in the United States.

(FAA: NPIAS)

enplanements. This means that 7 out of 10 passengers flying commercially in this country either begin or continue their journey at one of the 30 large hub airports (FAA, 2010b).

Medium Hubs

Airports categorized as **medium hubs** must serve between 0.25 percent and 1 percent of total U.S. passenger enplanements; based on 739 million enplanements nationwide in CY13, this would amount to 1.84 million to 7.39 million. The 37 medium hub airports in the United States typically account for 20 percent of all passenger enplanements (Figure 2-5). It is important to note that even though they are considered commercial service airports, medium hub airports (and smaller) also typically have a substantial amount of GA activity, in addition to commercial airline activity. In fact, two medium hubs in the United States (Dallas Love Field—DAL, and John Wayne Airport/Orange County—SNA) have an average of over 600 based aircraft. This is quite amazing considering that these airports are also projecting enplanements in 2013

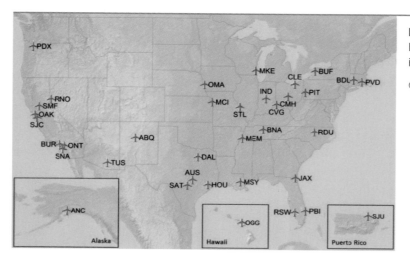

Figure 2-5.
Medium hub airports in the United States.

(FAA: NPIAS)

to total 4.2 million and 5.3 million, respectively. The remaining medium hub airports average a much lower 129 based aircraft. Still, it is clear that both commercial airline activity and general aviation activity can coexist to a certain degree at an airport (FAA, 2010b).

Small Hubs

Airports that are not as busy as medium hubs are categorized as **small hubs**. Specifically, small hubs are those airports enplaning 0.05 percent to 0.25 percent of all passenger enplanements; based on 739 million enplanements nationwide in CY13, this would amount to 369,000 to 1.84 million. There are currently 72 small hub airports in the United States that collectively account for 8 percent of all passenger enplanements (see Figure 2-6). Small hub airports, which typically are not congested and don't have any significant air traffic delays, also accommodate a large degree of general aviation activity. Although small hubs average 134 based aircraft, there are some airports, such as Long Beach Airport, with many more based aircraft and a substantial amount of general aviation activity. For instance, Long Beach Airport in California had 435 aircraft in 2013 (FAA, 2010b).

Figure 2-6.
Small hub airports in the United States.

(FAA: NPIAS)

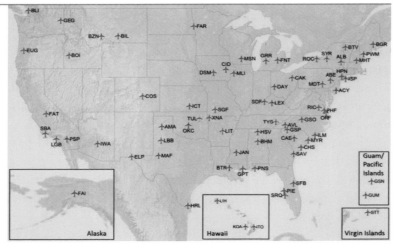

Nonhub Primary

There are some commercial service airports that are not categorized as hub airports, and yet still maintain their commercial service status. The first of these categories is **nonhub primary** (see Figure 2-7). Commercial service airports that enplane less than 0.05 percent of all commercial passenger enplanements and have at least 10,000 annual enplanements are categorized as nonhub primary airports. Although these airports collectively account for only 3 percent of all enplanements in the United States, they number 244. Generally, as the airport size decreases, the number of airports of a particular size increases. The United States has many more small airports than larger airports and that holds

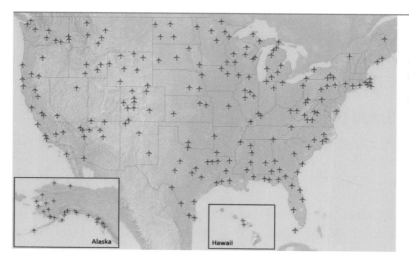

Figure 2-7.
Nonhub primary airports in the United States.

(FAA: NPIAS)

true with this category. Additionally, nonhub primary airports are extensively utilized by general aviation pilots, accounting for almost 11 percent of all U.S. based aircraft (FAA, 2010b).

Nonprimary Commercial Service

The final category of commercial service airports is known as **nonprimary commercial service**. These are the smallest commercial service airports with at least 2,500 annual passenger enplanements, but no more than 10,000. Although these airports account for only 0.1 percent of all enplanements, there are 139 airports in this category (see Figure 2-8). There are fewer airports in this category than in the nonhub primary category, but this is due to the narrow definition for this category of airport. It can be difficult to have commercial service and enplane fewer than 10,000 passengers per year. In effect, an airport in this category would likely have commuter service by only one carrier and would be enplaning less than 833 passengers per month, on average. On the one hand, this can be difficult to accomplish. In reality, these are mostly general

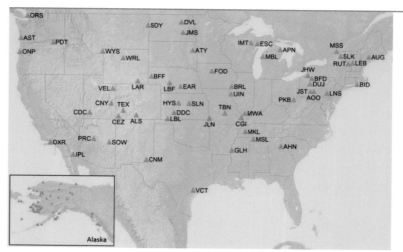

Figure 2-8.
Nonprimary commercial service airports in the United States.

(FAA: NPIAS)

aviation airports that also have a small amount of commercial airline service, possibly through the Essential Air Service Program (FAA, 2010b).

RELIEVER

Although a review of the commercial service categories just discussed makes it apparent that commercial aviation and general aviation can coexist at an airport, GA activity, especially in the form of small aircraft and flight-training activities, is generally not very compatible with the larger commercial service airports. This is due to several factors, including mix of aircraft (and subsequent approach speeds and wake turbulence), Class B and C airspace requirements for aircraft equipment and pilot qualifications, the large volume of commercial aircraft operations, and the lack of familiarity among some GA pilots with complex airfield layouts and procedures at these large commercial service airports. Some airports even prohibit touch-and-gos or other flight-training activities due to the conflict these would create with large commercial service aircraft present in high numbers.

In recognition of this, and to encourage the development of high-capacity general aviation airports in major metropolitan areas, the FAA has designated certain airports as **relievers**. These airports are attractive alternatives for GA pilots desiring access to a major metropolitan area, but also desiring to stay out of the busy, and possibly congested, commercial service airport. To be categorized as a reliever, the airport must have 100 or more based aircraft or 25,000 annual **itinerant operations**. Itinerant operations are those operations that are not local, meaning they are conducted by aircraft not based at the airport. The United States currently has 270 reliever airports with an average of 230 based aircraft (see Figure 2-9). This represents almost 30 percent of the country's GA fleet (FAA, 2010b).

Figure 2-9.
Reliever airports in the United States.

(FAA: NPIAS)

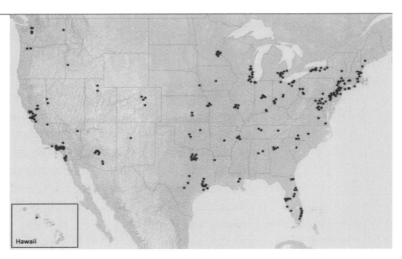

GENERAL AVIATION AIRPORTS

There is a plethora of airports in this country without commercial airline service (or with less than 2,500 annual passenger enplanements). General aviation is the category into which these airports fall (see Figure 2-10). The U.S. has some very active GA airports. For instance, Van Nuys Airport, located in the heart of the San Fernando Valley, ranks as the world's busiest general aviation airport. It averages nearly 400,000 takeoffs and landings annually. Interestingly, this airport is busier than many commercial service airports, in terms of number of operations. At the same time, there are also some very sleepy airports with no based aircraft. For instance, the majority of airports in Alaska have no based aircraft. Quite a few others have only a handful of based aircraft. Of course, with no based aircraft, these airports serve only itinerant operations (Van Nuys Los Angeles World Airports, 2011; FAA, 2010b).

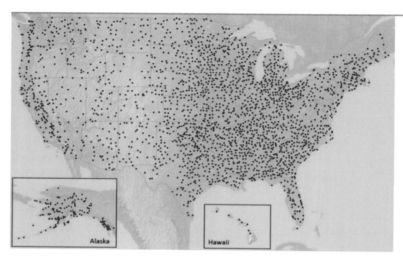

Figure 2-10.
General aviation airports in the United States.

(FAA: NPIAS)

The NPIAS, however, is not a complete document. It does not identify all airport capital development needs nationwide. The NPIAS is designed to "identify for Congress and the public those airports included in the national system, the role they serve, and the amounts and types of airport development eligible for federal funding under the Airport Improvement Program (AIP) over the next five years" (FAA, 2010b, p. 1). Only 65 percent of the 5,179 public-use airports throughout the United States are included in the NPIAS. This means that a large number of public-use airports (almost 1,800) are not included in the NPIAS. As stated in the NPIAS, "All primary and commercial service airports, all general aviation airports designated as reliever airports by the FAA, and selected general aviation airports are included in the plan" (NPIAS, 2009, p. 1).

To be included in the NPIAS, a GA airport must have at least 10 locally based aircraft and be at least 20 miles from the nearest NPIAS airport. The more than 2,500 GA airports included in the NPIAS tend to be distributed on a one-per-county basis in rural areas and typically located near the county seat.

These airports have an average of 35 based aircraft and account for 41 percent of the U.S. GA fleet. Of particular importance, these airports are the nearest source of air transportation for almost 20 percent of the U.S. population (FAA, 2010b).

JOINT USE

Although not specifically included in the NPIAS, there are also joint-use airports in this country. According to the **Bureau of Transportation Statistics (BTS)** Dictionary (available on the BTS website), a **joint-use airport** is a "military installation at which the Department of Defense permits some degree of civil aviation use" (Bureau of Transportation Statistics, n.d.). Stated another way, a joint-use facility is established by agreement to allow use of a military runway for a public airport. The degrees of civil aviation use include either all civil aviation under a joint-use agreement, or limited use. Strictly military airports do not qualify for primary or commercial service status. Table 2-1 presents the joint-use airports in the United States as of October 2012.

Table 2-1. U.S. joint-use airports as of 2012.

Air Force	
AF Plant 42, Palmdale, CA	Kelly/Lackland AFB, San Antonio, TX
Barter Island LRRS, Barter Island, AK	March ARB, Riverside, CA
Charleston AFB, Charleston, SC	Pt. Lay LRRS, Point Lay, AK
Dover AFB, Dover, DE	Scott AFB (Mid America), Belleville, IL
Eglin AFB, Valparaiso, FL	Sheppard AFB, Wichita Falls, TX
Grissom AFB, Peru, IN	Westover ARB, Chicopee, MA
Army	
Blackstone AAF (Ft. Pickett), VA	Grayling AAF (Camp Grayling), MI
Camp Guernsey AAF, Guernsey, WY	Libby AAF (Ft. Huachuca), Sierra Vista, AZ
Dillingham AAF, Waialua, HI	Sherman AAF (Ft. Leavenworth), KS
Forney AAF (Fort Leonard Wood), MO	Sparta/Fort McCoy (Sparta), WI
Robert Gray AAF, Ft. Hood/Killeen, TX	Wright AAF (Fort Stewart) Midcoast Rgnl, Ft Stewart/Hinesville, GA
Navy	
MCAS Yuma, Yuma, AZ	

Joint-Use Airport

One example of a joint-use airport that is currently owned by the U.S. Department of Defense is Yuma (Arizona) International Airport. The Marine Corps Air Station Yuma and the Yuma County Airport Authority have entered into a joint-use operating agreement to allow both civilian and military activity on the same airport. The agreement "formalizes the coexistence of two independent, but mutually operating parties legitimately sharing a single common airfield since 1956." Specifically, the agreement establishes procedures and outlines responsibilities for the joint civil/military use of Marine Corps Air Station Yuma and Yuma International Airport. The actual agreement is available for viewing on www.yumaairport.com.

(Yuma International Airport 2009)

Multi-Use Airport

An example of a former U.S. Department of Defense facility now owned by a municipality and used as a multi-use airport (as contrasted to a joint-use airport) is in Austin, Texas. In 1990, the Base Realignment and Closure Commission notified the City of Austin, Texas that Bergstrom Air Force Base, after nearly 50 years of service, would be decommissioned and the land would be returned to the City. Timing could not have been better for the City of Austin, which had been exploring alternative sites for building a new commercial service airport to replace land-locked Robert Mueller Municipal Airport, which was not prepared to handle the future needs of the city and had 30,000 residents living in noise impact areas. The base was only eight miles from the capitol, was large enough to meet the community's growing needs, and had runways and other facilities already in place. As an added incentive, the surrounding area was sparsely populated, which meant that relatively few residents and businesses would be affected by noise. As a result, the City initiated an airport master plan to study Bergstrom's feasibility as a civilian airport. The results proved the feasibility of the project, and the Austin City Council unanimously approved the proposal. The voters then overwhelmingly approved it in 1993. With a $585 million budget, one-fourth funded by the FAA, a second, 9,000-foot runway was added to complement the existing 12,250-foot runway, a new terminal was constructed, both surface and garage parking were added, and a new cargo facility was built. Interestingly, cargo carriers began operating at the new Austin-Bergstrom International Airport on June 30, 1997, two years before passenger operations began on May 23, 1999. A multi-use facility, Austin-Bergstrom International Airport hosts general aviation, the State Aircraft Pooling Board, and the Texas Army National Guard, as well as 10.7 million annual passengers in 2014.

(Austin-Bergstrom International Airport, 2005)

Ownership of Airports

The ownership of airports in the United States is quite varied. Indeed, just as airports range in size from very large commercial service airports to unattended landing strips, there is wide variation in how these airports are structured in terms of ownership. Even so, specific types of airport ownership structures exist that all airports must fall into.

PRIVATE

According to the NPIAS, there are over 14,000 airports in the United States that are closed to the public. These are termed **private-use** airports. Typically, these private-use airports are also privately owned. However, there are also privately-owned airports that are open to the public, also known as **public-use**. The NPIAS lists almost 1,000 of these. Privately-owned airports are owned by either a private individual or company. How this is accomplished varies. Many times, a private individual may build a runway on their land and open a private-use airpark. Other times, a for-profit company may build an airport with private funds and open a public-use airport. The main determinant is that no public funding was made available in building the airport, and as such, it can either remain private or be open for public-use.

 Privately-Owned, Public-Use, Commercial Service Airport

Although most airports in the United States are privately owned, building an airport with private funds (rather than federal grants) is not something to be undertaken lightly. One modern-day example is the Branson Airport, which opened in May 2009. This airport was built for $140 million, composed of $26.5 million in private equity and $114 million in revenue bonds. Located on a 922-acre site in Taney County, Missouri, the airport is considered the first privately financed and operated commercial airport in the United States. It is owned and operated by Branson Airport, LLC. Thus, this airport is a privately-owned, public-use airport.

As a privately-owned, public-use, commercial service airport, Branson Airport, LCC operates with a unique business approach to managing an airport. As a private enterprise, Branson Airport has flexibility not typically afforded to **federally-obligated** airports, meaning those airports that have accepted federal funds. For example, according to their website, Branson Airport "is able to offer exclusivity to airlines and vendors and develop unconventional revenue streams, such as offering naming rights and other sponsorship opportunities."

(Branson Airport, 2011)

PUBLIC-PRIVATE PARTNERSHIP

Yet another option in the ownership of airports is that of a public-private partnership. In this instance, the ownership is somewhat of a hybrid with a certain degree of both public and private ownership characteristics. In a public-private partnership, several options are available, not all of which fall under "ownership." First, an airport capital project could be partially funded or financed by a private firm. For instance, an airline could fund the construction of a new maintenance hangar from which the airline would operate. Another option is for an airport to enter into an agreement with a private firm for the joint operation of the airport. For example, the Orlando Sanford International Airport (SFB), although operated, maintained, and developed by the Sanford Airport Authority, is operated through a public-private partnership between the Sanford Airport Authority and TBI Airport Management, Inc. TBI Airport Management, Inc. has been contracted by the Sanford Airport Authority to manage both the international and domestic terminals, develop additional air service, and provide ground handling and cargo services. As stated by the airport, "This public/private partnership has created an environment with valuable service benefits for SFB customers and passengers" (Orlando Sanford International Airport, n.d.).

In fact, most of the world's airports, even though owned by local, regional, or national governments, are leased to private corporations that oversee the airports' operation. For example, BAA Limited operates seven of the commercial service airports in the United Kingdom, as well as several other airports outside of the UK. Germany's Frankfurt Airport is managed by the quasi-private firm Fraport. A third option, which is quite common at most U.S. commercial service airports, allows the airport to enter into an agreement with a private firm to operate concessions, ground handling, fueling, or other services at the airport. The airport may also enter into an agreement with a private firm to operate the **fixed base operator (FBO)**, which provides services to aircraft, typically in the form of fuel, maintenance, and other services (Figure 2-11). While smaller airports may operate the FBO, the parking lot, and aircraft **T-hangars**, the large, commercial service airports typically look to the private sector for assistance with managing the many services available at these airports. Whether it is automobile parking, rental car services, the FBO, fueling, or ground handling, there are firms in the private sector with experience and expertise useful to managing these activities. Airports recognize this and willingly pay for the services of these providers experienced in managing these services. This arrangement typically allows the airport to have one-third to one-half less employees than if all these services were handled in-house by employees (Prather, 2009).

LOCAL GOVERNMENT

The predominate form of public airport ownership in the United States is that of local government ownership. This is also referred to as municipal ownership. Indeed, there are variations of this concept, as local government may include city, county, multiple cities or counties, or parishes in the state of Louisiana. Regardless of the variation, this form of ownership allows a local government to own and operate an airport within its jurisdiction.

One of the main reasons why local government is the predominate form of public airport ownership is the 1946 Federal Airport Act. One intent of this Act was to transfer airfields built before World War II to state or local government entities. In other words, the military was transferring ownership of these assets and the federal government, in an agreement known as an **AP-4 agreement**, required the new owners to "assure" the federal government that the airport would continue to be operated and maintained as needed. Generally, with their financial resources and stability, a municipality could provide the best assurance that the airport would remain in operation and maintained as needed. Thus, numerous local governments became the owner and operator of airports throughout the United States. And while most AP-4 agreements have been superseded by AIP grants and their associated grant assurances, the local government form of ownership continues in popularity today.

Of course, there are pros and cons to the ownership of airports by local government. It usually works well for small airports that may need the support (financial and otherwise) of the municipality. These smaller airports may not be self-sustaining and the financial assistance of the municipality to fund both operating budgets and capital budgets is oftentimes a necessity. Additionally, the municipality has the power to tax and issue government bonds to fund the airport's operation and capital development.

On the other hand, with a municipally-owned airport, the airport manager must report to the city or county administrator just as, for example, the director of building and codes, director of city schools, director of planning and engineering, director of parks and recreation, and director of solid waste must. With this structure, the airport director is one of many voices all competing for the same finite resources. What makes the airport more important than the parks and recreation department, for instance? Depending on the views of the city or county administrator, the airport may be viewed as much less important. As a result, particularly with the local government form of airport ownership, it is incumbent upon the airport manager to impress upon local government officials the benefits (economic and otherwise) of the airport to the local community. Even so, during periods of financial constraint on the municipality, the airport will likely suffer the same budget reductions common to all municipal departments and services. Worse, the airport may be seen as a liability and a way to reduce expenses if it were closed and sold to a developer. Unfortunately, this last situation is quite common in this country.

STATE GOVERNMENT

Yet another option of airport ownership is that of state government ownership. In some states, such as Hawaii, all public-use airports are owned and operated by the state. In other states, such as Idaho, a large number of public-use airports are owned and operated by the state. For example, the state of Idaho has 30 state owned and operated airports. At the same time, the state has airports with other ownership structures, such as the Boise Airport, which is a division of the City of Boise Department of Aviation and Public Transportation and is overseen by a seven-member airport commission. Yet in other states, such as Arizona, only a handful of airports are owned and operated by the state. In Arizona specifically, the state owns and operates only one airport—the Grand Canyon National Park Airport (Arizona Department of Transportation, n.d.).

Generally, state ownership of airports is not too common in the United States, although it does occur more regularly in the western states. In any event, state ownership presents a unique set of challenges for states. As the state DOT is typically located in the capital city, and if no regional offices exist, how are airports to be managed on a daily basis by someone sitting in an office several hundred miles away? Unless the airport is rarely used, this is not a good solution. Thus, the state may assign a full-time state employee to the airport to serve as the airport manager, or may contract with a private firm to provide these services. If an FBO is present on the field, the FBO manager possibly could serve in this capacity. Regardless of who fills the position, the state-operated airport must compete with all of the other state-operated airports and state services and facilities for the funding of operations and maintenance, as well as capital development. It can be argued that although a state aviation department has a good grasp on the aviation infrastructure needs of the state and the manner in which airports comprise the entire state system, the state may not

In Hawaii, the State of Hawaii Department of Transportation's Airports Division has jurisdiction over and control of all State of Hawaii airports as well as air navigation facilities, and general supervision of aeronautics within the state. The Hawaii Airports Division operates and maintains 15 airports located throughout the state. An airports administrator is responsible for day-to-day operations of the division, including the four district offices that manage the day-to-day operations of the airports under their control. The mission of the Airports Division is to develop, manage and maintain a safe and efficient global air transportation organization.

(State of Hawaii, 2011)

be as knowledgeable regarding local airport issues and community concerns as would be possible by having a local airport manager on-site.

The State of Oregon is unique in that it has airports that fall under most of the ownership categories previously discussed. As shown in Table 2-2, airports in Oregon fall into one of eight distinct categories. The most popular of these categories is city ownership, with 30 airports throughout the state falling in this category. The next most common category is state owership, with the state owning and operating no fewer than 28 airports.

NATIONAL/FEDERAL GOVERNMENT

Although it's an option for ownership of U.S. airports, the national or federal government ownership structure is most popular at airports outside the United States. However, prior to June 7, 1987, Dulles International and Reagan National Airports were owned and operated by the FAA in the U.S. Department of Transportation. On June 7, 1987, Washington Dulles International and Washington National Airports were transferred to the Metropolitan Washington Airports Authority under a 50-year lease authorized by the Metropolitan Washington Airports Act of 1986. All property was transferred to the Airports Authority and the federal government holds title to the lease (Metropolitan Washington Airports Authority, 2011).

Currently, a large number of military airports, and some airports operated by the U.S. Department of the Interior, remain under federal government ownership and operation. For instance, Furnace Creek and Stovepipe Wells Airports in Death Valley National Park are operated by the Department of the Interior. Likewise, there are 440 military bases in the continental United States, but not all of these are considered military airports.

Table 2-2. Ownership categories of airports in the state of Oregon.

OREGON AIRPORTS BY TYPE OF OWNERSHIP	
City	
Albany Municipal	Lakeside
Arlington Municipal	Madras City - County
Ashland Municipal - Sumner Parker Field	Malin
Baker City Municipal	McMinnville Municipal
Bend Municipal	Miller Memorial Airpark
Burns Municipal	Monument Municipal
Columbia Gorge / The Dalles	Myrtle Creek Municipal
Corvallis Municipal	Newport Municipal
Creswell Hobby Field	Ontario Municipal
Eastern Oregon Regional @ Pendleton	Portland Downtown Heliport
Enterprise Municipal	Redmond Municipal—Roberts Field
Eugene Mahlon Sweet Field	Roseburg Regional
Florence Municipal	Salem McNary Field
Hermiston Municipal	Seaside Municipal
Klamath Falls / Kingsley Field	Vernonia Airfield
County	
Curry Coast Airpark	Lake County
Grant Couny Regional / Ogilvie Field	Lexington
Grants Pass	Paisley
Illinois Valley	Prineville
LaGrande / Union County	Rogue Valley International—Medford
Federal	
Memaloose (USFS)	
Silver Lake (USFS)	
Airport District	
Southwest Oregon Regional	
Other	
Christmas Valley	
Port	
Astoria Regional	Portland International
Boardman	Powers
Gold Beach Municipal	Scappoose Industrial Airpark
Hillsboro	Tillamook
Ken Jernstedt Airfield	Troutdale

Private	
Beaver Marsh	Sandy River
Chehalem Airpark	Sisters Eagle Air
Country Squire Airpark	Skyport
Davis	Sportsman Airpark
George Felt	Stark's Twin Oaks Airpark
Lake Billy Chinook	Sunriver
Lake Woahink Seaplane Base	Valley View
Lenhardt Airpark	
State	
Alkali Lake State	Mulino State
Aurora State	Nehalem Bay State
Bandon State	Oakridge State
Cape Blanco State	Owyhee Reservoir State
Cascade Locks State	Pacific City State
Chiloquin State	Pinehurst State
Condon State	Prospect State
Cottage Grove State	Rome State
Crescent Lake State	Santiam Junction State
Independence State	Siletz Bay State
Joseph State	Toketee State
Lebanon State	Toledo State
McDermitt State	Wakonda Beach State
McKenzie Bridge State	Wasco State

(oregon.gov)

AUTHORITIES OR COMMISSIONS

Although the local government ownership structure is the predominate form of airport ownership, especially among smaller airports, there has been a movement in recent decades toward authority ownership. There are several reasons for the increasing popularity of authorities:

1. By having a governing board that is specifically focused on airport matters, greater concentration on airport issues is possible, and as a result, less time is spent on non-airport issues. Further, an airport authority board is composed of members interested in the success of the airport and with specific expertise on airport issues. On the other hand, with a city-owned and operated airport, the city council must discuss issues and set policy on a number of municipal services, such as parks and recreation, public safety, education, and airports.

2. More efficient operation and enhanced economies of scale are obtained when several political jurisdictions, each with separate airport responsibilities,

choose to combine these responsibilities under one governing board. In essence, if two public-use airports exist in two contiguous counties, it may be in both counties' interest to create one airport authority with board representation from each county to manage the two airports. There are many airport authorities with responsibility for more than one public-use airport. Similarly, governing boards can have representation from several political jurisdictions. As an example, the Tri-Cities Airport Commission, charged with the operation of Tri-Cities Regional Airport located in Blountville, Tennessee, is governed by a 12-person commission appointed by the airport's owners: the Cities of Kingsport, Bristol, Johnson City, TN and Bristol, VA; and Washington and Sullivan Counties, TN (Tri-Cities Regional Airport, n.d.).

3. An authority can provide experienced decision makers located on airport who are able to operate the airport with less political interference than might be the case with a municipally-owned and operated airport. For instance, at a municipal airport, the airport manager answers to the city or county manager, mayor, or other (oftentimes) political appointee. However, the executive director of an authority reports directly to the authority board.

(AAAE, 2005)

An authority is generally in the form of either an airport authority or port authority. Airport authorities are specific to an airport (or airports), whereas port authorities also operate shipping terminals, railroads, seaports, and irrigation facilities. The Port Authority of New York & New Jersey, Massport, Port of Seattle, and Port of Portland are all examples of port authorities that also own and operate airports.

There are typical terms and provisions in place for autonomous airport or port authorities. Using Massport as an example, these provisions are outlined below:

1. The authority acts as the owner, manager, and operator of the facilities under its control, including all related property and services. As discussed above, the authority may also have responsibility for other transportation facilities and services. In Massport's case, airports including Boston Logan International, Hanscom Field, and Worcester Regional, as well as a container port, cruiseport, autoport, and other secondary facilities, are all owned and operated by Massport.

2. The authority is governed by a board of directors appointed by the state or local government (many times, the governor). Board members typically volunteer their time and expertise and normally receive no compensation. In the case of Massport, the authority is governed by a seven-member board, with members appointed by the governor. Governors are elected to four-year terms in Massachusetts. Thus, a governor elected to one four-year term will normally obtain a board with a majority of members appointed by him or her only during the last year of his or her tenure. The intent of this provision is to minimize the political forces on the Massport board and ensure some level of continuity and stability in its policies.

The Massachusetts Port Authority

The mission of the Massachusetts Port Authority, Massport, is to "promote economic growth and vitality throughout Massachusetts and New England by operating many of the region's largest transportation facilities safely, securely and efficiently while being mindful of the environment and our neighboring communities."

The authority is self-supporting and receives no state tax revenues to support its operations or facilities. A recent economic impact report estimated that Massport contributes $8.7 billion per year in total economic impact.

(Massport, 2011)

3. The authority operates on a not-for-profit basis and is exempt from taxes. Although this provision is not necessarily different than municipally-owned and operated airports, the unique aspect of authorities allows them to make "voluntary contributions" to its shareholders, typically the state or local government. In Massport's instance, part of the operating surplus it generates is allocated to providing financial assistance to a number of Boston-area cities and townships. Note that while this act of "voluntary contributions" may occur with port authorities, it is prohibited by airport authorities that are federally obligated. This creates a condition of revenue diversion, in which airport revenues are diverted to some non-airport use. Revenue diversion is prohibited by the DOT/FAA.

4. The authority, as a legal entity, is permitted to acquire land and property at fair market value, and may undertake construction projects and other enhancements to its property and facilities. Clearly, Massport has acquired a great deal of land and property and commences various capital improvement projects to maintain and expand its facilities.

5. The authority may issue **tax-exempt bonds** secured by future airport revenues (known as revenue bonds) to fund capital improvements. Although bonds and other airport funding mechanisms are presented in-depth in Chapter 14, it should be noted that tax-exempt bonds, while also available to municipally-owned and operated airports, allow the authority to issue bonds at lower interest rates. This has the effect of reducing the cost to borrow money. In essence, an investor in a high tax bracket may be willing to accept a lower interest rate on their bond investment if the interest will be tax-free.

6. Just as with all federally-obligated airports, the authority must strive toward economic self-sufficiency. This concept includes the ability to fund capital improvements from its own revenues. In reality, many of the nation's smaller airports have difficulty obtaining self-sufficiency. For an airport offering only fuel, fuel sales alone make it difficult to cover all operating expenses, let alone fund any capital improvements. Authorities, however,

are typically managing commercial service airports at which it is easier to achieve economic self-sufficiency. User charges may be adjusted to achieve this objective.

7. A final provision common to authorities provides for all of the authority's property to be returned to the shareholders (state or local government) at some future time if the authority is ever dissolved. It is rare for an authority to dissolve; nonetheless, this provision may be present. In Massport's case, the property would be returned to the Commonwealth of Massachusetts. (DeNeufville and Odoni, 2003)

ADVISORY BOARDS

Although not truly an ownership form, airport advisory boards do play an important role in the affairs of many local airports. Typically, the airport manager is hired by the city council, board of county commissioners, or the city or county administrator directly. The airport manager is oftentimes expected to be an expert in airport operations, capital development, land-use planning, community concerns, etc. To provide additional input to the airport manager to facilitate the decision-making process, a municipality may establish an airport advisory board. These boards are just that—advisory in nature. They do not promulgate rules or polices, but the board will generally provide an alternative view, while bringing up community concerns, to the airport manager. This advising may be seen by the airport manager as very helpful—or as a hindrance. The view often depends upon the board's perceived role in advising. Some advisory boards feel they should direct the work of the airport manager, which of course can make life difficult for the airport manager, when the manager is in fact expecting only advisement on various issues. Board members should be from diverse backgrounds, preferably with either experience in, or a connection to, aviation. However, it should be noted that all too often, this is not the case.

PRIVATIZATION

Although airports quite often privatize certain functions and services, as discussed in the previous section entitled "public-private partnership," the outright privatizing of an entire airport is a rare act in the United States—and for good reason. FAA grant assurances, which are the "strings attached" to federal AIP grants, prohibit revenue diversion, the sale of land acquired with federal funds to private interests, and other acts related to privatization.

However, in response to increasing interest about the benefits of airport privatization, an Airport Privatization Pilot Program was included in the 1996 FAA Reauthorization Act. The Airport Privatization Pilot Program, which began in September 1997, allowed only a select number of participants—one

Figure 2-16.
The job search.

(©iStock.com/wdstock)

(ACI) website. Both of these sites are free for those searching for positions, although employers pay a reasonable fee to post an advertisement. Any position posted on these sites may be seen by anyone searching the sites, which includes airport personnel nationwide as well as college students, recent graduates, and others interested in airport positions. Posting a vacancy on such a specialized job board provides the best "bang for the buck" for airports. Indeed, executive search firms hired by an airport often utilize the AAAE and/or ACI site to advertise the opportunity.

One last method to advertise airport vacancies is the tried-and-true "word of mouth" method. Although some job searchers do not believe in the value of this method, and thus do not take advantage of it, it clearly does pay to know individuals in hiring positions. Whether referred to as networking, "schmoozing," or simply introducing yourself, getting to know those individuals currently working in the field in which you wish to gain employment or advance your career is a worthy exercise. Many times someone has become aware of a vacancy simply as a result of shaking hands or speaking to someone at a conference.

METHODS TO OBTAIN EMPLOYMENT

Although methods used to obtain employment in the airport industry closely relate to where vacancies are advertised, certain methods can be used to obtain employment. First, before graduating college, it is very beneficial to contact the airport manager or department director at the local airport and request an informational interview. In practical terms, this involves meeting with the individual to ask a few questions and find out how they entered the industry. In practical terms, a resume should be brought to this meeting and after asking questions to find out about the individual's career history, the resume can be presented for feedback on how it may be improved. This places the resume in front of a high-level decision maker, yet without any pretense. This method has produced internship opportunities, entry-level employment, and advance notice of airport vacancies for those who have taken the time to implement it.

Airport internships are yet another method useful for gaining airport employment. In fact, this may be the only way for someone to gain airport experience, at least initially. Whether for the summer or the entire year, and whether paid or unpaid, if at all possible, airport internships should be given serious consideration by the job seeker, especially those still in college. Airport internships have opened doors to permanent full-time employment for many interns over the years. If nothing else, having some airport experience on a resume greatly enhances the success of a job search.

Even with informational interviews and internships, the main method used to obtain airport employment is to formally apply for a permanent position. This can be done simply by emailing a resume, completing an online employment application, or completing a hard copy employment application and mailing it in. The method used depends on the employer, and the applicant must be careful to follow all directions presented by the employer. If the employer requests that a resume and cover letter be emailed by January 31, then the applicant should do this—nothing more, nothing less. The airport business is built around RFPs, RFQs, specifications, rules and regulations, grant assurances... the list goes on and on. Thus, the hiring airport expects applicants to follow directions precisely. Airport management reasons that if an applicant cannot follow simple directions during the application process, they'll likely have difficulty following directions and paying attention to detail on the job.

Concluding Thoughts

There is a great variety of airports throughout the United States. Whether categorized by NPIAS category, type of ownership, organizational structure, or the departments that exist within the airport's organizational structure, many variations exist. Indeed, it has been said that if you've seen one airport, you've seen one airport. This chapter has highlighted these many variations and revealed the diverse nature of the dynamic airport industry.

Chapter Summary

- The five categories of commercial service airports (large hub, medium hub, small hub, nonhub primary, and nonprimary commercial service) are determined by the number of annual enplaned passengers and the degree to which this number accounts for the total U.S. passenger enplanements on a percentage basis.

- Reliever airports are classified by the FAA and are so designated due to their role in reducing demand by GA aircraft at commercial service airports.

- The GA airport category contains the most airports and although many of these are quite small, some GA airports are busier in terms of number of operations than many commercial service airports.

- Joint-use airports are military installations at which the Department of Defense permits some degree of civil use.

- Airports may be privately or publicly owned and available for private or public use.

- Airport advisory boards do not promulgate rules or policies, but do advise the airport manager by providing an alternative view and bringing up community concerns.

- Although a small GA airport may have only one employee—the airport manager—larger commercial service airports may have employees numbering in the hundreds or even thousands.

- Although it varies by airport, larger airports generally have numerous departments which allow employees with specific skills and expertise to focus in distinct areas, such as air service development and international commerce, human resources, governmental and legal affairs, public information and community relations, performance management and internal audit, planning and development, operations, public safety, properties and contracts administration, maintenance, marketing, information technology, finance, and customer service.

- Airports generally offer either in-house training or external training, or both, to their employees.

- There are a number of methods used by airports to advertise position vacancies, and word-of-mouth remains effective even with the technological options available today.

- Informational interviewing and internships are effective methods used to enter the airport profession.

Review Questions ↘

1. How many total airports are there in the U.S., and what is the breakdown of public and private use versus public and private ownership?

2. What are the criteria for an airport to be included in the National Plan of Integrated Airport Systems (NPIAS)?

3. What condition must be met for an airport to be categorized as a large hub airport?

4. What condition must be met for an airport to be categorized as a medium hub airport?

5. What condition must be met for an airport to be categorized as a small hub airport?

6. What condition must be met for an airport to be categorized as a nonhub primary?

7. What condition must be met for an airport to be categorized as a nonprimary commercial service?

8. What is the role of a reliever airport in the nation's air transportation system?

9. What condition must be met for an airport to be categorized as a general aviation airport?

10. Explain the differences between private-use and public-use, as well as privately-owned and publicly-owned airports.

11. What is the predominate form of airport ownership in the United States?

12. What are the reasons for the increasing popularity of airport authorities?

13. Explain the role of the airport advisory board and the challenges this may present to the airport manager.

14. Explain the FAA Airport Privatization Pilot Program.

15. Why would a municipality pursue airport privatization?

16. Describe the typical organization chart of a municipality with no airport manager.

17. Describe the typical organization chart of a GA airport.

18. Describe the typical organization chart of a small hub airport.

19. Describe the typical organization chart of a large hub airport.

20. Explain the roles and responsibilities of the following airport departments:

    a. Air service development and international commerce
    b. Human resources
    c. Governmental and legal affairs
    d. Public information and community relations
    e. Performance management and internal audit
    f. Planning and development
    g. Operations
    h. Public safety
    i. Properties and contracts administration
    j. Maintenance
    k. Marketing
    l. Information technology
    m. Finance
    n. Customer service

1. The City of Oak Bluff and the governor of the state feel it is time for a new airport in the Oak Bluff area. The City Council proposes a small GA airport with one runway and one FBO on the field. As you currently own an airport consulting firm, the City of Oak Bluff has contracted with your firm to provide expert guidance on the creation of this new airport. First, they have asked you how the airport ownership should be structured (i.e., city, county, authority, etc.). Additionally, they are seeking input into the organizational structure of the airport, which will have an estimated eight employees. Please provide them with an organization chart to visually convey your recommended structure.

2. As the executive director of an aviation authority with responsibility for both a large hub airport and GA airport, you are surprised to hear that the airport authority board is considering privatizing the GA airport under authority control. Their intention is to sell the airport to a private investor through the FAA Airport Privatization Pilot Program. This would raise funds to support the large hub airport's capital improvement program. However, as executive director, the board is asking for your advice on this proposal. What are the pros and cons to privatization? What do you recommend and why?

3. You are currently the director of public works for a small city, which has a small GA airport. In this city structure, there is no airport manager. In fact, the director of public works manages the airport, roads and streets, and solid waste. The new city manager is considering hiring an airport manager dedicated to managing the airport and growing the facilities. He has asked for your opinion on this and has made it clear that if the city decides to hire an airport manager, you will first be considered for the position.

4. As a newly hired director of human resources, you have been asked to create position announcements for the following positions: (a) operations manager, (b) director of finance, and (c) director of maintenance. Utilize the internet to explore currently available airport job opportunities and write position announcements to be advertised online for these three vacant positions.

5. As airport manager of a small, non-primary commercial service airport with 50,000 flight operations per year and an FBO, consider the typical airport departments one would see at an airport. Which departments presented in this chapter would you desire to have staffed for your airport? Considering a reduced budget, what innovative methods would you consider to ensure the responsibilities of these departments are carried out for your airport, even if all departments are not represented?

References and Resources for Further Study

American Association of Airport Executives. 2005. Body of Knowledge Module 1. "History, the Regulation of Air Transportation, Airports, and the Federal Aviation Administration." Washington, DC: AAAE.

Arizona Department of Transportation. n.d. "Grand Canyon Airport." Retrieved from http://www.grandcanyonairport.org/

Austin-Bergstrom International Airport. 2005. "Austin's Aviation History, Awards, and Accomplishments." Retrieved from http://www.ci.austin.tx.us/austinairport/default.htm

Branson Airport. 2011. "About Branson Airport." Retrieved from http://flybranson.com/about.php

Bureau of Transportation Statistics. n.d. "Dictionary." Retrieved from www.bts.gov/dictionary/index.xml

De Neufville, R. and A. Odoni. 2003. Airport Systems: Planning Design and Management. New York: McGraw Hill.

Federal Aviation Administration. 2010a. "FAA News." Retrieved from http://www.faa.gov/news/fact_sheets/news_story.cfm?newsId=14174

————. 2010b. National Plan of Integrated Airport Systems (NPIAS) 2011–2015. Retrieved from http://www.faa.gov/airports/planning_capacity/npias/reports/historical/

————. 2011. "Airport Privatization Pilot Program." Retrieved from http://www.faa.gov/airports/airport_compliance/privatization/

————. 2012. "Joint Civilian/Military (Joint-Use) Airports." Retrieved from http://www.faa.gov/airports/aip/military_airport_program/index.cfm?sect=joint

Hartsfield-Jackson International Airport. 2006. "2006 Annual Report: Focused on the Future." Retrieved from http://www.atlanta-airport.com/docs/Financial/2006_Annual_Report.pdf

Massport. 2011. "History." Retrieved from http://www.massport.com/massport/about-massport/Pages/AboutMassport.aspx

Metropolitan Washington Airports Authority. 2011. "About the Authority: History." Retrieved from http://www.metwashairports.com/263.htm

Orlando Sanford International Airport. n.d. "Airport organization." Retrieved from http://www.orlandosanfordairport.com/organization.asp

Prather, C.D. 2009. *General Aviation Marketing and Management: Operating, Marketing, and Managing an FBO*. Malabar, FL: Krieger.

State of Hawaii. 2011. "State Airport System." Retrieved from http://hawaii.gov/ogg/airport-information/state-airport-system

State of Oregon. n.d. "Oregon Airports by Type of Ownership." Retrieved from http:// www.oregon.gov/Aviation/docs/aplistbyown.pdf

Tri-Cities Regional Airport. n.d. "Airport Authority." Retrieved from http://www. triflight.com/about-tri/airport-commission/

Van Nuys Los Angeles World Airports. 2011. "Airport Information." Retrieved from http://www.lawa.org/welcome_VNY.aspx?id=92

Yuma International Airport. 2009. "Joint-Use Operating Agreement." Retrieved from http://www.yumainternationalairport.com/yuma/airportreflibrary.nsf/4ee27e9b609 182af0725723b0018389f/36b643751ee6e071072575ac002e9ecd?OpenDocument

Chapter 3

Air Traffic, Capacity, and Delay

Objectives ↘

Upon completion of this chapter, you should:

- Understand the role of the air traffic control system, including its history.
- Be able to explain the various classes of U.S. airspace.
- Understand various NAVAIDs.
- Understand airfield lighting.
- Understand airfield signage and markings.
- Understand proper radio communication.
- Understand the Federal Contract Tower program.
- Understand NextGen.
- Understand aspects of capacity and delay.
- Understand components of demand management.

Key Terms ↘

air operations area (AOA)
airport surface detection equipment (ASDE)
airport surveillance radar (ASR)
air traffic control
Air Traffic Control System Command Center
alert area
approach lights
automatic direction finder (ADF)
available landing distance (ALD)

boundary signs
CAT I ILS
CAT II ILS
CAT III ILS
Class A airspace
Class B airspace
Class C airspace
Class D airspace
Class E airspace
Class G airspace
clearance bars

Key Terms ↘

clearance delivery
common traffic advisory frequency (CTAF)
congestion pricing
contact approach
controlled firing area
crossbar lights
declared capacity
demand management
destination signs
direction signs
Federal Contract Tower Program
global positioning system (GPS)
ground-based augmentation system (GBAS)
ground control
high-intensity runway lights (HIRL)
information signs
instrument approach
instrument landing system (ILS)
instrument meteorological conditions (IMC)
land and hold short lighting
land and hold short operations (LAHSO)
localizer (LOC)
localizer directional aid (LDA)
location signs
low-intensity runway lights (LIRL)
mandatory instruction signs
marker beacons
maximum takeoff weight (MTOW)
maximum throughput capacity
medium-intensity runway lights (MIRL)
microwave landing system (MLS)
military operations areas (MOA)
National Airspace System Plan
navigational aids (NAVAIDs)
Next Generation (NextGen)
non-directional beacon (NDB)
non-precision instrument approach

obstruction light
practical hourly capacity (PHCAP)
precision approach path indicator (PAPI)
precision instrument approach
prohibited areas
radio detection and ranging (RADAR)
ramp control
restricted areas
rotating beacon
runway centerline lighting
runway distance remaining signs
runway end identifier lights
runway end lights
runway guard lights
runway occupancy time (ROT)
runway visual range (RVR)
sequence flashing lights
simplified directional facility (SDF)
slot
stop bars
stopway edge lights
sustained capacity
tactical air navigation (TACAN)
taxiway centerline lights
taxiway edge lights
taxiway edge reflectors
taxiway ending marker
threshold end lights
touchdown zone lights
tower
vehicle roadway signs
very high frequency omnidirectional range (VOR)
visual approach
visual approach slope indicator (VASI)
visual meteorological conditions
warning area
wide area augmentation system (WAAS)

In Chapter 3

FEATURES

Tampa International Airport Informal Runway Use Program 143

By adopting an informal runway use program, the airport and airport users cooperate in reducing noise impacts to surrounding communities.

Introduction

The efficiency of the nation's air transportation system depends, to a large degree, on the efficiency of the air traffic control system. Whether this system operates with the ability to fully accommodate all users with minimal delay depends upon many factors, such as weather, airport and airspace characteristics, and aircraft mix. Nonetheless, there are specific areas that, if properly addressed by both airports and the FAA, can lead to a more efficient system. This chapter addresses those areas, as well as techniques to minimize delay and manage demand.

ATC System Overview

The **air traffic control** (ATC) system in the United States is made up of many components. These components are interrelated and interact to ensure a safe and efficient national airspace system. Today's modern ATC system, however, had very humble beginnings.

HISTORY

The history of the air traffic control system actually begins in Europe. Although there were aircraft being flown in the United States, so few aircraft were in the skies that ground-based control of aircraft was not needed. In Europe, however, aircraft were flying between countries and a standardized system was called for. Thus, in 1919, the International Commission for Air Navigation (ICAN) was created to develop "General Rules for Air Traffic." The United States was not party to ICAN, but later developed U.S. air traffic rules after the passage of the Air Commerce Act of 1926 directed the Department of Commerce to "establish air traffic rules for the navigation, protection, and identification of aircraft." (U.S. Centennial of Flight Commission, n.d.)

Although these basic air traffic rules were initially effective, it soon became clear that more control over aircraft would be needed to prevent collisions between aircraft. Some airport operators began using ground-based, visual signals involving "air traffic controllers" standing on the field waving flags to communicate with pilots. Archie League was one of the system's first flagmen, beginning in the late 1920s at the airfield in St. Louis, Missouri. As has been the case with aviation, even this system would soon become outdated (U.S. Centennial of Flight Commission, n.d.).

As more aircraft were being equipped with radio communication, the flagmen were soon replaced by airport traffic control towers. In 1930, the first of these radio-equipped towers began operating at Cleveland Municipal Airport. Only two years later, virtually the entire fleet of airline aircraft had been equipped for radio-telephone communication. By 1935, approximately 20 radio control towers were in operation throughout the United States. Up to this point, the control of air traffic was focused on airport areas. Yet the safety and control of aircraft en route was also becoming a concern. As a result, in 1935, the major airlines using the Chicago, Cleveland, and Newark airports decided to coordinate the handling of aircraft between these cities. In December of that year, the first airway traffic control center opened at Newark, New Jersey. The following year, additional centers opened at Chicago and Cleveland (U.S. Centennial of Flight Commission, n.d.).

During these early days, aircraft were tracked by controllers using maps, blackboards, and small boat-shaped weights that became known as "shrimp boats" (Figure 3-1). Conrollers had no direct radio link with aircraft, but stayed in touch with airline dispatchers, airway radio operators, and airport traffic controllers via the telephone to stay abreast of aircraft position and progress on their route of flight (U.S. Centennial of Flight Commission, n.d.).

By the summer of 1936, the federal government assumed the responsibility for enroute air traffic control. However, airport towers continued to be operated by airports. This began to change in 1941 as the Civil Aeronautics Administration (CAA) began constructing and operating ATC towers. Once constructed, the CAA began operating these towers and was responsible for the operation of 115 towers by 1944. The CAA soon began taking over the operation of existing towers at airports as well (U.S. Centennial of Flight Commission, n.d.).

The first revolution to occur in air traffic control after WWII was the introduction of **radio detection and ranging (RADAR)**. By using radio waves to detect distant objects, radar technology allowed controllers the unique ability

Figure 3-1.
Early days of controlling air traffic with shrimp boats.

(FAA)

to "see" the position of aircraft on an electronic display. This technology was first used by the CAA in an experimental fashion in 1946, but by 1952 the CAA implemented routine use of radar technology for approach and departure control. In 1956, the CAA placed a large order for long-range radars that were to be used in enroute ATC (U.S. Centennial of Flight Commission, n.d.).

In an effort to consolidate some airport traffic control towers at smaller airports, the CAA began combining them with airway communication stations in 1950. These communications stations were the forerunners of flight service stations. By 1958, the CAA operated 84 of these combined station-towers, the last of which closed in 1981 (U.S. Centennial of Flight Commission, n.d.).

Radar beacons, or aircraft transponders, were first tested by the FAA in 1960. Aircraft operating in certain "positive control" areas were required to have a transponder, be piloted using instruments, and remain in contact with controllers. With the aid of transponders and these additional rules, controllers were able to reduce the separation between aircraft by as much as half the standard distance (U.S. Centennial of Flight Commission, n.d.).

In 1964, in an effort to minimize the complex web of airways that existed at the time, the FAA developed two layers of airways: one from 1,000 to 18,000 feet above ground level and the second from 18,000 to 45,000 feet above ground level. It also standardized aircraft instrument settings and navigation checkpoints to reduce the workload of controllers (U.S. Centennial of Flight Commission, n.d.).

The next breakthrough in ATC advances occurred with the adoption of computer technology. Although experimental use of computer technology by the FAA had begun as early as 1956, the period of 1965–1975 was characterized by a deliberate effort to apply this technology throughout the ATC system. Specifically, the FAA developed complex computer systems designed to replace the "shrimp boats" used to track aircraft. The system allowed controllers to view aircraft identification and position formation on a simulated three-dimensional radar screen. The automation this provided allowed controllers to focus on providing separation services to aircraft (U.S. Centennial of Flight Commission, n.d.).

In 1970, the FAA, in an effort to minimize the consequences of system congestion, established a Central Flow Control Facility. By analyzing clusters of congestion at a national level, this facility allows the FAA to implement programs (such as ground delay programs) to temporarily reduce demand in certain regions or metropolitan areas. In essence, this allows the FAA the ability to adopt a proactive approach to managing demand with capacity in the national airspace system. In 1994, the FAA opened a new **Air Traffic Control System Command Center** outside Washington, DC, which is considered to be the largest and most sophisticated facility of its kind in the world (U.S. Centennial of Flight Commission, n.d.).

In 1982, the **National Airspace System Plan** was introduced by the FAA. This plan was characterized by modernization and included goals of modernizing flight service stations, the ATC system, and ground-to-air surveillance and communication. Additionally, computers and software were modernized, air route traffic control centers were consolidated, and the number of flight service stations was reduced. In addition, new Doppler radars and advanced transponders complemented automatic radio broadcasts of surface and flight conditions (U.S. Centennial of Flight Commission, n.d.).

In an effort to further modernize ATC, in 1988 the FAA selected IBM to develop a new multi-billion dollar Advanced Automation System for the nation's enroute centers. By 1993, little had been accomplished and IBM was behind schedule and over budget. In response, the FAA revaluated its needs and in 1994 selected new contractors. Although additional delays were experienced, in 1999, controllers first began using an early version of the Standard Terminal Automation Replacement System, which included new displays and capabilities for approach control facilities. During the following year, the FAA finished replacing all of the display systems, which provided more efficient workstations for en route controllers (U.S. Centennial of Flight Commission, n.d.).

CLASSES OF AIRSPACE

There are two categories of airspace in the United States: regulatory and nonregulatory. Within these two categories of airspace, there is controlled, uncontrolled, special use, and other airspace. Regulatory airspace includes Class A, Class B, Class C, Class D, Class E, restricted areas, and prohibited areas (Figure 3-2). Nonregulatory airspace includes Military operations areas (MOAs), Warning areas, Alert areas, and Controlled firing areas. Controlled airspace refers to airspace in which air traffic control services are provided to both IFR flights and VFR flights in accordance with the airspace classification. Uncontrolled airspace is airspace within which air traffic control service is not provided.

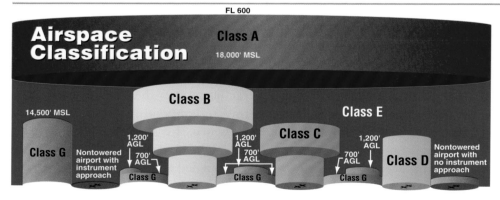

Figure 3-2.
Classes of U.S. airspace.

(FAA *Pilot's Handbook of Aeronautical Knowledge*)

AIRPORT MANAGEMENT

Controlled Airspace

Class A airspace is that airspace from 18,000 feet mean sea level (MSL) up to and including flight level (FL) 600, including the airspace overlying the waters within 12 nautical miles of the coast of the 48 contiguous states and Alaska. Unless otherwise authorized, each pilot operating aircraft in Class A airspace must operate under instrument flight rules (IFR) (FAA, 2011b).

Class B airspace is, generally, that airspace from the surface to 10,000 feet MSL surrounding the nation's busiest airports in terms of IFR operations or passenger enplanements. The configuration of each Class B airspace area is individually tailored and consists of a surface area and two or more layers, with some Class B airspace areas resembling upside-down wedding cakes. Each Class B airspace area is designed to contain all published instrument procedures once an aircraft enters the airspace. An ATC clearance is required for all aircraft to operate in the area, and all aircraft that are so cleared receive separation services within the airspace. The cloud clearance requirement for VFR operations is "clear of clouds" (FAA, 2011b).

Class C airspace is, generally, that airspace from the surface to 4,000 feet above the airport elevation surrounding those airports that have an operational control tower, are serviced by a radar approach control, and that have a certain number of IFR operations or passenger enplanements. Although the configuration of each Class C airspace area is individually tailored, the airspace usually consists of a surface area with a 5 nautical mile (NM) radius, and an outer circle with a 10 NM radius that extends from 1,200 feet to 4,000 feet above the airport elevation. Each pilot must establish two-way radio communications with the ATC facility providing air traffic services prior to entering the airspace and thereafter maintain those communications while within the airspace. This communication must begin within 20 miles of the Class C airport. Approach control frequencies are given in the *Airport/Facility Directory* (A/FD) and on sectional charts in magenta-bordered white boxes. VFR aircraft are only separated from IFR aircraft within the airspace (FAA, 2011b).

Class D airspace is, generally, that airspace from the surface to 2,500 feet above the airport elevation surrounding those airports that have an operational control tower. The configuration of each Class D airspace area is individually tailored and when instrument procedures are published, the airspace will normally be designed to contain the procedures. Arrival extensions for instrument approach procedures may be Class D or Class E airspace. Unless otherwise authorized, each pilot must establish two-way radio communications with the ATC facility providing air traffic services prior to entering the airspace and thereafter maintain those communications while in the airspace. No separation services are provided to VFR aircraft (FAA, 2011b).

Class E airspace is, generally, that controlled airspace not designated as Class A, Class B, Class C, or Class D. Class E airspace extends upward from either the surface or a designated altitude to the overlying or adjacent controlled airspace. When designated as a surface area, the airspace will be configured to contain all instrument procedures. Also in this class are federal airways, airspace beginning at either 700 or 1,200 feet AGL used to transition to or from the terminal or enroute environment, and enroute domestic and offshore airspace areas designated below 18,000 feet MSL. Unless designated at a lower altitude, Class E airspace begins at 14,500 MSL over the United States, including that airspace overlying the waters within 12 nautical miles of the coast of the 48 contiguous states and Alaska. Class E airspace does not include the airspace 18,000 MSL or above (FAA, 2011b).

Uncontrolled Airspace

Class G airspace is the only category of uncontrolled airspace. It includes that airspace not designated as Class A, Class B, Class C, Class D, or Class E. Although Class G airspace is uncontrolled and mainly the domain of VFR flights, pilots may operate on an IFR flight plan within Class G airspace for the purpose of arriving into or departing from an airport under IFR conditions with an instrument approach (FAA, 2011b).

Special Use Airspace

Special use airspace is that airspace where activities must be confined because of their nature, or where limitations are imposed on aircraft operations that are not a part of those activities, or possibly both. **Prohibited areas** contain airspace of defined dimensions identified by an area on the surface of the earth within which the flight of aircraft is prohibited. Such areas are established for security or other reasons associated with the national welfare. **Restricted areas** contain airspace identified by an area on the surface of the earth within which the flight of aircraft, while not wholly prohibited, is subject to restrictions. Activities within these areas must be confined because of their nature or limitations imposed upon aircraft operations that are not a part of those activities, or both. Restricted areas denote the existence of unusual, often invisible, hazards to aircraft such as artillery firing, aerial gunnery, or guided missiles. A **warning area** is airspace of defined dimensions, extending from three nautical miles outward from the coast of the United States that contains activity that may be hazardous to nonparticipating aircraft. **Military operations areas** (MOAs) consist of airspace of defined vertical and lateral limits established for the purpose of separating certain military training activities from IFR traffic. **Alert areas** are depicted on aeronautical charts to inform nonparticipating pilots of areas that may contain a high volume of pilot training or an unusual type of aerial activity. **Controlled firing areas** (CFAs) contain activities which, if not conducted in a controlled environment, could be hazardous to nonparticipating aircraft.

NAVAIDS

Any navigational approach made by an aircraft to an airport is conducted either with visual reference (**visual meteorological conditions**) or use of instruments (**instrument meteorological conditions**). A **visual approach** is an approach when either part or all of an instrument approach procedure is not completed (or was never initiated) and the approach is executed with visual reference to the terrain. This type of approach can be made anytime ATC approves it, when the destination airport meets visibility requirements of three statute miles or greater, and the cloud ceiling height is at least 1,000 feet above the ground level. A **contact approach** is a procedure that results from an instrument approach when the visibility is greater than one mile. In such cases, a pilot is cleared by ATC to make an instrument approach to land, and the pilot then uses visual reference to complete the approach when conditions allow. An **instrument approach** is an approach using horizontal and/or vertical guidance and is a procedure established by the FAA that outlines the routes and altitudes to be flown by an aircraft for safe flight from takeoff to landing. Instrument approaches can be either precision or non-precision. **Precision instrument approaches** provide both vertical and horizontal guidance, whereas **non-precision instrument approaches** provide only horizontal guidance.

To support these various types of approaches, **navigational aids (NAVAIDs)** are installed on or near airports. Many of these NAVAIDs can be used for both enroute and approach guidance. Although most are usable for non-precision approaches, some are also usable for precision approaches.

The most widely used precision NAVAID is the **instrument landing system (ILS)** (see Figure 3-3). This system provides both vertical and horizontal electronic guidance information to the pilot for purposes of aligning an aircraft with the centerline of a runway at the proper approach angle (typically 3 degrees). An ILS consists of a localizer beam (which provides horizontal guidance); a glide slope transmitter (which provides vertical guidance); an outer marker; a middle marker, and possibly an inner marker (providing distance information); an FAA-determined decision height (at which point a missed approach is executed if the runway environment is not in sight); and an approach lighting system (which allows the pilot to transition from instrument flight to visual flight). Functionally, aircraft guidance is provided by the localizer and glide slope, aircraft range information is provided by the marker beacons and distance measurement equipment (DME), and pilot visual information is provided by the approach and runway lighting systems (including touchdown, centerline, and runway light systems, as well as visual approach slope indicators [VASI] or precision approach path indicators [PAPI]).

The localizer antenna is usually located on the extended runway centerline outside the runway safety area between 1,000 to 2,000 feet beyond the end of the runway. The localizer equipment shelter is located at least 250 feet to either side of the antenna array and within 30 degrees of the extended longitudinal axis of the antenna array. The glideslope antenna may be located on either side of the runway, but is preferably located on the side providing the least

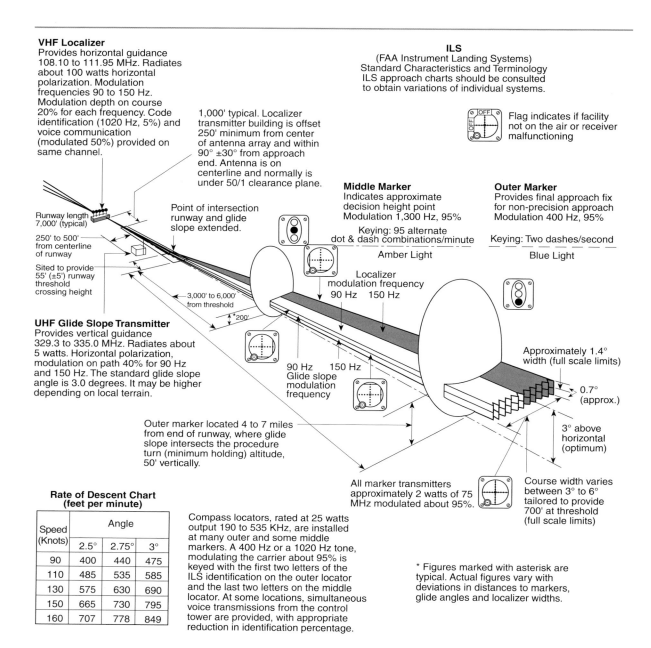

VHF Localizer
Provides horizontal guidance 108.10 to 111.95 MHz. Radiates about 100 watts horizontal polarization. Modulation frequencies 90 to 150 Hz. Modulation depth on course 20% for each frequency. Code identification (1020 Hz, 5%) and voice communication (modulated 50%) provided on same channel.

1,000' typical. Localizer transmitter building is offset 250' minimum from center of antenna array and within 90° ±30° from approach end. Antenna is on centerline and normally is under 50/1 clearance plane.

Runway length 7,000' (typical)

250' to 500' from centerline of runway

Sited to provide 55' (±5') runway threshold crossing height

Point of intersection runway and glide slope extended.

ILS
(FAA Instrument Landing Systems)
Standard Characteristics and Terminology
ILS approach charts should be consulted to obtain variations of individual systems.

Flag indicates if facility not on the air or receiver malfunctioning

Middle Marker
Indicates approximate decision height point
Modulation 1,300 Hz, 95%
Keying: 95 alternate dot & dash combinations/minute
Amber Light

Outer Marker
Provides final approach fix for non-precision approach
Modulation 400 Hz, 95%
Keying: Two dashes/second
Blue Light

Localizer modulation frequency
90 Hz   150 Hz

3,000' to 6,000' from threshold

*200'

UHF Glide Slope Transmitter
Provides vertical guidance 329.3 to 335.0 MHz. Radiates about 5 watts. Horizontal polarization, modulation on path 40% for 90 Hz and 150 Hz. The standard glide slope angle is 3.0 degrees. It may be higher depending on local terrain.

90 Hz   150 Hz
Glide slope modulation frequency

Approximately 1.4° width (full scale limits)

0.7° (approx.)

3° above horizontal (optimum)

Outer marker located 4 to 7 miles from end of runway, where glide slope intersects the procedure turn (minimum holding) altitude, 50' vertically.

All marker transmitters approximately 2 watts of 75 MHz modulated about 95%.

Course width varies between 3° to 6° tailored to provide 700' at threshold (full scale limits)

Rate of Descent Chart
(feet per minute)

Speed (Knots)	Angle		
	2.5°	2.75°	3°
90	400	440	475
110	485	535	585
130	575	630	690
150	665	730	795
160	707	778	849

Compass locators, rated at 25 watts output 190 to 535 KHz, are installed at many outer and some middle markers. A 400 Hz or a 1020 Hz tone, modulating the carrier about 95% is keyed with the first two letters of the ILS identification on the outer locator and the last two letters on the middle locator. At some locations, simultaneous voice transmissions from the control tower are provided, with appropriate reduction in identification percentage.

* Figures marked with asterisk are typical. Actual figures vary with deviations in distances to markers, glide angles and localizer widths.

Figure 3-3. Instrument landing system (ILS).

(From the FAA *Aeronautical Information Manual*)

interference from buildings, power lines, vehicles, and aircraft. The glideslope equipment shelter is located 10 feet behind the antenna and a minimum of 400 feet from the runway centerline. **Marker beacons** associated with the ILS may include an outer marker (OM), middle marker (MM), and inner marker (IM). The OM beacon is located four to seven nautical miles from the runway threshold to mark the point at which the glideslope altitude is verified or at which the descent without glideslope begins. The MM beacon is located 2,000 to 6,000 feet from the runway threshold. It marks the approximate decision point of a CAT I ILS approach. Finally, the IM beacon may be used to locate the decision point of a CAT II or III ILS approach, normally 1,000 feet from the threshold. Inner marker beacons are not used for CAT I ILS approaches (FAA, 2014a).

A standard ILS Category **(CAT) I** approach consists of a localizer, glide slope, final approach fix (FAF) or compass locator, marker system (outer and middle), an approach light system, and runway marking and lighting. Runways equipped with an ILS **CAT II** approach also require an inner marker and have specific RVR requirements. Likewise, a **CAT III** approach requires an inner marker along with specific RVR requirements, and is the most stringent and expensive of ILS systems because of the equipment involved. However, the CAT III approach also allows landings during the poorest visibility. Within the CAT III approach category, there are sub-categories consisting of **CAT IIIA**, **IIIB**, and **IIIC** (see Table 3-1).

Table 3-1. ILS decision height and visibility requirements.

ILS Category	Decision Height	Visibility or RVR
I	200 feet	1/2 mile (2400 feet)
I (with centerline and TDZ lights and RVR)	200 feet	1800 feet
II	100 feet	1200 feet
IIIA	*	700 feet
IIIB	*	150 feet
IIIC	*	+

* Decision height not specified, only visibility limits apply
+ Aircraft must have autoland capabilities and a qualified pilot

Runway visual range (RVR) equipment allows for measurement of horizontal visibility, although the exact number of RVRs required will depend on the runway approach category and physical runway length. ILS CAT I runways only require one touchdown RVR. CAT II runways with visibility minimums down to 1,600 feet require one touchdown RVR, while a CAT II runway with minimums below 1,600 RVR require touchdown and rollout RVRs. All CAT II runways require a touchdown RVR, with a rollout sensor also required for CAT II operations below 1,600 feet RVR. When the runway is in excess of 8,000 feet in length, a midpoint RVR sensor is also required in addition to the touchdown and rollout sensors for CAT II operations below RVR 1600.

CAT II runways greater than 8,000 feet in length, as well as CAT III runways with visibility minimums below 1,200 RVR, require touchdown, rollout, and midpoint RVRs. Touchdown RVRs are located 750 to 1,000 feet from the runway threshold, generally behind the MLS elevation antenna or ILS glideslope antenna. Midpoint RVRs are located within 250 feet of the center of the runway. Rollout RVRs are located 750 to 1,000 feet from the rollout end of the runway. Although older systems are composed of two separate parts (a projector and receiver), newer units are single-point and contain the projector and receiver on the same pole. Laterally, single-point units are located at least 400 feet from the runway centerline and 150 feet from a taxiway centerline. Older, dual-point units contain a transmissometer projector that is located 400 feet from the runway centerline and 150 feet from a taxiway centerline, and a receiver that is located 250 to 1,000 feet from the runway centerline (FAA, 2009; FAA, 2014a).

Although the localizer is part of the ILS, an airport may have a localizer-only approach. The **localizer** (**LOC** or LLZ) or **localizer directional aid (LDA)** projects a radio frequency beam down the runway from the departure end toward the approach end. The signal fans out narrowly along its path toward the centerline of the runway. This component provides lateral guidance, assisting the pilot in aligning the aircraft with the runway centerline. A localizer-only approach is considered a non-precision approach. The normal operation and use of a localizer result in what is known as a front course approach. On some localizer installations, the installed equipment and terrain allow for a reverse approach to the airport, or what is known as a non-precision localizer back course approach. Most of these approaches are being phased out of service. Newer localizers are more stable in their signal generation and do not normally generate a signal that can be used as a back course localizer approach.

A **non-directional beacon (NDB)** is used for air navigation primarily where bad terrain exists or if cost considerations dictate its use. Because NDBs are generally inexpensive and occupy little ground space, they can be situated almost anywhere (Figure 3-4). In fact, only a single short vertical antenna and normal electrical power are required for its operation. Non-directional refers to the type of radio signal transmitted. The transmitted signal is omnidirectional and can be received by an aircraft instrument known as an **automatic direction finder (ADF)** in the cockpit. In essence, the signal acts as a homing device for an aircraft.

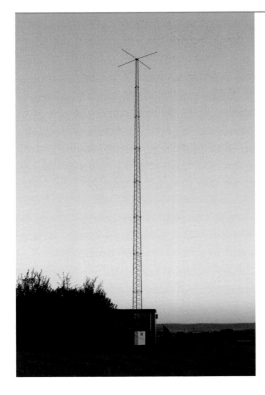

Figure 3-4.
Non-directional beacon.

(Wikimedia Commons; see credit on page 623)

NDBs are subject to environmental disturbances such as lightning, precipitation static, and interference from other radio stations, especially at night.

The **very high frequency omnidirectional range (VOR)**, which broadcasts 360-degree bearing information from the station using VHF signals, provides considerably greater accuracy and reliability than NDBs. VHF is used because it is not greatly affected by lightning static or reflection from terrain. The VOR located on an airport is typically a terminal VOR (TVOR). With this NAVAID, a distance of at least 500 feet from the centerline of any runway and 250 feet from the centerline of any taxiway should be maintained. Additionally, if an airport has intersecting runways, the TVOR should be located adjacent to the intersection to provide approach guidance to both runways. However, the TVOR antenna should be located at least 1,000 feet from any structures to avoid signal distortion. Metal fences should be at least 500 feet from the antenna (FAA, 2014a).

Tactical air navigation (TACAN) is the military's version of the VOR system. If VORs and TACANs are co-located within the same facility, it is known as a VORTAC (see Figure 3-5).

Figure 3-5. Very high frequency omnidirectional range (VOR) collocated with Tactical Air Navigation (TACAN), also known as VORTAC.

At those airports where siting or cost factors preclude installation of an ILS system, a **simplified directional facility (SDF)** may be installed to provide increased runway use during inclement weather. An SDF provides course information similar to a localizer, but it is less accurate, while also being more flexible given the surrounding environment. The approach techniques and procedures used in an SDF instrument approach are essentially the same as those employed in executing a standard localizer approach, except the SDF course may not be aligned with the runway and the course may be wider, resulting in less precision.

There was great effort during the 1970s and 1980s to develop an alternative instrument landing system that would resolve some of the problems experienced by the standard ILS. As a result, the **microwave landing system (MLS)** was developed. The MLS would alleviate standard ILS problems associated with terrain interference, long straight approaches into an airport, and growing radio frequency congestion. The MLS signal is fan-shaped and up to 60 degrees either side of the centerline (see Figure 3-6). The MLS signal provides continuous DME information to the pilot and allows for any number of multiple curved and segmented approaches to a runway. However, the FAA halted further development of MLS in 1994 with the recognition of GPS capability.

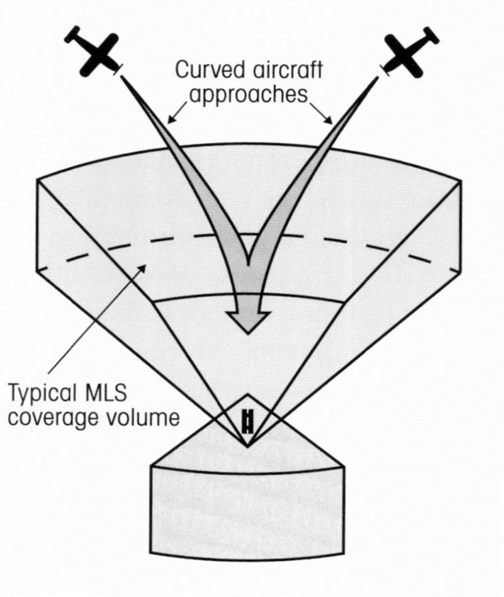

Figure 3-6.
Typical approaches into a microwave landing system-based approach.

(Wikimedia Commons; see credit on page 623)

The most advanced NAVAID is the **global positioning system (GPS)**. GPS is a satellite-based navigation system designed to eventually replace most of the current ground-based navigational systems in the United States. GPS achieves better accuracy than most land-based systems in that it provides velocity information and is less susceptible to ground-derived interference or error. GPS is not without faults, however. It is dependent on line-of-sight availability and unless augmented with ground-based stations, can only be used for non-precision approaches. For instance, signals from four satellites are necessary to provide a three-dimensional position. The loss of even one satellite signal can affect the integrity of the approach (Figure 3-7).

To obtain the precision guidance necessary for instrument approaches, an augmentation signal on the ground is necessary to ensure that the GPS signal is accurate, reliable, and available to everyone using the approach or enroute signal. The **Wide Area Augmentation System (WAAS)** is designed to enhance the capabilities of GPS signals to allow the system to be used for precision approaches without the need for on-airport equipment. The installation of a ground-based reference station improves GPS accuracy to within 30 feet. The FAA has determined that approximately 24 ground-based stations are required in the United States to meet the requirements for safety of flight. When coupled with the existing 24 orbiting satellite stations, WAAS is expected to satisfy the Category I instrument approach needs of most U.S. airports.

Figure 3-7.
Global positioning system satellite.

(Wikimedia Commons; see credit on page 623)

A **Ground-Based Augmentation System (GBAS)** places a ground-based transmitter in close proximity to, if not on, an airport. It performs the same function as the WAAS, which is to augment the satellite transmitters and to verify the satellite signals. However, it is of a lower power and range, as its purpose is to satisfy the need for accuracy and the number of transmitters for an aircraft to make a Category II or III approach to a runway.

LIGHTING

Airfield lighting systems may utilize incandescent lighting, tungsten-halogen lighting, fluorescent lighting, or light-emitting diodes (LEDs). The oldest lamp type in use, the longevity of incandescent lighting is primarily based upon the temperature generated. The higher the lumen output, the shorter the lifespan and hence the more frequent replacement requirement. Commonly called a "quartz lamp," tungsten-halogen bulbs produce a much hotter filament, and the quartz lens is better able to withstand the heat. However, the quartz bulb system is very sensitive to temperature variation and lens contamination. Fluorescent lamps generate light through low-pressure gas discharge. A ballast that is matched to the electrical requirements of the lamp is used to limit the current to the lamp electrodes. Florescent lamps are used for internal lighting of airfield signs. They are used only at airports where low ambient temperatures are not routinely experienced. Otherwise, incandescent or tungsten-halogen bulbs must be used, due to their heating characteristics. Lastly, a light-emitting diode (LED) has the benefits of a brighter emitting light, a longer lamp life, and lower power consumption. A drawback to LED lamps is that they do not generate heat to melt snow or ice accumulation. For this reason, LED installations may require supplemental heater coils in colder areas. LED technology is becoming more common at airports.

According to FAA Advisory Circular (AC) 150/5340-30, *Design and Installation Details for Airport Visual Aids*, airfield lighting can be grouped into the following categories:

1. Runway and taxiway edge lighting systems
2. Runway centerline and touchdown lighting systems
3. Taxiway lighting systems
4. Land and hold short lighting systems
5. Miscellaneous airfield aids
6. Approach lighting
   (FAA, 2011a)

Runway edge lights define the edge of the runway (see Figure 3-8). Runway edge lighting systems may be **low-intensity runway lights (LIRL)**, **medium-intensity runway lights (MIRL)**, or **high-intensity runway lights (HIRL)**. LIRL runway edge lights emit white light. MIRL and HIRL runway edge lights emit white light, except in the caution zone, which is the last 2,000 feet of runway or one-half the runway length, whichever is less. In the caution zone, yellow lights are substituted for white lights in the

Figure 3-8.
Runway edge lights.

direction facing the instrument approach threshold, with white lights in the opposite direction. Further, MIRL and HIRL have varying lighting intensities, or "steps," depending on intensity of lighting required (FAA, 2011a).

Threshold and **runway end lights** are installed in combination and emit green light outward from the runway toward the approach and red light toward the runway to mark the ends of the runway (see Figure 3-9). The green lights indicate the landing threshold to landing aircraft and the red lights indicate the end of the runway to both landing and departing aircraft (FAA, 2011a).

Stopway edge lights are unidirectional red lights oriented toward the takeoff direction of the runway. They are placed along its full length in two parallel rows that are equidistant from the runway centerline and coincident with the rows of runway edge lights (FAA, 2011a).

Taxiway edge lights define the edge of the taxiway and are blue in color (see Figure 3-10). The standard taxiway edge lighting system for airports is MITL—medium-intensity taxiway lights (FAA, 2011a).

Taxiway edge reflectors may be installed (a) in lieu of taxiway edge lights or (b) to enhance taxiway edge lights (see Figure 3-11). Reflectors are permitted in lieu of edge lights where a centerline system is installed. 14 CFR §139.311 actually requires airports

Figure 3-9.
Threshold end lights.

(Brett Fay, Lakeland Linder Regional Airport.)

Figure 3-10.
Taxiway edge lights.

(Brett Fay, Lakeland Linder Regional Airport.)

Figure 3-11.
Taxiway edge reflectors.

(Adam Lunn, Lakeland Linder Regional Airport.)

to have one taxiway lighting system installed, which can consist of centerline lights, centerline reflectors, edge lights, or edge reflectors (FAA, 2011a).

Runway centerline lighting is required for CAT II and CAT III runways and for CAT I runways used for landing operations below 2,400 feet RVR. Runway centerline lights are required on runways used for takeoff operations below 1,600 feet RVR. The last 3,000-foot portion of the runway centerline lighting system is color coded to warn pilots of the impending runway end. Alternating red and white lights are installed, starting with red, as seen from 3,000 feet to 1,000 feet from the runway end, and red lights are installed in the last 1,000-foot portion (FAA, 2011a).

Touchdown zone lights consist of two rows of transverse light bars located symmetrically about the runway centerline. Each light bar consists of three unidirectional lights facing the landing threshold. The touchdown zone lights extend to 3,000 feet, or one-half the runway length for runways less than 6,000 feet, from the threshold with the first light bars located 100 feet from the threshold (FAA, 2011a).

Taxiway centerline lights provide taxi guidance between the runway and apron areas (see Figure 3-12). A taxiway centerline lighting system consists of unidirectional or bidirectional in-pavement lights installed parallel to the centerline of the taxiway. Taxiway centerline lights are green, with the exception of lead-off lights,[1] lead-on lights,[2] and taxiway centerline lights that cross a runway[3] (FAA, 2011a).

Runway guard lights (RGL) provide a visual indication to pilots and ground vehicle operators approaching the runway holding position that they are about to enter an active runway (see Figure 3-13). They can be elevated or in-pavement (FAA, 2011a).

Stop bars provide a distinctive "stop" signal to a pilot or ground vehicle operator approaching a runway, in the form of a row of unidirectional in-pavement red lights and an elevated red light on each side of the taxiway. In low-visibility conditions, controlled stop bars are used to permit access to the active runway. Uncontrolled stop bars protect the active runway at taxiway/runway intersections that are not part of the low-visibility taxi route (FAA, 2011a).

---

[1] Alternating green and yellow lights are installed from the runway centerline (beginning with a green light) to one centerline light position beyond the runway hold or ILS/MLS critical area hold position, ending with a yellow light.

[2] Color-coded with the same yellow/green color pattern as lead-off lights.

[3] Color-coded yellow/green, ending with a bidirectional yellow/green light fixture one centerline light position beyond the runway holding position painted marking or ILS/MLS critical area holding position painted marking.

Figure 3-12.
Taxiway centerline lights.

(Wikimedia Commons; see credit on page 623)

Clearance bars are designed to (a) advise pilots and vehicle drivers that they are approaching a hold point (other than a runway holding position), and (b) advise pilots and vehicle drivers that they are approaching an intersecting taxiway. Clearance bars consist of a row of three in-pavement yellow lights to indicate a low visibility hold point (FAA, 2011a).

Figure 3-13.
Elevated runway guard lights.

Land and hold short lighting systems are installed to indicate the location of hold-short points on runways approved for **land and hold short operations (LAHSO)**. LAHSO is an air traffic control procedure that requires pilots to land and hold short of a point (typically an intersecting runway being used), allowing the airport to balance the needs for increased airport capacity and system efficiency, consistent with safety. The pilot-in-command should determine if the aircraft can safely land and stop within the **available landing distance (ALD)**, a distance published in the *Airport/Facility Directory* (A/FD). If unable, the pilot-in-command should not accept a LAHSO clearance. To provide a visual of the LAHSO point, the land and hold short lighting system consists of a row of six or seven in-pavement unidirectional pulsing white lights installed across the runway at the hold-short point (see Figure 3-14) (FAA, 2011a).

Figure 3-14.
Land and hold short lighting.

(Brett Fay, Lakeland Linder Regional Airport.)

Airport **rotating beacons** are designed to indicate the location of a lighted airport; as such, the rotating beacon is an integral part of an airfield lighting system (see Figure 3-15). All airport rotating beacons project a beam of light in two directions, 180 degrees apart. For civil land airports only, the beacon flashes an alternating white (clear) and green light at 24–30 flashes per minute. Beacons should be installed within 5,000 feet of a runway and in an area that will not (a) create light interference for pilots or controllers and (b) obstruct the projection of the rotating beacon light beam. Generally, rotating beacons are located on airport property (FAA, 2011a; FAA, 2014).

Obstruction lights are installed on all obstructions that present a hazard to air traffic, warning pilots of the presence of an obstruction during hours of darkness and during periods of limited daytime visibility (see Figure 3-16). An obstruction's height, size, shape, and the area in which it is located determine the position of lights on the obstruction and the number of lights required to

Figure 3-15. (left) Rotating beacon.

Figure 3-16. (right) Obstruction lights.

adequately light the obstruction to assure visibility of such lighting from an aircraft at any angle of approach (FAA, 2011a).

In addition to various types of airfield lighting, approach lighting systems are utilized to allow the pilot to transition from instrument flying within the cockpit to visually locating the runway outside the cockpit (Figure 3-17). Approach lighting systems are oriented on the extended runway centerline, and extend from the runway threshold toward the approach. All approach lighting systems require a space 400 feet wide extending 200 feet beyond the outermost light of the approach lighting system. According to FAA categorization, the following are common approach lighting system configurations:

1. High intensity approach lighting system with sequenced flashing lights (ALSF-2)—A high intensity ALS that is 2,400 feet in length with sequenced flashing lights. Required for CAT II and III precision approaches.

2. Medium intensity approach lighting system with runway alignment indicator lights (MALSR)—A medium intensity ALS that is 2,400 feet in length with runway alignment indicator lights (RAILS). Approved for CAT I approaches, the MALS portion is 1,400 feet in length, while the RAIL portion extends outward an additional 1,000 feet.

3. Medium intensity approach lighting system (MALS)—A medium intensity ALS that is 1,400 feet in length. It enhances nonprecision instrument and night visual approaches.

4. Medium intensity approach lighting system with sequence flashing lights (MALSF)—A medium intensity ALS that is identical to MALS, with the exception of sequenced flashing lights that are added to the outer three light bars. The purpose of the sequenced flashing lights is to improve recognition of the ALS by pilots when there is light pollution/distraction in the local airport vicinity.

Figure 3-17.
Approach lighting system.

(hkratky/Bigstock.com)

5. Omnidirectional approach lighting systems (ODALS)—Typically installed on a nonprecision instrument runway that is difficult to identify due to light pollution in the local airport vicinity. It consists of seven lights, with five of these seven serving as sequence flashing omnidirectional lights. These five lights are located on the extended runway centerline beginning 300 feet from the runway threshold and spaced at 300-foot intervals. The remaining two lights are installed on either side of the runway threshold. ODALS require a 400-foot-wide area that extends 1,700 feet from the threshold. (FAA, 2014a)

Depending upon the system, the approach lighting system may consist of the following components:

1. Sequence flashing lights
2. Approach lights
3. Crossbar lights
4. Runway end identifier lights (REIL)
5. Visual approach slope indicators (VASI)
6. Precision approach path indicators (PAPI)

Sequence flashing lights are a series of five lights that extend past the 1,000-foot mark of the approach lights. Flashing in sequence and in one direction, they are commonly referred to as "the rabbit" because they lead the aircraft toward the runway, just as a mechanical rabbit leads greyhounds around a race track (FAA, 2011a).

The **approach lights** are a series of lights uniformly extending from the threshold out to a point where the pilot can make a timely transition from instrument to visual reference. Approach lighting varies based on the operational requirements of a particular approach. Their purpose is to allow the pilot to visually verify the runway environment in low visibility conditions, which is made easier by extending approach lighting closer to the pilot on approach (FAA 2011a).

White **crossbar lights** are a series of lights positioned perpendicular on both sides of the primary approach lights. They are used by a pilot as a visual aid for leveling the aircraft's wings. They also provide information on distance to the runway, since they are positioned at fixed distances from the threshold (FAA, 2011a).

Additionally, **runway end identifier lights (REIL)** aid in early identification of the runway and runway end. These lights, in the form of two flashing lights located near the end of the runway, are mostly used at airports located in areas with significant light pollution.

Visual approach slope indicators (VASI) provide a visual approach path on proper glide slope to the runway (Figure 3-18). These lights are visible from 3–5 miles during the day and up to 20 miles or more at night. The visual glide path of the VASI provides safe obstruction clearance within plus or minus 10 degrees of the extended runway centerline and up to 4 nautical miles from the runway threshold. They come in different arrays of 2- or 3-bar systems that have 2, 4, 6, 12, or 24 lights each. The most common VASI type is a 2-bar, 4-light unit (FAA, 2011a).

Precision approach path indicators (PAPI) serve the same purpose of VASI but are generally more standard. They are installed in a single row of either two or four light units (Figure 3-19). These lights are visible from about 5 miles during the day and up to 20 miles at night. The visual glide path of the PAPI typically provides safe obstruction clearance within plus or minus 10 degrees of the extended runway centerline and to 4 nautical miles from the runway threshold.

Figure 3-18.
Visual approach slope indicator (VASI).

Figure 3-19.
Precision approach path indicator (PAPI).

(Nan Phanitsuda Sophonpanasak, Denver International Airport)

Figure 3-29. Runway landing designator marking.
(iofoto.com/Bigstock.com)

Figure 3-30. Runway centerline marking.

Figure 3-31. Runway threshold marking.

Figure 3-32. Runway aiming point marking.
(iofoto.com/Bigstock.com)

Figure 3-33. Runway touchdown zone marking.
(shutterrudder/Bigstock.com)

Figure 3-34. Runway edge marking.

Figure 3-35. Runway displaced threshold marking.
(©iStock.com/DraganSaponjic)

- *Chevron markings*—This marking, yellow in color, identifies paved blast pads, stopways, and EMAS (engineered materials arresting systems) in relation to the end of the runway (Figure 3-36).
- *Runway shoulder marking*—This marking is used, when needed, as a supplement to further delineate a paved runway shoulder that pilots have mistaken or are likely to mistake as usable runway. This marking is used only in conjunction with the runway edge marking (Figure 3-37).

Figure 3-36. Chevron markings.

Figure 3-37. Runway shoulder marking.

(Diana Fernandez, San Diego International Airport)

In addition to runways, taxiways also provide guidance and direction information to pilots and operators of ground vehicles. This is done primarily through markings. Taxiway markings include:

1. *Holding position markings*—This marking is designed to prevent aircraft and vehicles from entering into critical areas associated with a runway safety area and from entering into critical areas associated with navigational aids, or to control traffic at the intersection of taxiways. There are six operational situations (cases) in which three different holding position marking schemes may be used. The most common application is used for an aircraft that will need to hold short prior to entering an active runway (Figure 3-38).

2. *Taxiway centerline markings*—Designed to provide pilots and ground vehicle operators continuous visual guidance along a designated path, this marking—unlike the runway centerline marking—has no gaps, except in certain situations. To reinforce situational awareness before entering a runway, taxiway centerlines are enhanced for 150 feet prior to a runway holding position marking on those taxiways that directly enter a runway. This enhancement creates a triple-wide marking, with a row of dashed yellow markings on each side of the standard taxiway centerline marking. (Figure 3-39).

3. *Taxiway edge marking*—This marking can be either a dual continuous or dashed marking and is used along a taxi route to alert pilots where the demarcation line exists between usable pavement for taxi operations and

unusable pavement. The dashed taxiway edge marking is used on pavement that permits pilots to cross over this surface marking (Figure 3-40).

4. *Surface painted holding position signs*—This surface painted sign provides supplemental visual cues that alert pilots and vehicle drivers of an upcoming holding position location and the associated runway designator as another method to minimize the potential for a runway incursion. This surface sign painted is identical to the mandatory sign located adjacent to each taxiway entering a runway. It has a red background with white numbers (and letters if required to indicate the runway designation) (Figure 3-41).

5. *Taxiway shoulder marking*—Although optional, this marking indicates the non-usable paved shoulders. The taxiway shoulder marking is yellow, with straight lines painted perpendicular to the taxiway on the paved shoulder. (Figure 3-42).

Figure 3-38. Holding position marking.

Figure 3-40. Taxiway edge marking.

Figure 3-39. Taxiway centerline markings.

Figure 3-41. Surface painted holding position signs.

Figure 3-42. Taxiway shoulder marking.

6. *Surface painted taxiway direction signs*—The surface painted taxiway direction sign is used with an arrow to provide directional guidance at an intersection (Figure 3-43).

7. *Surface painted taxiway location signs*—This surface painted sign identifies the taxiway upon which the aircraft is located. This marking is used to supplement other signs located along the taxiway system (Figure 3-44).

8. *Surface painted gate destination signs*—This surface painted sign is used to assist pilots in locating their assigned terminal gate, especially useful for low-visibility operations.

9. *Surface painted apron entrance point sign*—This surface painted sign is used to assist pilots in locating their position along the edges of a large, continuous apron serving the terminal gates. The marking is especially useful for identifying both the entrances and exits in and along the terminal complex.

10. *Geographic position marking*—This marking is used repeatedly along a designated taxi route to serve as an indicator of a location or spot so that pilots can confirm holding points or report their location while taxiing during periods of low-visibility operations. It is generally used along low-visibility taxi routes associated with a surface movement guidance and control system (SMGCS) plan. It is known as a pink spot and is the only airfield marking with pink paint. It is circular and outlined by a white border and a black border, with black number/letter designation (Figure 3-45).

11. *Ramp control markings*—This optional marking is used to facilitate the local ramp tower or the FAA airport traffic control tower in the movement of aircraft and vehicles to designated areas of ramps, aprons, and other paved areas between non-movement areas and the movement area. These markings may be either circular or triangle-shaped and consist of a black inscription on a yellow background.

Other markings include:

1. *Vehicle roadway markings*—These consist of (a) roadway edge lines to delineate each edge of the roadway, (b) a dashed line to separate lanes within the edges of the roadway, and, where appropriate, (c) a roadway stop line (bar) (Figure 3-46).

2. *Very high frequency omnidirectional range (VOR) receiver checkpoint marking*—The VOR receiver checkpoint marking is used by pilots to check their aircraft instruments with navigational aid signals. It consists of a painted circle with a painted directional arrow that is aligned toward the azimuth of the VOR facility.

3. *Non-movement area boundary marking*—This marking is used to delineate the movement areas under direct control by the airport traffic control tower from the non-movement areas that are not under their control. It is a marking important for everyone with driving privileges at the airport to properly

Figure 3-43. Surface painted taxiway direction sign.

(Lee Brown, Fort Lauderdale-Hollywood International Airport)

Figure 3-44. Surface painted taxiway location sign.

Figure 3-45. Geographic position marking.

(Nan Phanitsuda Sophonpanasak, Denver International Airport)

Figure 3-46. Vehicle roadway markings.

identify. In essence, it appears as a smaller marking very similar to the mandatory holding position marking. With one solid yellow marking and one dashed yellow marking, the solid line is always on the non-movement side, signifying that permission must be received prior to crossing over the marking. (Figure 3-47).

4. *Runway and taxiway closure markings*—For runways and taxiways that are permanently closed, the lighting circuits are disconnected. For closed runways, all markings for runway thresholds, runway designations, touchdown aiming points, and touchdown zones are obliterated. Only solid yellow "X" markings are painted to indicate closed pavement. For runways that closed only temporarily, lighted X markings are typically used. These hydraulically raised lighted Xs are powered by a generator and provide significantly enhanced visibility of the closure marking both in day and night situations. Lights can be steady or flashing (Figure 3-48).

Figure 3-48. Lighted X used for temporary runway closures.
(Nan Phanitsuda Sophonpanasak, Denver International Airport)

Figure 3-47. Non-movement area boundary marking.

Radio Communications

In aviation, effective communication is critical. To ensure safety, this communication must occur in both controlled and uncontrolled airspace. This communication generally involves ATC, and involves both pilots and ground vehicle operators. First, aircraft communicate with ATC at controlled airports. At uncontrolled airports, pilots communicate with each other via the **common traffic advisory frequency (CTAF)**. Likewise, drivers of vehicles (such as ARFF, operations, or maintenance) communicate with ATC at controlled airports and with aircraft at uncontrolled airports via the CTAF.

Whether contact is initiated by a pilot or driver of a vehicle, proper radio communication requires the person to identify who is being contacted, who is contacting, location, and intention. For instance, "Tampa Ground [who is being contacted], this is Airport 8 [who is contacting] on the west ramp [location], requesting permission to start airfield inspection [intention]." Generally, a newly hired airport operations employee will find radio communication much easier if they already have experience (such as may have been acquired while pursuing a private pilot certificate). If not, it can be quite intimidating to both learn the airfield layout at a major international airport and properly communicate with ATC. It takes patience and plenty of practice.

Airfield Capacity

One of the determining factors that clearly plays a role in the success of any airport is the capacity of the airfield. Although the majority of airports in the United States are not challenged in this area, there are also many (mostly in the commercial service category) that regularly see demand approach and even exceed capacity, especially during certain times of the day (Figure 3-53). The capacity of an airfield is, therefore, integral in allowing that airport to meet demand for air traffic.

The concentration of aircraft arrivals and departures at an airport can create congestion and result in delay. Delay is an indicator that activity levels are approaching or exceeding capacity levels. The impacts of delays can be measured in many ways, and include direct costs (such as increased fuel use and crew time), indirect costs (such as the extra travel time for passengers and missed connections, resulting in delays on other airlines and their passengers), and increased air emissions (FAA, 2010).

Airfield capacity can be explained using an interstate as an example. If the capacity (i.e., number of lanes) is not sufficient to accommodate the demand (i.e., rush hour traffic), congestion and, subsequently, delays will result. Similarly, if an airport does not have the runway, taxiway, and gate capacity to accommodate the number of aircraft operations scheduled for that airport during a specific period of time, demand will exceed capacity, resulting in congestion and delays.

Figure 3-53.
Airfield congestion.

(Wikimedia Commons; see credit on page 623)

MEASURES OF CAPACITY

Although several measures of runway capacity are in use, each is designed to estimate the number of aircraft operations (arrivals and/or departures) that can be accommodated on the runway system during some specified time period. It is important to note, however, that runway capacity is not static. It changes depending on the circumstances involved, and there are many factors (to be discussed next) that affect capacity. Thus, when discussing runway capacity, it is important to remember that numbers typically refer to the average number (or stated another way, the expected number) of movements that can be performed in a given time period.

Maximum Throughput Capacity

Considered the most fundamental and least subjective measure of runway capacity, the **maximum throughput capacity** is defined as the expected number of movements (or operations) that can be performed in one hour on a runway system without violating air traffic rules. It assumes continuous aircraft demand. In essence, how many aircraft operations can the runway system handle when the system is maxed out? Also known as saturation capacity, this measure of capacity requires various conditions—such as separation requirements, aircraft mix, mix of movements, and allocation of movements among runways—to be defined. One significant disadvantage of this measure is that it does not take into account any service criteria. In other words, the measure only specifies the number of aircraft movements that can be processed on average per hour, if the runway system is utilized at its maximum potential and considering continuous aircraft demand. Delays, whether they are several minutes or several hours, are not a concern with this measure (de Neufville and Odoni, 2003).

Practical Hourly Capacity

The **practical hourly capacity (PHCAP)** is a measure of capacity that has been in use by the FAA since the 1960s. PHCAP is defined as the expected number of movements that can be performed in one hour with some average delay per movement (typically defined as 4 minutes). This measure differs from maximum throughput capacity because it defines a level of service (average delay of four minutes per movement). The runway system is considered at capacity when that delay threshold is exceeded. Generally, the PHCAP of a runway system is approximately 80 to 90 percent of its maximum throughput capacity. Of course, at most major airports today, delays often greatly exceed 4 minutes per movement. As a result, these airports are operating at a level of service that is much lower than what was considered acceptable in 1960 (de Neufville and Odoni, 2003).

Sustained Capacity

Sustained capacity is a measure of runway capacity defined as the number of movements per hour that can be reasonably sustained over a period of several hours. The term "reasonably sustained" refers to the air traffic control system, including the workload of controllers. Although it is preferable for the air traffic system to operate at full potential all the time, this is not realistic. Indeed, such a level of full potential and maximum efficiency can often only be sustained for periods of one to several hours. As a result, sustained capacity only considers what can be sustained over this period of several hours. As a rule of thumb, the sustained capacity is equal to approximately 90 percent of maximum throughput capacity when runway configurations with high maximum throughput capacity are in use. Likewise, the sustained capacity is equal to approximately 100 percent of maximum throughput capacity with configurations with low maximum throughput capacity (de Neufville and Odoni, 2003).

Declared Capacity

A final measure of runway capacity is known as **declared capacity**. This measure is defined as the number of aircraft movements that can be accommodated per hour at a reasonable level of service. Even though this measure is mostly relied upon at airports outside the United States (especially in connection with schedule coordination and slot allocation), there is no standard definition of declared capacity, nor a standard methodology for setting it. Although declared capacity may be determined by the capacities of the terminals or gate areas (which may be more constraining than the capacity of the runway system), it is typically equal to approximately 85 to 90 percent of the maximum throughput capacity (de Neufville and Odoni, 2003).

FACTORS AFFECTING CAPACITY

The capacity of an airfield is very dynamic, often varying throughout the day. This variation is caused by a number of factors that interact in an oftentimes complex manner. Although airport management may be able to control some aspects of airfield capacity, other factors, such as weather and airspace characteristics, are impossible to control. This section details many of the factors affecting the capacity of airports.

Number and Geometric Layout of Runways

One of the most important factors affecting the capacity of an airfield is the number and geometric layout of runways. Simply having a certain number of runways is not enough; these runways must be in use. Therefore, the number of "simultaneously active runways" must be considered. The runway configuration in use is also important. Although an airport may have two parallel runways, is each used for both arrivals and departures, or is one dedicated to arrivals while the other is dedicated to departures? What about the types of aircraft? This allocation of types of aircraft and movements may change throughout the day, for reasons such as noise, weather, operational needs, etc. For example, Boston/ Logan International Airport can operate in about 40 different configurations, although it only has five runways. Finally, the separation between parallel runways and the runway intersections will determine the degree of dependence among runways. Independent runways are preferred, but not always a reality. Although an airport can greatly enhance capacity by constructing a new runway, this is an expensive option that requires available land and political support (de Neufville and Odoni, 2003).

Separation Requirements

To ensure safety within the airspace system, the FAA has developed certain separation standards that apply to aircraft flying under instrument flight rules (IFR). These separation requirements, however, effectively determine the maximum number of aircraft that can safely operate in a given amount of airspace or a runway system at one time. In the United States, aircraft belong to one of the following classes, according to their **maximum takeoff weight (MTOW)**:

- MTOW greater than 255,000 pounds: Class H—Heavy
- MTOW between 41,000 pounds and 255,000 pounds: Class L—Large
- MTOW less than 41,000 pounds: Class S—Small
- Boeing 757—due to strong and unique wake vortices that were the factor in several accidents

Based on the class, there are minimum separation standards that must be maintained at all times between two aircraft operating successively. The distance (in nautical miles) that must be maintained will vary based on whether a single runway or parallel runways are in use. Additionally, the sequencing of movements will affect the separation requirements. Specifically, sequencing can include arrival followed by arrival, arrival followed by departure, departure followed by departure, and/or departure followed by arrival (de Neufville and Odoni, 2003).

Visibility, Cloud Ceiling, Precipitation, Winds

Of all weather conditions that most affect airfield capacity, cloud ceiling and visibility have the most impact. As stated in 14 CFR §91.155, no person may operate an aircraft under VFR when the flight visibility is less, or at a distance from clouds that is less, than shown in Table 3-2. Generally, capacity improves as the weather improves. Under visual meteorological conditions (VMC), ATC often requests that pilots maintain visual separation from preceding aircraft during final phases of flight, which greatly increases capacity per runway compared to what can be achieved under IFR.

Winds also affect airfield capacity in a number of ways. A runway can be used only when crosswinds are within certain limits and tailwinds do not exceed 5 or 6 knots. This means, of course, that the specific runway configuration in use is often dictated by prevailing winds. At some airports, prevailing winds can greatly reduce capacity. Consider Boston/Logan International Airport. When winds are strong out of the northwest, only runway 33L is available for arriving turbojet aircraft because runway 33R is only 2,557 feet long. In these conditions, arrivals into Boston/Logan may be delayed up to two hours. At airports with winds less than 5 knots (calm or light and variable), the airfield configuration in use is at the discretion of ATC (de Neufville and Odoni, 2003).

Aircraft Mix

The mix of aircraft types will also influence runway capacity. For instance, consider a mix of 50 percent each of heavy and small aircraft arriving into a single runway. This nonhomogeneous mix of aircraft will require increased separation standards and will negatively impact the capacity of that runway. If, however, a relatively homogenous mix of aircraft is the norm, capacity will improve and the work of air traffic controllers will be simplified.

Table 3-2. Flight rules related to ceiling and visibility.

Airspace			Flight Visibility	Distance from Clouds
Class A			Not applicable	Not applicable.
Class B			3 statute miles	Clear of clouds.
Class C			3 statute miles	500 feet below.
				1,000 feet above.
				2,000 feet horizontal.
Class D			3 statute miles	500 feet below.
				1,000 feet above.
				2,000 feet horizontal.
Class E	Less than 10,000 feet MSL		3 statute miles	500 feet below.
				1,000 feet above.
				2,000 feet horizontal
	At or above 10,000 feet MSL		5 statute miles	1,000 feet below.
				1,000 feet above.
				1 statute mile horizontal.
Class G	1,200 feet or less above the surface (regardless of MSL altitude)	Day*	1 statute mile	Clear of clouds.
		Night*	3 statute miles	500 feet below.
				1,000 feet above.
				2,000 feet horizontal.
	More than 1,200 feet above the surface but less than 10,000 feet MSL	Day	1 statute mile	500 feet below.
				1,000 feet above.
				2,000 feet horizontal.
		Night	3 statute miles	500 feet below.
				1,000 feet above.
				2,000 feet horizontal.
	More than 1,200 feet above the surface and at or above 10,000 feet MSL		5 statute miles	1,000 feet below.
				1,000 feet above.
				1 statute mile horizontal.

*except as provided in §91.155(b)

Sequencing of Movements

Yet another factor that influences airfield capacity is the sequencing of movements on a runway. This specifically refers to the mix of arrivals and departures, particularly when a runway is used for both operations. Generally, the capacity of a runway used only for departures is higher than the capacity of a runway used only for arrivals, given the same mix of aircraft. In reality, airports tend to see clusters of arrivals or departures, depending on the time of day. Even with a steady stream of arrivals, ATC may "squeeze" in one or more departures between arrivals, especially when there is a significant separation between arriving aircraft, as would occur with a small aircraft landing behind a heavy aircraft. At Los Angeles International Airport, for example, the outboard parallel runways (7R-25L and 6L-24R) are generally used for arrivals, while the inboard parallel runways (7L-25R and 6R-24L) are used for departures.

Taxiway Exits

The presence and location of taxiway exits also affect runway capacity. The longer an aircraft stays on the runway, the less capacity that runway has over a given time period. Therefore, it is important for well-placed taxiway exits to be part of any runway. **Runway occupancy time (ROT)** is defined as the time between when an aircraft touches down on the runway until it is clear of that runway. Most important to reducing runway occupancy time is the appropriate use of high-speed exits. Rather than the 90-degree angle of a typical exit, the 30-degree high-speed exit allows an aircraft to exit a runway at a speed faster than that required for a 90-degree exit. However, constructing a high-speed exit requires more land and engineering and construction expense. Generally, however, a runway will need no more than two or three high-speed exits for a single direction of runway operation.

Air Traffic Control System

To ensure efficient use of an airfield resulting in greater capacity, properly trained air traffic controllers must operate within an efficient and functional ATC system. For example, with an ATC system that provides accurate position information on aircraft to skilled controllers, tight separations between successive aircraft on final approach can be achieved. The role of the ATC system to maximize airfield capacity should continue to improve with the implementation of NextGen. Indeed, NextGen is designed to accommodate the growing number of users expected in the air transportation system of tomorrow with continued safety and reduced delays.

Noise and Other Environmental Considerations

Of the various environmental considerations that affect airports and airport capacity, noise tends to be the most significant. Many airports have noise-restricted runways spelled out in a noise abatement program. Noise curfews and

The informal runway use program at Tampa International Airport is a voluntary program that seeks pilot cooperation to minimize the impact of aircraft noise (specifically from turbojet aircraft) in the surrounding community. The program is in the form of a Letter to Airmen, which is an agreement between the airport and ATCT. In general, the program is based on a priority runway use assignment for turbojet aircraft operations dependent on the direction of the prevailing wind, weather, and operational constraint. Specifically, from 6:00 a.m. to midnight, if on a south operation, runway 19R for departures is preferred. If on a north operation, runway 1L for arrivals is preferred. During the evening hours of midnight to 6:00 a.m., if traffic, wind, weather, and field conditions permit, runway 19R will be used for turbojet departures and 1L for turbojet arrivals. Additionally, after departure, south operations will be assigned a heading of 200 if departing runway 19R and a heading of 210 if departing runway 19L. Although noise complaints are still recorded, this program has significantly reduced noise-affected areas of Tampa and generally created better community relations for the airport.

aircraft stage restrictions may also be in force. As such, air traffic controllers use noise criteria in determining which runway configurations to use, affecting airport capacity. Noise-related restrictions, therefore, negatively impact airfield capacity by reducing the frequency with which various high-capacity configurations can be used.

Airfield Delay

When airfield capacity is insufficient to meet aircraft demand, airfield delay results, and these delays can be significant. Rather than being rare, flight delays at the nation's major airports are quite common. A great deal of effort is expended in measuring airfield delay and enacting solutions to minimize delay at the nation's airports. Currently, we know that delays:

- May be present even when the demand rate is lower than capacity
- Depend in a nonlinear way on changes in demand and/or capacity, becoming very sensitive to even very small changes when demand is very close to or greater than capacity
- Display a complex dynamic behavior over any time span when the runway system is heavily utilized

(de Neufville and Odoni, 2003, p. 435)

Delay is measured and tracked in different ways. For example, the U.S. Department of Transportation tracks the on-time performance of airlines and the reasons for flights arriving after their scheduled arrival times. Air traffic controllers track instances in which aircraft are delayed 15 minutes or more in a given flight segment. The FAA then uses this information to monitor the day-to-day operation of the air traffic control system. Airport planners typically use the average delay per aircraft operation as a measure of congestion. This statistic can be forecast and translated into a dollar cost of delay (FAA, 2010).

ACCEPTABLE LEVELS OF DELAY

It is often impossible to eliminate all delays; therefore, airports and aircraft operators have generally considered a certain average level of delay to be acceptable. Although this level varies among stakeholders, acceptable delay is a judgment involving several factors. First, stakeholders must realize that some level of delay is unavoidable due to factors (such as weather) that simply cannot be controlled. Next, the demand for service is often quite random and affected by many different stakeholders (such as when airlines choose to schedule arrivals and departures). It should also be recognized that some delays would be too costly to eliminate (such as constructing an additional runway). Finally, due to the previously mentioned random nature of demand, there will typically be some aircraft experiencing delay that has been deemed acceptable (AAAE, 2005).

Based on these considerations, what is an acceptable average level of delay? Although this will vary by airport, and even throughout a 24-hour period, delays generally average from 4–6 minutes per operation at the point when practical capacity is reached. If average delays are greater than 9 minutes per operation, the airport would be considered severely congested. There is no defined acceptable level of delay, although the U.S. Department of Transportation specifically records delays of 15 minutes or greater.

CAUSES OF DELAY

Aircraft experience delays due to a number of factors. These factors, some of which are controllable, can be grouped into airfield characteristics, airspace characteristics, air traffic control, meteorological conditions, and demand characteristics. These same factors affect capacity (as previously discussed), but as capacity is reached and demand begins to exceed capacity, delays result (AAAE, 2005).

According to the U.S. DOT, in February 2015, air carriers reported that 6.88 percent of their flights were delayed by aviation system delays, 7.76 percent by late-arriving aircraft, 6.44 percent by factors within the airline's control (such as maintenance or crew problems), 1.07 percent by extreme weather, and 0.03 percent for security reasons. Weather was a factor in both the extreme-weather category and the aviation-system category. This included delays due to the re-routing of flights by the FAA in consultation with the carriers involved. Weather is also a factor in delays attributed to late-arriving aircraft, although

References and Resources for Further Study

American Association of Airport Executives. 2005. "Body of Knowledge Module 2. Planning, Construction and Environmental." Washington, DC: AAAE.

———. 2010. "U.S. Contract Tower Association Annual Report, 2010." Retrieved from http://www.contracttower.org/ctaannual/USCTAAR10.pdf

de Neufville, R. and A. Odoni. 2003. *Airport Systems: Planning Design and Management.* New York: McGraw Hill.

Federal Aviation Administration (FAA). n.d. NextGen 101 video. Retrieved from http://www.faa.gov/nextgen/

———. 2002. "High Density Airports; Notice of Adopted Lottery Allocation Procedures for Slot Exemptions at LaGuardia Airport." *Federal Register*, 67 FR 65826. Retrieved from http://federalregister.gov/a/02-27381

———. 2009. "Procedures for the Evaluation and Approval of Facilities for Special Authorization Category I Operations and All Category II and III Operations." FAA Order 8400.13D.

———. 2010. "2011–2015 National Plan of Integrated Airport Systems."

———. 2011a. *Design and Installation Details for Airport Visual Aids.* AC 150/5340-30. Washington, DC: FAA.

———. 2011b. *Pilot/Controller Glossary.* Retrieved from http://www.faa.gov/air_traffic/publications/atpubs/PCG/introduction.htm

———. 2012. "Contract Towers Continue to Provide Cost-effective and Safe Air Traffic Services, but Improved Oversight of the Program is Needed." Retrieved from https://www.oig.dot.gov/sites/default/files/FAA%20Federal%20Contract%20Tower%20Program%20Report%5E11-5-12.pdf

———. 2014a. *Airport Design.* AC 150/5300-13A. Washington, DC: FAA.

———. 2014b. "The Business Case for the Next Generation Air Transportation System, FY 2014." Retrieved from http://www.faa.gov/nextgen/media/BusinessCaseForNextGen-2014.pdf

———. 2014c. "Nextgen Implementation Plan." Retrieved from http://www.faa.gov/nextgen/library/media/nextgen_implementation_plan_2014.pdf

Jones, T. R. 2013. "FAA Contract Tower (FCT) Program Office Update." Retrieved from http://www.contracttower.org/FCT_Program_Office_Update_12413_Final.pdf

U.S. Centennial of Flight Commission. n.d. "Air Traffic Control." Retrieved from http://www.centennialofflight.net/essay/Government_Role/Air_traffic_control/POL15.htm

Chapter 4

Planning

Objectives ↘

Upon completion of this chapter, you should:

- Understand the role of the National Plan of Integrated Airport Systems (NPIAS).
- Understand the role of regional aviation system plans.
- Understand the role of state aviation system plans.
- Understand the role of airport master plans and airport layout plans.
- Understand the purpose of business plans.
- Understand the purpose of strategic plans.
- Be able to explain the forecasting steps.
- Understand the various types of forecasting used in aviation activity forecasting.
- Be able to explain the various uses of forecasts.

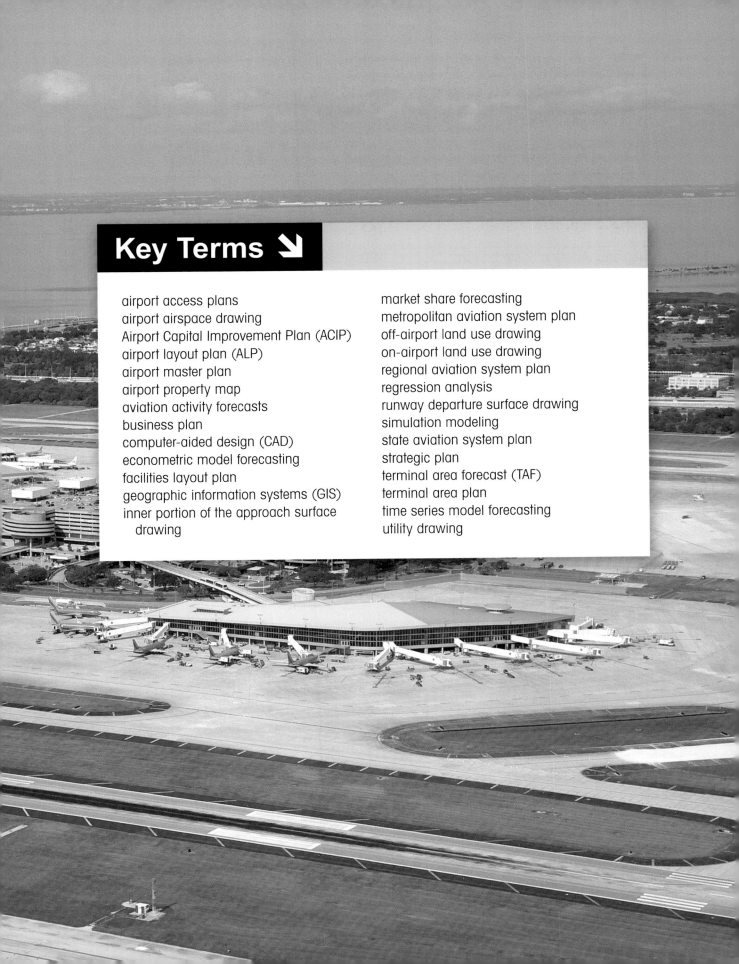

Key Terms ⬂

airport access plans
airport airspace drawing
Airport Capital Improvement Plan (ACIP)
airport layout plan (ALP)
airport master plan
airport property map
aviation activity forecasts
business plan
computer-aided design (CAD)
econometric model forecasting
facilities layout plan
geographic information systems (GIS)
inner portion of the approach surface
   drawing

market share forecasting
metropolitan aviation system plan
off-airport land use drawing
on-airport land use drawing
regional aviation system plan
regression analysis
runway departure surface drawing
simulation modeling
state aviation system plan
strategic plan
terminal area forecast (TAF)
terminal area plan
time series model forecasting
utility drawing

In Chapter 4

FEATURES

A plan to utilize Boston Logan Airport and under-utilized regional airports could support air carrier service in the New England region.

Examples from airports of these three statements, which are key elements in the strategic planning process.

The components of a SWOT Analysis.

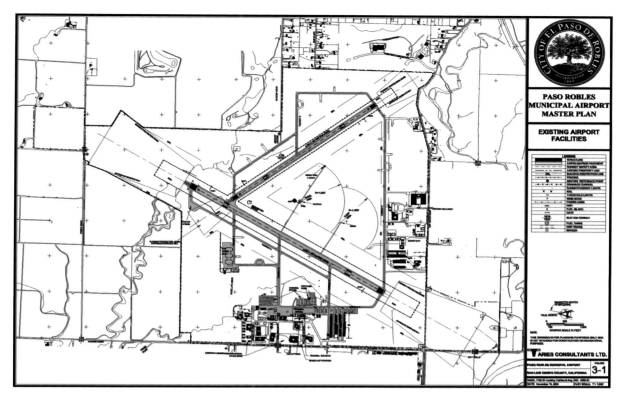

Figure 4-4. Facilities layout plan, Paso Robles Municipal Airport.

(Paso Robles Municipal Airport)

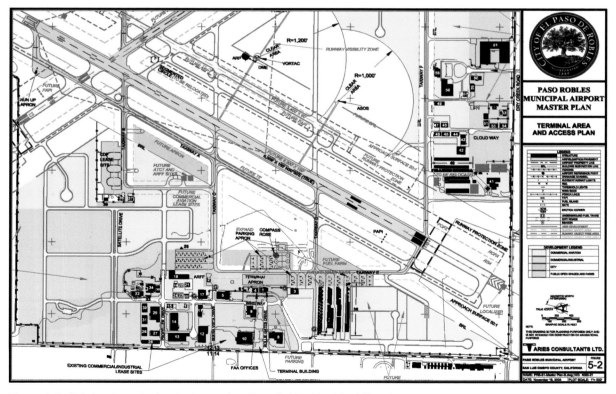

Figure 4-5. ALP drawing set—terminal area plan, Paso Robles Municipal Airport.

(Paso Robles Municipal Airport)

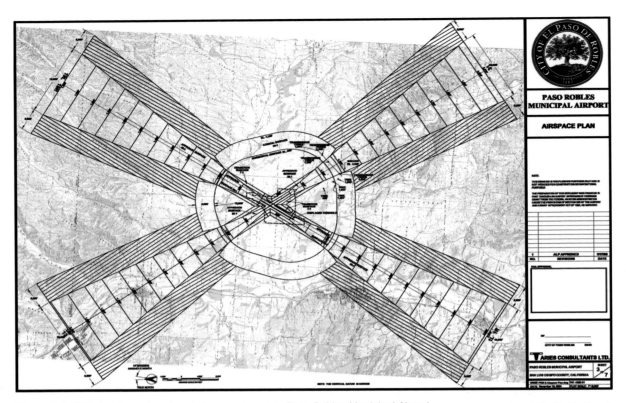

Figure 4-6. ALP drawing set—airport airspace drawing, Paso Robles Municipal Airport.

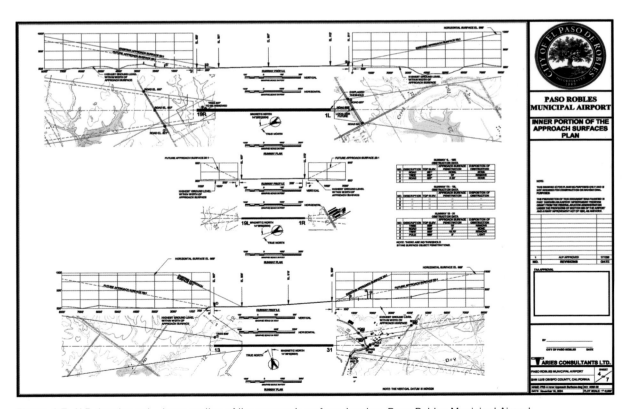

Figure 4-7. ALP drawing set—inner portion of the approach surface drawing, Paso Robles Municipal Airport.

Review Questions ↘

1. How many airports are included in the NPIAS?

2. Within what must airports be included to be eligible for federal grants under the Airport Improvement Program (AIP)?

3. What type of plan provides the foundation for a regional strategy to meet air transportation needs of an entire region?

4. What do state aviation system plans enable planners to do?

5. What is one example of a metropolitan area in the United States with several commercial service airports that are closely linked?

6. What are the products that are part of a completed master plan?

7. What are the fourteen components of the ALP drawing set?

8. Which statement contains a brief description of the goals of the organization and the ideal state that the organization aims to achieve in the future?

9. What is the difference between a strategic plan and a business plan?

10. Why do airports engage in forecasting future aviation activity?

11. Which factors affect aviation activity?

12. Which aviation demand elements are required when conducting aviation activity forecasts?

13. What are the steps to follow in forecasting aviation activity?

14. What five characteristics are necessary for an effective forecast?

15. What are the four main categories of forecasting methods?

16. Define market share forecasting.

17. Define time series modeling.

18. What two questions must be asked when selecting an appropriate forecasting method?

19. What are some examples of short-term operational needs that can be forecast?

20. What are some examples of financial planning needs that can be forecast?

Scenarios ↘

1. As airport director of a large hub commercial service airport, you have been approached by the metropolitan planning organization in your area about participating in the development of a regional aviation system plan. This plan would include two other GA airports and one additional commercial service airport. How would you respond and why?

2. The city manager (to whom you report as airport manager of the local GA airport) has mentioned that the airport should be more strategic in the future. What do you think this means? How can you best do this? Would you attempt to provide this strategic focus yourself or rely on a consultant?

3. Recently hired to increase revenues, traffic, and passengers at a small commercial service airport, you would like to forecast revenues, traffic, and passengers based on current numbers with no improvements being implemented. How would you do this?

4. Select a local airport and conduct a SWOT analysis. This will likely require you to meet with the airport manager, select staff, and possibly a few tenants. Do your research. You cannot expect that everyone you speak to will have knowledge of all strengths, weaknesses, opportunities, and threats at the airport.

5. As the newly hired airport manager at a small GA airport, you become aware of a 20-year-old master plan. In short order, you decide a master plan update is long overdue. How do you begin this process? What steps would you expect to take to see this project through to completion?

References and Resources for Further Study

Central Region Airports Division (FAA). 2010. "AIP Sponsor Guide." Retrieved from http://www.faa.gov/airports/central/aip/sponsor_guide/media/0500.pdf

Federal Aviation Administration (FAA). 2000. "Field Formulation of the National Plan of Integrated Airport Systems (NPIAS)." FAA Order 5090.3C.

———. 2001. "Forecasting Aviation Activity by Airport." Retrieved from www.faa.gov/data_research/aviation_data_statistics/forecasting/media/af1.doc

———. 2007. *Airport Master Plans*. AC 150/5070-6B. Washington, DC: FAA.

———. 2010. "National Plan of Integrated Airport Systems, 2011–2015."

New England Airport Coalition. 2006. New England Regional Airport System Plan. http://www.faa.gov/airports/new_england/planning_capacity/airport_system_plan/media/nerasp_complete.pdf

Ricondo & Associates, Booz Allen Hamilton, George Mason University, and National Service Research. 2009. "ARCP Report 20. Strategic Planning in the Airport Industry." Washington, DC: Transportation Research Board.

Small Business Administration. n.d. Retrieved from http://www.sba.gov/writing-business-plan

Spitz, W. and R. Golaszewski. 2007. "ACRP Synthesis 2: Airport Aviation Activity Forecasting." Washington, DC: Transportation Research Board.

Chapter 5

Design and Construction

Upon completion of this chapter, you should:

- Understand the purpose of predesign, prebid, and preconstruction conferences.

- Understand the components of a construction safety and phasing plan.

- Understand the responsibilities of the airport and contractor(s) in ensuring safety during construction.

- Be able to discuss the main components of the Airport Design advisory circular.

- Be able to determine runway design code.

- Understand the factors which affect the layout and configuration of runways.

- Understand when additional runways may be justified.

- Understand various runway separation criteria and object clearing criteria/areas.

- Understand taxiway design principles.

- Understand various taxiway characteristics.

- Be able to discuss the two types of pavement in use at airports.

- Understand the purpose and design considerations of runway and taxiway bridges.

- Understand the basic configurations of terminals.

- Be able to discuss the three major components of airport traffic and the issues associated with airport ground access.

- Understand common-use facilities.

- Understand the role of EMAS.

- Understand the purpose of 14 CFR Part 77 and the imaginary surfaces.

- Understand the purpose of TERPs.

- Understand the role of avigation easements.

- Understand the selection process, to include RFP, RFQ, the bid process, and contractor selection and negotiation.

- Be aware of ICAO requirements in the area of airport design.

Key Terms ↘

14 CFR Part 77
acute-angled exit taxiway
aircraft approach category (AAC)
airplane design group (ADG)
airport access problem
approach surface
bid
change order
clearway
cockpit over centerline steering
common-use
common-use terminal equipment (CUTE)
conical surface
construction phase
design aircraft
design phase
end-around taxiway
engineered materials arresting system (EMAS)
exclusive use
exit taxiway
finger pier terminal
flexible pavements
foreign object debris (FOD)
hazardous materials (HAZMAT)
horizontal surface

judgmental oversteering
midfield passenger terminal
modification to standards
notice to proceed
obstacle free zone (OFZ)
pavement overlays
prebid conference
preconstruction conference
predesign conference
primary surface
request for proposal (RFP)
request for qualifications (RFQ)
rigid pavements
runway blast pads
runway design code (RDC)
runway object free area (ROFA)
runway safety area (RSA)
runway shoulders
safety plan compliance document (SPCD)
satellite passenger terminal
simple linear terminal
stopway
taxiway design group (TDG)
Terminal Instrument Procedures (TERPS)
transitional surface
transporter

In Chapter 5

FEATURES

The nation's first end-around taxiway at Hartsfield-Jackson Atlanta International Airport.

The adoption of common-use technology has allowed virtual expansion without physical expansion of the terminal.

Introduction

Airports are developed according to specific design criteria set forth by the FAA. The specific criteria with which a specific airport must comply are based, in large part, on the design aircraft that will be utilizing the airport. This chapter provides insight into the design and construction of airports.

Construction Standards

Airports often have ongoing construction projects. Especially at larger commercial service airports, it seems that a construction project is always in progress. As a result, specific construction standards must be developed and adhered to. Typically, construction projects within the terminal area or on the landside of the airport are subject to different construction standards than those in place for projects on the AOA or airside of the airport. Regardless, construction standards are important to ensuring a safe project with minimal impact on airport activity (Figure 5-1).

The airport is responsible for all project engineering, including the preparation of plans and specifications, construction supervision, and inspection and testing for acceptability and quality of the work performed. If there is not sufficient or qualified airport staff to perform these services, it is in the best interest of the airport to retain a consulting engineering firm. The consultant will represent the airport's interest and assume overall responsibility for reporting on the acceptability and quality of the work. As with all contracted work, a written agreement will clearly define the role of the consultant.

Figure 5-1.
Airport construction.

PREDESIGN, PREBID, AND PRECONSTRUCTION CONFERENCES

Prior to commencement of the construction project, various conferences or meetings are held. A **predesign conference**, coordinated by the airport or an authorized agent, is used to discuss design parameters, airport safety, routing of aircraft and equipment, sequencing of construction operations, environmental considerations, and civil rights requirements. This meeting is also the proper forum to resolve potential conflicts between construction activities and airport activities. Held soon after sufficient preliminary design work has been completed and prior to the preparation of the final plans and specifications, invited parties may include the airport's design engineer, airport staff, Air Transport Association (ATA) regional representatives, Air Line Pilots Association (ALPA) representatives, fixed base operators (FBOs), airline representatives, FAA airport certification inspectors, and representatives of the FAA Airports Regional Office (FAA, 2009).

A **prebid conference** may also be conducted, usually by the airport's engineer. Typically held for large projects or projects with unique features, the purpose of a prebid conference is to help clarify and explain construction methods, procedures, and safety measures required by the contract. Usually held at least 10 days before the bid opening date, this conference enables all potential contractors to be fully knowledgeable about the airport's expectations and requirements for the project to enable a successful bid to be developed. Participants normally include prospective bidders, subcontractors, and material suppliers. Generally, the FAA's participation in the prebid conference is neither expected nor required (FAA, 2009).

Finally, once a contractor has been selected and a contract has been negotiated, the **preconstruction conference** is held. This meeting is conducted soon after the contract has been awarded and before issuance of the **notice to proceed**. This important meeting is coordinated by the airport or an authorized agent, and provides an opportunity to discuss operational safety, testing, quality control, quality acceptance, security, safety, labor requirements, environmental factors, and other issues with the contractor and any subcontractors. All airport expectations are spelled out in this meeting. Attendees may include the airport's engineer; resident engineer; airport staff; testing laboratory representative; contractor and subcontractor(s); contractor's project superintendent; contractor's project clerk; various airport users, including airline representatives, fixed base operators, Air Line Pilots Association (ALPA) representative, Air Transport Association (ATA) regional representative, and military representative (joint-use airport); utility companies affected by the proposed construction; federal, state, or local agencies affected by the proposed construction; and representatives of the FAA Airports regional or field office (FAA, 2009).

To know which specific design criteria apply to a specific airport, the **design aircraft** must first be determined. The design aircraft represents the most demanding aircraft (in terms of tail height, wingspan, approach speeds, width of aircraft main gear, and distance from the cockpit to the main gear) that is intended to be accommodated by the airport. Airports with multiple runways designate a design aircraft for each runway, which may or may not be the same aircraft type.

Technically, the design aircraft designation is actually driven by three parameters:

- Aircraft Approach Category (AAC)
- Airplane Design Group (ADG)
- Visibility minimums
- Taxiway Design Group (TDG)

The **Aircraft Approach Category (AAC)** relates to aircraft approach speed (operational characteristics) (see Table 5-1).

Table 5-1. Aircraft approach categories.

AAC	Approach Speed
A	Approach speed less than 91 knots
B	Approach speed 91 knots or more but less than 121 knots
C	Approach speed 121 knots or more but less than 141 knots
D	Approach speed 141 knots or more but less than 166 knots
E	Approach speed 166 knots or more

The **Airplane Design Group (ADG)** relates to either the aircraft wingspan or tail height (physical characteristics), whichever is most restrictive, of the largest aircraft expected to operate on the runway and taxiways (see Table 5-2).

Table 5-2. Airplane design groups.

ADG	Tail Height (in feet)	Wingspan (in feet)
I	Less than 20'	Less than 49'
II	20' to less than 30'	49' to less than 79'
III	30' to less than 45'	79' to less than 118'
IV	45' to less than 60'	118' to less than 171'
V	60' to less than 66'	171' to less than 214'
VI	66' to less than 80'	214' to less than 262'

The visibility minimums refers to visibility expressed by runway visual range (RVR) values. Visual runways do not have visibility minimums, indicated by VIS. See Table 5-3.

Table 5-3. Visibility minimums.

RVR (in feet)	Instrument Flight Visibility Category (in statute miles)
5000	Not lower than 1 mile
4000	Lower than 1 mile but not lower than 3/4 mile
2400	Lower than 3/4 mile but not lower than 1/2 mile
1600	Lower than 1/2 mile but not lower than 1/4 mile
1200	Lower than 1/4 mile

The **Taxiway Design Group (TDG)** relates to the undercarriage dimensions of the aircraft. Taxiway/taxilane width and fillet standards, and in some instances, runway to taxiway and taxiway/taxilane separation requirements, are determined by TDG. In application, the TDG will affect the taxiway width, taxiway edge safety margin, and taxiway should width, among other dimensions.

Generally, runway standards are related to aircraft approach speed, aircraft wingspan, and designated or planned approach visibility minimums. Runway to taxiway and taxiway/taxilane to taxiway/taxilane separation standards are related to ADG, TDG, and approach visibility minimums.

The selected AAC, ADG, and approach visibility minimums are combined to form the **runway design code (RDC)** of a particular runway. The RDC provides the information needed to determine certain design standards that apply in each situation. The RDC is a combination of the three components presented above, presented in an AAC-ADG-Vis fashion. For example, an airport's air carrier runway may have an RDC of C-IV-1200. The same airport's smaller runway used for general aviation activity may have an RDC of B-II-2400.

It should be noted that although AC 150/5300-13A presents the standards for airport design, an airport is allowed to request a "**modification to standards.**" In essence, local conditions may require modification to airport design standards for a specific airport. The request for modification must show that the modification will provide an acceptable level of safety, economy, durability, and workmanship. An example would be a request to allow a Group VI aircraft (Airbus 380) to operate at a Group V airport (Figure 5-3). Although the FAA has granted a modification to standards for some airports in this same situation, not all requests are approved (FAA, 2014).

Part 77 defines various imaginary surfaces for the purpose of determining whether or not an object is an obstruction to air navigation (see Figure 5-20 and Table 5-4). These surfaces are identified as:

1. **Primary surface**—Centered on the runway centerline and extends 200 feet past the runway end. The width of this surface varies from 250 feet to 1,000 feet, depending on the type of approach to the runway. This is the only imaginary surface that exists solely at ground level.

2. **Transitional surface**—Starts at the edges of the primary surface, perpendicular to the runway centerline, and transitions to the horizontal surface. The slope of the transitional surface is 7:1.[5]

3. **Approach surface**—Starts 200 feet from the runway end at the edge of the primary surface and extends outward from the end of the primary surface. The approach slope can vary from 20:1 for a visual runway for a distance of 5,000 feet; to ratios 20:1, 34:1, and 50:1 for a non-precision runway, for a distance of 10,000 feet; or to 50:1 for a precision runway for the first 10,000 feet and 40:1 thereafter to 40,000 feet.

4. **Horizontal surface**—A level plane 150 feet above the runway elevation. The surface area is determined by connecting tangents of radii extended from the edges of the primary surface area at the runway ends. The length of the surface area of the radii is dependent upon the approach category for the runway. For utility or visual runways it is 5,000 feet and for all others it is 10,000 feet. The area is intended to accommodate the safe operation and maneuvering of aircraft that are performing circle-to-land or missed approaches.

5. **Conical surface**—Starts at the perimeter of the horizontal surface and continues upward at a slope ratio of 20:1 for a horizontal distance of 4,000 feet.

Table 5-4. Part 77 imaginary surface angles.

Ratio	Percent	Angle	Surface
7:1	14.3	8.1°	Transitional
20:1	5.0	2.9°	Conical, visual approach
34:1	2.9	1.7°	Non-precision approach
40:1	2.5	1.4°	Precision (outer)
50:1	2.0	1.1°	Precision

---

[5] Run:Rise

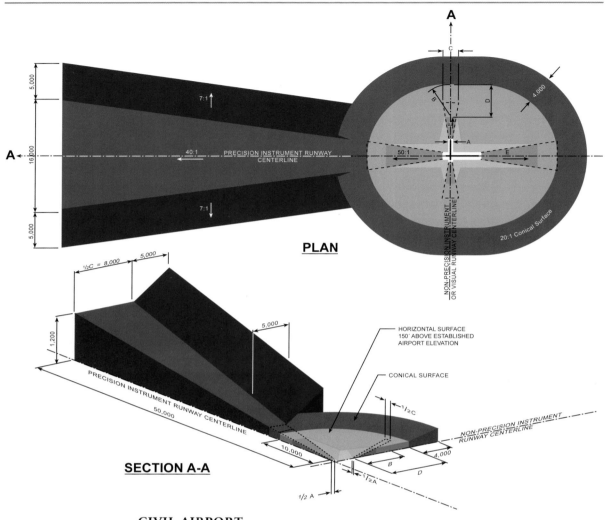

PLAN

SECTION A-A

CIVIL AIRPORT IMAGINARY SURFACES

DIM.	ITEM	DIMENSIONAL STANDARDS (FEET)					
		VISUAL RUNWAY		NON-PRECISION INSTRUMENT RUNWAY			PRECISION INSTRUMENT RUNWAY
		UTILITY	LARGER THAN UTILITY	UTILITY	LARGER THAN UTILITY		
					X	Y	
A	WIDTH OF PRIMARY SURFACE AND APPROACH SURFACE WIDTH AT INNER END	250	500	500	500	1,000	1,000
B	RADIUS OF HORIZONTAL SURFACE	5,000	5,000	5,000	10,000	10,000	10,000
		VISUAL APPROACH		NON-PRECISION INSTRUMENT APPROACH			PRECISION INSTRUMENT APPROACH
		UTILITY	LARGER THAN UTILITY	UTILITY	LARGER THAN UTILITY		
					X	Y	
C	APPROACH SURFACE WIDTH AT END	1,250	1,500	2,000	3,500	4,000	16,000
D	APPROACH SURFACE LENGTH	5,000	5,000	5,000	10,000	10,000	*
E	APPROACH SLOPE	20:1	20:1	20:1	34:1	34:1	*

X - VISIBILITY MINIMUMS GREATER THAN 3/4 MILE
Y - VISIBILITY MINIMUMS AS LOW AS 3/4 MILE
* - PRECISION INSTRUMENT APPROACH SLOPE IS 50:1 FOR INNER 10,000 FEET AND 40:1 FOR AN ADDITIONAL 40,000 FEET

SURFACE SLOPE KEY

- HORIZONTAL SURFACE
- 20:1
- 7:1
- 7:1
- VARIES (SEE "E" VALUE IN TABLE)
- 40:1 (PRECISION INSTRUMENT RUNWAY ONLY)

AVIATION DIVISION

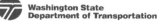

Washington State Department of Transportation

Figure 5-20. Part 77 imaginary surfaces.

(Carter Timmerman, Aviation Planner, WSDOT)

Upon receipt of any proposed construction via Form 7460-1, the FAA conducts a Part 77 study by analyzing the impact a proposed object would have on the airspace surrounding an airport. A Part 77 study concludes with one or more of six possibilities:

1. The obstruction to air navigation is a hazard to air navigation.
2. The object or activity on or in the vicinity of an airport is objectionable.
3. The need exists to alter, remove, mark, or light the object.
4. The airport layout plan is approved.
5. The proposed construction, enlargement, or modification to the airport would have an adverse effect on the safe and efficient use of navigable airspace.
6. A change in operational procedure is feasible or required.

When penetration to an approach surface exists, the airport operator must take one of five actions:

1. Remove or lower the object to acceptable threshold siting requirements.[6]
2. Displace the threshold, thereby shortening the landing distance.
3. Revise the glide path angle or threshold crossing height.
4. Raise the visibility minimums on the runway approach.
5. Restrict night operations.

It is important to understand that Part 77 does not provide the FAA with authority to prevent constructing or altering a structure, regardless of the results of the study. This authority to prevent construction or alteration is reserved for the states and resides with the local regional or municipal zoning authorities. For this reason, the FAA insists upon land use planning in and around airports to promote compatible land uses and to protect the FAA's investment in the airport and the airways. If a community does not protect its approaches under federal grant assurances, future federal AIP funding for the airport may be in jeopardy. Many airports have had to displace thresholds due to obstructions that were erected after the airport was built, indicating a lack of proper height zoning regulations at the local level.

Additionally, 14 CFR Part 157, Notice of Construction, Alteration, Activation, and Deactivation of Airports, requires those proposing to construct, activate, or deactivate an airport to provide notice to the FAA at least 30 days prior to the proposed alteration or deactivation. This notice requires a completed Form 7480-1, a layout sketch, and a location map. Additionally, 14 CFR Part 77, Safe, Efficient Use, and Preservation of the Navigable Airspace, requires notice to the FAA by those proposing any construction or alteration described in §77.13. Specifically, this includes any construction or alteration of structures more than 200 feet in height above ground level or at a height that will penetrate any of the imaginary surfaces defined in Part 77 (FAA, 2014).

---

[6] May not be possible if proposed object is not under control of the airport.

TERPS

A stated objective of the airspace system is for instrument procedures to be provided at civil airports open to the public whenever a need is shown. Although a minimum number of potential instrument approaches is not specified, an instrument procedure must be beneficial to more than a single user or interest. It is the responsibility of the FAA to establish and approve instrument procedures for civil airports. Within the 495-page FAA Order 8260.3B, "United States Standard for **Terminal Instrument Procedures (TERPS)**," the criteria by which these instrument procedures are established and approved are found.

TERPS refers to the methods for use in designing instrument flight procedures. This includes procedures for instrument approaches—including straight-in and simultaneous precision approaches, and straight-in non-precision approaches—as well as departure procedures (FAA, 2007b).

AVIGATION EASEMENTS

Often, it is not feasible for airports to own all parcels of land in areas affected by aircraft noise. Therefore, it may be prudent for an airport to purchase avigation easements. With this type of easement, airports purchase the "right" for aircraft to overfly a particular property, thus avoiding future noise complaints and the liability associated with such complaints from the property owner.

Selection Process

For airport planning and design projects, construction projects, and other consulting work, airports must undergo a process to develop project specifications, advertise for the project, and select a contractor to perform the work.[7]

SPECIFICATIONS

Once an airport has a project in mind, the first step is to develop the specifications for that project. In other words, this is the stage during which the airport staff clearly develop the concept of the work to be performed by the contractor. The specifications become the written directions and requirements for completing the contract work, including standards for specifying materials or testing. The specifications are often very detailed, and become an essential part of the RFP, RFQ, or bid documents. Without specifications for the project (or equipment, as would be developed for an ARFF truck), a potential contractor would

---

[7] The contractor is the individual, partnership, firm, or corporation primarily liable for the acceptable performance of the work contracted.

not be able to adequately determine costs associated with the project, which would result in proposals or bids which are not very useful to the airport.

RFP

Once the project specifications have been developed, it is necessary to advertise for the work to be performed. The published advertisement will state the time and place for submitting sealed proposals; a description of the proposed work; instructions to bidders for obtaining proposal forms, plans, and specifications; proposal guaranty required; and the airport's right to reject any and all bids. Additionally, the airport may hold either a mandatory or optional prebid conference for interested bidders. This conference (or meeting) allows airport staff to explain more about the project and answer questions from potential bidders. A site visit is also usually included, allowing potential bidders the opportunity to see the project site and better understand the requirements of the work to be performed.

One manner in which this advertisement is carried out is via a **request for proposal (RFP)**. An airport will issue an RFP, which is a document that specifically spells out the work to be performed, the required format of the proposal, the date on which the proposal is due, and the criteria for selection. The RFP will clearly inform a potential contractor about all aspects of the project and will provide all information necessary for the potential contractor to effectively respond to the RFP by developing a proposal detailing their qualifications, how they intend to carry out the project, and possibly (if requested) the monetary amount they are willing to accept for completion of the project. Proposals generally must also include statements covering the bidder's past experience on similar work, a list of equipment that would be available for the work, a list of key personnel that would be available for the project, and evidence of financial strength. Further, each proposal may be required to include a certified check, or other acceptable collateral, in the amount specified in the proposal form. Such financial guaranties are returned once the contract is awarded.

RFQ

Similar in purpose to an RFP, a **request for qualifications (RFQ)** is an airport's way of seeking the most qualified contractor to carry out a task. If an RFQ is issued, the airport is requesting the qualifications of a potential contractor. This will include resumes of key personnel, company experience with similar projects, location of the company, etc. Generally, with an RFQ, no dollar amount is included in the potential contactor's statement of qualifications. Once the most qualified contractor is chosen, the airport and the contractor will then negotiate a dollar amount for the work to be performed.

BIDS

The **bid** process requests potential contractors or vendors/suppliers to bid a specific monetary amount to supply the piece of equipment requested (such as a new ARFF truck), perform the work requested (such as a terminal demolition), or provide the expertise requested (such as an updated master plan). Usually, the airport has a pre-calculated budget in mind, meaning it knows what to expect as a reasonable bid for the project, equipment, or expertise. Although jokes abound about projects being awarded to the "lowest bidder," it should be noted that award of contracts are made to the lowest, qualified bidder whose proposal conforms to the requirements as spelled out in the bid documents. Even so, if a bid is submitted at 50 percent below the expected cost, for instance, an airport will need to evaluate whether the potential contractor did not understand the specifications or if the contractor is willing to realize a loss simply to win the contract. In either case, red flags will be raised requiring further evaluation by airport staff prior to awarding the project. Additionally, bids can be considered non-responsive if the bid is not submitted by the deadline or does not meet any other requirements spelled out in the bid advertisement. To be fair, airports must hold all proposers to the published deadlines.

CONTRACTOR SELECTION

All proposals, qualifications, or bids received by the deadline are opened, and read, publicly at the time and place specified in the advertisement. Bidders, their authorized agents, and other interested persons are welcome to attend the opening. Proposals that have been withdrawn by the bidder or not received by the deadline are returned unopened to the bidder (FAA, 2011b).

CONTRACT NEGOTIATION

Once a contractor is successful in securing a project, the airport will enter into a contract with the contractor. A contract is the written agreement covering the work to be performed. The contract usually includes the advertisement; contract form; proposal; performance bond; payment bond; any required insurance certificates; specifications; plans, and any addenda issued to bidders. The contract time refers to the number of calendar days or working days allowed for completion of the project. Finally, the contractor will be given a written notice, or notice to proceed, to begin the actual contract work on a previously agreed-to date (FAA, 2011b).

Review Questions ⬊

1. What components should be included in the construction safety and phasing plan?

2. Explain what occurs during the design phase of a project.

3. Explain what occurs during the construction phase of a project.

4. What is the runway design code?

5. For what purpose would an airport request a modification to standards?

6. The layout and configuration of runways depends on what factors?

7. Explain the two types of pavement.

8. Explain the simple linear passenger terminal building.

9. Explain the finger pier terminal.

10. Explain the satellite passenger terminal.

11. Explain the midfield passenger terminal.

12. Explain the purpose of transporters.

13. Explain the three major components of airport traffic.

14. What are the benefits to adopting common-use at airports?

15. Explain engineering materials arresting system.

16. Explain the imaginary surfaces of Part 77.

17. What is the purpose of a request for proposal?

18. What is the purpose of a request for qualifications?

19. Explain the bid process.

Scenarios ↘

1. As director of operations at Johnson International Airport, you have been instructed by the senior director of operations and maintenance to determine how the airport (which is an ARC DV) can accommodate an A-380. Apparently, Singapore Airlines is considering bringing their A-380 into your airport three times weekly. How do you approach this task? What are some options available to the airport? How would you seek FAA approval?

2. You are the airport director of a commercial service airport that tends to be overly congested. In discussions with the ATC tower chief, she feels that aircraft are remaining on the runway too long. What can be done about this? Can the airport actually enhance capacity without building a new runway? If so, how?

3. Looking for a challenge and an opportunity to utilize your 30 years of airport management experience in a unique way, you have been hired by a newly established airport authority that is in the design phase of building a new commercial service airport for a beachfront community. Preliminary air service studies have shown the region can produce demand for 2–3 million enplaned passengers annually, with the vast majority being domestic. The design firm is seeking your thoughts on the terminal configuration. Considering the possible types of terminals, what would you recommend and why?

4. As the airport manager at a GA airport, you desire to retain a management consultant to (a) develop a strategic plan, (b) perform an air service analysis, and (c) assist with other tasks that may require the need of this consultant. How would you select such a consultant?

5. You have been hired as an engineering/design consultant for a new commercial-service airport to replace an older commercial-service airport that is now landlocked. The airport will be located in northern Florida and serve no less than 4 airlines and 5 million enplaned passengers annually. Discuss how you would decide on the pavement type, the runway design, the terminal design, whether common-use would be appropriate, etc.

References and Resources for Further Study

American Association of Airport Executives. 2005. "Body of Knowledge Module 2. Planning, construction, and environmental." Washington, DC: AAAE.

Belliotti, R. 2008. "ACRP Synthesis 8: Common Use Facilities and Equipment at Airports." Washington, DC: Transportation Research Board.

de Neufville, R. and A. Odoni. 2003. *Airport Systems: Planning Design and Management.* New York: McGraw Hill.

Federal Aviation Administration (FAA). 2005a. *Engineering Materials Arresting Systems for Aircraft Overruns.* AC 150/5220-22A. Washington, DC: FAA.

———. 2005b. *Runway Length Requirements for Airport Design.* AC 150/5325-4B. Washington, DC: FAA.

———. 2007a. *Quality Control of Construction for Airport Grant Projects.* AC 150/5370-12A. Washington, DC: FAA.

———. 2007b. "United States Standard for Terminal Instrument Procedures." FAA Order 8260.3B.

———. 2009. *Predesign Prebid, and Preconstruction Conferences for Airport Grant Projects.* AC 150/5300-9B. Washington, DC: FAA.

———. 2011a. *Operational Safety on Airports During Construction.* AC 150/5370-2F. Washington, DC: FAA.

———. 2011b. *Standards for Specifying Construction of Airports.* AC 150/5370-10F. Washington, DC: FAA.

———. 2014. *Airport Design.* AC 150/5300-13A. Washington, DC: FAA.

Los Angeles World Airports. 2012. "Comprehensive Annual Financial Report." Retrieved from http://www.lawa.org/uploadedFiles/LAWA/pdf/LAWA_Comprehensive_Annual_Financial_Report_2012.pdf

Richards, J. 2008. "Common Use Technology Trumps Physical Expansion at Fresno." Retrieved from http://www.airportimprovement.com/article/common-use-technology-trumps-physical-expansion-fresno

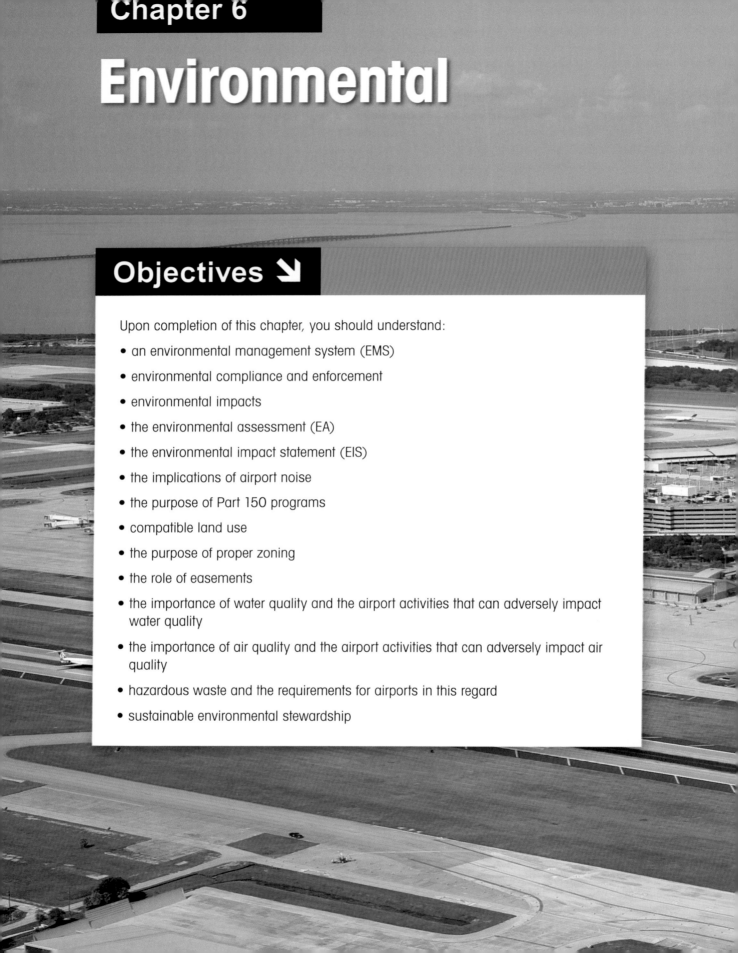

Chapter 6

Environmental

Objectives ↘

Upon completion of this chapter, you should understand:

- an environmental management system (EMS)
- environmental compliance and enforcement
- environmental impacts
- the environmental assessment (EA)
- the environmental impact statement (EIS)
- the implications of airport noise
- the purpose of Part 150 programs
- compatible land use
- the purpose of proper zoning
- the role of easements
- the importance of water quality and the airport activities that can adversely impact water quality
- the importance of air quality and the airport activities that can adversely impact air quality
- hazardous waste and the requirements for airports in this regard
- sustainable environmental stewardship

Key Terms ↘

best management practices (BMPs)
biochemical oxygen demand (BOD)
Conditionally Exempt Small Quantity
  Generators (CESQGs)
day-night sound level (DNL)
environmental assessment (EA)
environmental impact statement (EIS)
environmental management system
  (EMS)
Environmental Protection Agency (EPA)
facility response plan
finding of no significant impact (FONSI)
Integrated Noise Model (INM)
International Organization for
  Standardization (ISO)
Large Quantity Generators (LQGs)
Leadership in Energy and Environmental
  Design (LEED)

leaking underground storage tanks (LUST)
material safety data sheet (MSDS)
National Pollution Discharge Elimination
  System (NPDES)
National Response Center (NRC)
noise compatibility plan (NCP)
noise exposure map (NEM)
notice of intent (NOI)
personal protective equipment (PPE)
Small Quantity Generators (SQGs)
Spill Prevention, Control, and
  Countermeasure (SPCC)
stormwater pollution prevention plan
  (SWPPP)
total suspended solids (TSS)
underground storage tanks (USTs)

In Chapter 6

FEATURES

By adopting a proactive approach to soundproofing residential homes and schools, Boston Logan is minimizing the impact of aircraft noise on the surrounding communities.

A glycol recovery system has allowed the airport to meet new EPA rules while accommodating airline needs for aircraft deicing.

By becoming the first airport terminal to achieve LEED Gold status, SFO has shown a commitment to sustainability.

Environmental Regulations

Environmental impacts can result from a number of activities and facilities on airports, such as stormwater discharge, weed and pest control, runway and taxiway deicing, aircraft rescue firefighting training, various underground and aboveground fuel storage tanks, electrical equipment and vaults, aircraft maintenance, vehicle maintenance, asbestos in buildings, restaurant or building maintenance, and grease, solvents, and other chemicals. Airports must be aware of—and strive to maintain compliance with—the numerous local, state, and federal environmental regulations and policies. It is important to remember that even though an airport typically has numerous tenants, such as airlines, fixed base operators, and maintenance providers, the airport acts as the landlord and is responsible for ensuring that tenants comply with the various regulations and policies on airport property. Additionally, airports can be forced to remediate environmental issues on property returned to the airport via lease expirations, terminations, or bankruptcy. In the end, the airport operator is responsible for what occurs on airport property.

Environmental Management System

FAA Advisory Circular (AC) 150/5050-8, *Environmental Management Systems for Airport Sponsors*, provides guidance to airports in developing a comprehensive **environmental management system (EMS)**. An EMS, which serves as the foundation for a strategic and proactive approach to ensuring environmental compliance, is generally based on the **International Organization for Standardization (ISO)** 14001 EMS standard. Based on the principles of process control, reduced consumption of resources, and environmental compliance, an EMS is designed to allow airports to balance environmental performance with business objectives through a process of continual improvement. Specifically, it incorporates the "Plan-Do-Check-Act" (P-D-C-A) cycle. During the "Plan" phase, the airport's overall environmental program is defined. During the "Do" phase, the strategies of the EMS (including training) are fully implemented. The "Check" phase involves monitoring environmental program performance to verify results and the achievement of objectives. Finally, during the "Act" phase, elements needing improvement are identified and a plan is developed and committed to for improving upon these areas (FAA, 2007; McGormley et al., 2011). Benefits of an EMS include:

1. Increased overall efficiency and accountability
2. Reduced costs and reduction of potential liability
3. Increased employee awareness of environmental responsibilities
4. Improved community relations
   (AAAE, 2010, p. 135)

To develop an effective EMS, airports take the following steps:

1. Establish an environmental compliance philosophy.
2. Communicate compliance goals to employees, tenants, and the community.
3. Identify and assess the current level of compliance through an audit.
4. Establish programs to attain compliance.
5. Create processes and procedures to correct and maintain compliance.
6. Establish and implement strategies for building environmental capacity (AAAE, 2010, p. 135)

Similar to a safety management system (SMS), the EMS is becoming a standard practice at airports desiring to formalize their approach to proactive environmental management. Although the EMS is voluntary, airports are aware of the potential for environmental liability and the EMS is a best management practice in the airport industry to minimize this liability.

Compliance and Enforcement

Compliance with environmental regulations is imperative for airports. It is important for airports to effectively manage this compliance to avoid any liability associated with non-compliance. A good-faith effort is important in environmental compliance. If an airport has made such an effort, liability is minimized, even decreasing the likelihood of an airport manager being prosecuted for noncompliance by either the government or a private citizen. It is also crucial that the airport manager know the regulatory requirements and implement policies and procedures to ensure compliance. These two items are integral to a comprehensive environmental management program (AAAE, 2010).

The foundation of a good-faith effort requires airports to ensure tenant and contractor compliance through initial bid specifications and/or requests for proposals, periodic inspections and audits, and lease and contract agreements. Although requiring compliance initially through bid specifications and lease and contract agreements is a step in the right direction, airports must regularly ensure compliance through inspections and audits. An audit involves examining the current level of environmental compliance both within the organization and among various airport tenants. The audit should reveal any areas of non-compliance so that these areas can be addressed in light of the environmental requirements. Without an audit, no baseline (current level of compliance) can be established and continued oversight of environmental compliance is not possible. Additionally, providing an employee/tenant training program and maintaining good records is important (AAAE, 2010).

Additionally, airports typically maintain environmental impairment liability insurance. Even with good-faith efforts and a comprehensive environmental management program in place, airports may experience environmental liability the community along with the specific needs of the airport. In essence, it is not in the best interest of homeowners or the airport to locate a residential area in a noise-affected area. Thus, proper zoning can prevent this from occurring. Rather than being viewed negatively, zoning can and should be viewed positively. It can be used constructively to increase the value and productivity of affected land. For zoning to be viable, however, there should be a reasonable present or future need for each designated use (FAA, 1983).

Although proper zoning is highly recommended in order to prevent incompatible land use around airports, zoning is not without pitfalls. First, zoning is not a permanent solution to the land use compatibility issue around airports. Requests for zoning changes can be applied for, with zoning changed by local officials. Also, zoning can actually allow incompatible land use around an airport, such as in the case of communities adopting cumulative zoning in which all "higher" uses of land (residential) is permitted in "lower" use districts (such as commercial or industrial). Zoning is also typically not retroactive, meaning that changing zoning primarily to prohibit a use that is already in existence is normally not possible. Lastly, airport noise impacts may span more than one jurisdiction, requiring a coordinated approach to zoning between these various communities (FAA, 1983).

It is imperative for the airport manager to work collaboratively with the municipal zoning commission or planning department to ensure that zoning regulations are adopted to prevent incompatible land use in the proximity of the airport. For instance, to prevent a cellular phone tower from being erected two miles away from the airport in the approach corridor (which could interfere with 14 CFR Part 77 surfaces), the airport must educate the local zoning commission or planning department as to land uses that would be incompatible with the operation of the airport. If successfully carried out, the municipality would deny the request to erect a cell phone tower at that location. If not successfully carried out, the tower may be erected and the FAA may determine it to be a hazard to air navigation, requiring the airport to displace a threshold, for instance. Clearly, this is not in the airport's best interest. Therefore, a proactive approach to zoning is absolutely necessary for airports (FAA, 1983).

Easements

Somewhat related to zoning, an easement is a right held by one person to make use of the land of another for a limited purpose. An avigation easement allows for flights of aircraft over the property, whereas a noise easement allows for aircraft to generate noise over the property. Easements can be quite effective in assuring compatible land use around airports. Airports may acquire easements via purchase, condemnation, and dedication. Although the concept of purchase is obvious, the concepts of condemnation and dedication are more novel. Condemnation for an easement is similar to full condemnation via eminent domain. The condemnation process involves court action (resulting in higher costs) and generates significant negative publicity and ill will on the part of the home or land owner. Dedication refers to the concept of subdivision regulations including a provision for dedicating private land or easements on private land for public purposes.

A significant advantage of easements is their permanent nature, in contrast to the temporary nature of land use zoning. Additionally, easements can typically be obtained for a fraction of the total value of the land, making them much less expensive than acquisition of the land. However, an easement does not reduce the noise impacts on people or convert incompatible land uses to compatible uses (FAA, 1983).

Water Quality

Maintaining the quality of water, especially in the nation's rivers and lakes, is the main purpose of the Clean Water Act of 1977. The Clean Water Act, through presidential executive order, prohibits the discharge of pollutants into a waterway from a point source unless a permit (issued by the **Environmental Protection Agency [EPA]** or other authorized agency) allows such a discharge. The **National Pollution Discharge Elimination System (NPDES)** permit program is the means of regulating point source discharge of pollutants into the nation's navigable waterways. In contrast to non-point source pollution (which results from runoff, precipitation and drainage), point-source discharges of industrial process water, noncontact cooling water, and collected or channeled stormwater runoff require a NPDES permit (see Figure 6-5). In essence, discharges or runoff that are made directly to surface waters require a NPDES permit.

Figure 6-5.
Runoff with environmental pollutants being discharged to waterways can affect water quality.

(Wikimedia Commons; see credit on page 624)

AIRPORT MANAGEMENT

- **Conditionally Exempt Small Quantity Generators (CESQGs)**—Generate less than 100 kg per month. Authorized to accumulate no more than 1,000 kg at any time.

- **Small Quantity Generators (SQGs)**—Generate more than 100 kg per month, but less than 1,000 kg per month. Authorized to accumulate no more than 6,000 kg in any 180-day period.

- **Large Quantity Generators (LQGs)**—Generate more than 1,000 kg of waste per month. Authorized to accumulate no more than 6,000 kg in any 90-day period.

Special permits may allow for greater accumulation limits. Additionally, stored waste is required to be taken off-site or treated within 180 days (270 days if the treatment plant is 200 miles or further away), unless a permit allows for storage, treatment, and disposal on-site. An airport is prohibited from disposing of waste on the airport unless a permit allowing for such disposal has been obtained. Of course, if hazardous waste is generated and/or stored on the airport, it is imperative for the airport to prevent accidental release of the hazardous substances into the environment. Prevention of a hazardous substance release is most effectively ensured with a preparedness and prevention plan. This plan will detail emergency communication methods, firefighting equipment and response, and the types of hazardous waste to be generated and the storage locations on airport (McGormley et al., 2011).

In addition, the 1984 Hazardous and Solid Waste Amendments to RCRA address **underground storage tanks (USTs)**, specifically establishing requirements for tank design, release/leak detection, and **leaking underground storage tanks (LUSTs)**. USTs at airports typically contain jet fuel, used oil, fuel oil, diesel, or gasoline. Although most states have developed state-specific UST requirements, the EPA regulates the states without such a program. Owners of USTs are required to register their tanks with either their state or the EPA (in the absence of a state program). In addition to registering the tank ownership, location, facility type, and contact information, owners of USTs must provide evidence of financial ability to address leaks and other environmental concerns associated with the UST, as well as compensate third parties for accidental releases of petroleum and CERCLA hazardous substances from the UST. For the installation of new USTs, owners must certify compliance with tank and piping installation requirements, cathodic protection, financial responsibility, and release/leak detection (Figure 6-9) (McGormley et al., 2011).

If there is an accidental release of a hazardous substance (covered under CERCLA) or an extremely hazardous substance (covered under EPCRA) in excess of its reportable quantities and anticipated to affect areas that are beyond the facility boundaries, airports are required to notify their local emergency planning committee and the state emergency response commission. Releases of hazardous substances (under CERCLA) also require notification to the **National Response Center (NRC)**. Notification will contain the name of

the substance, an estimate of the quantity released, time and duration of the release, known or anticipated acute or chronic health risks associated with the substance, etc. If a release is solely within the airport boundaries or federally permitted, this reporting is not required (McGormley et al., 2011).

Federal regulations have also been adopted to manage the registration, manufacturing, transportation, sale, labeling, storage, application, and disposal of pesticides in the United States. The Federal Insecticide, Fungicide, and Rodenticide Act of 1947 (as amended) (FIFRA) addresses these aspects of pesticide management. Airports typically apply pesticides to control vegetation and pests. Although an airport may contract out these services, if an airport handles pesticides in-house, airport management must ensure that FIFRA is complied with. For airports, the most applicable aspects of FIFRA include storage and labeling, as well as application and disposal. The regulation requires

pesticides to be stored in an approved container/package and be properly labeled with the pesticide registration number, health hazards, and warnings. Individuals applying pesticides classified as "restricted-use" must either be certified as a commercial or private applicator or be supervised by a certified commercial or private applicator. Additionally, any individual applying pesticides should wear proper **personal protective equipment (PPE)** as specified on the product labeling (see Figure 6-10). Disposal of containers used to apply pesticides must be triple rinsed or pressure rinsed prior to disposal. Unused pesticides may be recycled by adhering to universal waste management procedures (McGormley et al., 2011).

Sustainable Environmental Stewardship

Proactive environmental stewardship offers numerous environmental, social, and financial benefits, including:

- Reduced life cycle costs of capital assets
- Reduced operating costs
- Reduced environmental footprint
- Optimization for new and better technologies
- Reduced costs of asset development
- Enhanced bond ratings
- Reduced environmental, health, and safety risks
- Improved work environment for employees, leading to higher productivity
- Better customer service and satisfaction
- Enhanced relationships with the surrounding community

Airport sustainability has been defined as "a holistic approach to managing an airport so as to ensure the integrity of economic viability, operational efficiency, natural resource conservation, and social responsibility of the airport." (McGormley et al., 2011, p. 101). Sustainability planning at airports incorporates a proactive approach to environmental stewardship and affects every effort the airport takes. Sustainability planning involves:

- *Developing a sustainability vision or policy*—In concert with the airport mission, this will set forth the direction of the airport regarding environmental stewardship.

- *Conducting a baseline assessment/gap analysis*—Determining the airport's current environmental impacts is essential in identifying opportunities for improvement. By examining current conditions and then determining where gaps exist, it is easier to determine areas for improvement.

- *Establishing goals and objectives*—Goals and objectives flow from the sustainability vision and are developed on consultation with stakeholders.

- *Setting performance targets*—Setting performance targets and metrics is important to meet established goals and objectives. Typical environmental performance metrics include potable water use per square foot of building area or passenger, electricity consumption per square foot of building area or passenger, and rate of recycling waste as a percentage of total waste generated.

- *Identifying sustainability practices*—This involves identifying reasonable and practical sustainability practices considering the airport's available resources. In evaluating which initiatives would be most beneficial, useful criteria include the priorities of the airport, benefits and costs of each practice, resources required to implement and maintain each practice, and the potential cost savings or return on investment.

- *Implementing practices*—This involves implementing the selected initiatives by identifying priority projects, funding them, and developing schedules and individual responsibilities.

- *Regularly measuring, reporting, and reevaluating*—Using metrics previously developed, the airport is able to measure progress and ascertain the performance of its sustainability program.

(McGormley et al., 2011, pp. 102–103)

A number of airports have adopted specific environmental stewardship practices that have proven successful in generating both positive environmental benefits and positive goodwill and community relations. One such practice is the pursuit of **Leadership in Energy and Environmental Design (LEED)** accreditation. Developed by the U.S. Green Building Council (USGBC), LEED provides building owners and operators with a framework for identifying and implementing practical and measurable green building design, construction, operations and maintenance solutions. Specifically, LEED certification provides independent, third-party verification that a building, home or community was designed and built using strategies aimed at achieving high performance in key areas of human and environmental health: sustainable site development, water savings, energy efficiency, materials selection, and indoor environmental quality. Among airports, Terminal 2 at San Francisco International Airport was the first airport terminal in the United States to achieve LEED Gold certification. Highlights include dining options that feature locally grown and organic foods, hydration stations, eco-friendly child play areas, natural light, cleaner air, connection to mass transit, zero waste, water conservation, paperless ticketing, and use of sustainable building materials. Since Terminal 2 at San Francisco International Airport, other airports have developed new LEED facilities. For example, in January 2014, the newly constructed aircraft rescue and firefighting station at Southwest Florida International earned the LEED Gold Certification due to energy-efficient lighting and mechanical systems, low-flow water fixtures, a rainwater reclamation system that collects and stores water to be used for landscaping irrigation, recycling and separating of construction debris and

San Francisco International Airport Terminal 2

In 2011, San Francisco International Airport's Terminal 2 (T2) was the first airport terminal in the United States to achieve LEED Gold status. LEED references the Leadership in Energy and Environmental Design by the U.S. Green Building Council (USGBC). The 640,000 square foot T2 has many unique features, including a wide array of natural and organic culinary offerings; more than 400 computer plug-in outlets and intuitive, comfortable work-station seating; eco-friendly art installations from local artists that highlight the natural world and double as children's play areas; and convenient "hydration stations" that allow travelers to refill reusable water bottles post-security. Additionally, T2 produces cleaner air due to a special displacement ventilation system; natural sunlight enhances the interior lighting; and a paperless ticketing system reduces waste and adds convenience. T2 provides a car-free connection with direct connection to Bay Area Rapid Transit (BART); is zero-waste, replacing traditional garbage cans with waste stations incorporating compartments for composting, recyclables and trash; and conserves water via a dual plumbing system that allows for reclaimed water from the airport's water treatment facility to be used for toilets and other uses throughout the airport, as well as plumbing fixtures that use 40 percent less water than typical fixtures.

(San Francisco International Airport, 2011)

waste, and the use of reflective building materials and allowance of natural light into the building (McCarron, 2011).

Another practice involves encouraging alternative transportation means for employees and passengers. For example, airports may encourage more frequent use of public transportation by providing public transit incentives for employees and ensure convenient connections to public transportation by passengers. Additionally, bicycle lanes, special parking areas for electric/hybrid vehicles, and storage racks for bicycles could be installed. Airports have also encouraged use of compressed natural gas-powered buses, electric vehicles, and three-wheeled bikes for maintenance employees.

Yet another practice involves encouraging biodiversity. Airports can do this by planting native, non-wildlife attracting landscaping that needs less irrigation than non-native species. Airports may also partner with local environmental organizations.

Airports may also adopt measures to counteract climate change and reduce the airport's carbon footprint by becoming more energy efficient. By conducting an energy audit, the airport can determine where energy is used at the airport. Examples of energy efficient measures include escalator sleep-mode settings, motion-activated lighting in infrequently used areas, Energy Star computers and equipment, and fluorescent and LED lighting.

A relatively new trend among airports involves capitalizing on renewable energy sources such as solar, wind, and geothermal. Often the most visible of these are installations of photovoltaic (PV) module installations. Quite a few airports have installed PV arrays, including Denver International Airport (DIA), Fresno Yosemite International Airport (FAT), and Tallahassee Regional Airport (TLH). PV installations can be quite expensive, however, in essence requiring that 20+ years of electricity is paid for up front. In the case of TLH, in 2010 the purchase and installation of a 25 kilowatt (kW) system was $125,000, while a 75 kW system was $350,000 to $400,000. Return on investment (ROI) was estimated at 40 years for a 25 kW system and 34 years for a 75 kW system, although these timeframes will be significantly lessened (to 8.6 years and 23.8 years, respectively) with an energy efficiency and conservation block grant. At Fresno Yosemite International Airport, the solar installation is expected to supply 40 percent of the airport's energy needs, saving the airport $13 million over 20 years. Regardless of which environmental stewardship practices are adopted, airports can directly lessen their impact on the environment in a publicly acceptable way by pursuing sustainable environmental stewardship (McGormley et al., 2011).

Concluding Thoughts

Airports are responsible for complying with numerous environmental regulations. Whether it be noise, land use compatibility, zoning, water quality, air quality, or hazardous waste, it is imperative for airport managers to understand the importance of environmental compliance and develop policies and procedures to ensure that all businesses on the airport meet environmental requirements.

Chapter Summary

- An environmental management system (EMS) is the foundation for a strategic and proactive approach to ensuring environmental compliance and is becoming a standard practice at airports desiring to formalize their approach to proactive environmental management.
- The foundation of a good-faith effort requires airports to ensure tenant and contractor compliance through initial bid specifications and/or requests for proposals, periodic inspections and audits, and lease and contract agreements.
- Environmental regulations are "without regard to fault," meaning that an airport manager or other personnel can be found guilty of noncompliance even if there was not intent to commit a crime.

- The National Environmental Policy Act of 1969 required airports (among other industries) to completely consider the environmental impacts of a proposed project prior to initiating it.

- A project may be categorically excluded from the environmental impact study requirements if, according to FAA Order 5050.4B, projects of that type have been found under normal circumstances to have no potential for significant environmental impact.

- If a project is either not categorically excluded or is categorically excluded but likely to involve extraordinary circumstances, then an environmental assessment may be required.

- The EA results in one of two findings—either no significant impacts or significant impacts. If the former, a finding of no significant impact (FONSI) is prepared. If, on the other hand, the impacts of the proposed project are determined to be significant, an environmental impact statement (EIS) may be required.

- The FAA has adopted a cumulative noise metric—the average day-night sound level (DNL) in A-weighted decibels. DNL is the 24-hour average sound level in A-weighted decibels for the period midnight to midnight.

- 14 CFR Part 150 contains the procedures, standards, and methodology addressing the development, submission, and review of noise exposure maps and noise compatibility plans.

- According to Part 150, all types of land use are considered to be compatible with noise levels less than 65 dB DNL.

- The reduction of airport noise is generally accomplished via (a) reduction of noise at the source, (b) relocation of the source of the noise in either space or time, and (c) acoustical changes to the area receiving the noise.

- Although voluntary, Part 150 programs are strongly recommended by the FAA if the airport has (a) significant amounts of noise-affected incompatible land use, (b) the receipt of serious noise complaints, (c) a threat from urban development pressure to increase incompatible land use near the airport, or (d) the introduction of major changes in airport facilities or operations that are likely to shift or increase noise patterns.

- The standard prediction analysis tool for use by airports, the FAA's Integrated Noise Model, calculates the total impact of aircraft noise at or around airports. The INM produces noise exposure contours that are used to produce NEMs and aid the airport in land use compatibility planning.

- Maintaining the quality of water, especially in the nation's rivers and lakes, is the main purpose of the Clean Water Act of 1977.

- The National Pollution Discharge Elimination System permit program is the means of regulating point source discharge of pollutants into the nation's navigable waterways.

- The Oil Pollution Act of 1990 requires the development of (a) a facility response plan that addresses a worst-case discharge of oil into the environment and (b) a Spill Prevention, Control and Countermeasure (SPCC) plan if the airport has an aboveground oil storage capacity greater than 1,320 gallons or a buried oil storage capacity greater than 42,000 gallons, and a reasonable potential for a discharge into or upon navigable waters of the United States.

- Airports are required by the National Pollution Discharge Elimination System permit program to obtain an NPDES permit for stormwater discharge. Prior to obtaining a permit, an airport must develop a stormwater pollution prevention plan.

- The FAA has approved both fluid and solid deicers/anti-icers for use on pavements. Approved fluids include glycol-based, potassium acetate-based, and potassium formate-based fluids. Approved solid compounds include airside urea, sodium formate, and sodium acetate.

- Chemicals used in aircraft deicing include propylene glycol and ethylene glycol.

- The EPA approves state air quality plans; develops regulations and polices pertaining to air pollution; designates areas with respect to attainment of outdoor air quality standards; enforces violations of federal air quality regulations; sets air emissions standards for engines, fuels, and other emissions sources; and sets outdoor air quality standards for air pollutants.

- The Comprehensive Environmental Response, Compensation, and Liability Act of 1980, also known as "Superfund," and subsequent modifications (Superfund Amendments and Reauthorization Act of 1986) established criteria for closed and abandoned hazardous waste sites, allowed for the liability of individuals and/or companies found responsible for the release of hazardous waste, and created a funding source that provides for the cleanup of hazardous waste sites when the responsible individuals and/or companies either cannot be located or are no longer in existence.

- Under the Occupational Safety and Health Act of 1970, airports are required to have material safety data sheets for each hazardous chemical present on the airport. MSDS are intended to provide workers and emergency personnel with procedures for handling that substance in a safe manner, and include information on the chemical's physical properties, toxicity, health effects, first aid, etc.

- The 1984 Hazardous and Solid Waste Amendments to RCRA address underground storage tanks, specifically establishing requirements for tank design, release/leak detection, and leaking underground storage tanks.

- Sustainability planning involves developing a sustainability vision or policy, conducting a baseline assessment/gap analysis, establishing goals and objectives, setting performance targets, identifying sustainability practices, implementing practices, and regularly measuring, reporting, and reevaluating.

Review Questions ↘

1. What are some of the airport activities that can result in environmental impacts?

2. Explain an environmental management system, including the benefits and steps in development.

3. What is required of airports by the National Environmental Policy Act of 1969?

4. Explain the environmental impact statement.

5. Explain the decibel scale.

6. What standard noise metric is used to measure aircraft noise?

7. Explain the purpose of 14 CFR Part 150.

8. What is the purpose of a noise compatibility plan?

9. What are the most common noise mitigation measures?

10. Explain how a continuous airport noise monitoring system works.

11. Under what conditions is a Part 150 program strongly recommended?

12. Explain the Integrated Noise Model (INM).

13. Explain compatible land use.

14. Explain the purpose of easements.

15. What are the typical components of a Spill Prevention, Control and Countermeasure plan?

16. Explain the chemicals used in maintaining airport pavements during snow and icing conditions.

17. Explain the chemicals used in deicing aircraft.

18. What is the purpose of material safety data sheets?

19. Under what situations would the National Response Center (NRC) be notified?

20. Explain what sustainability planning involves.

Scenarios ↘

1. As the new environmental manager at Blue Junction Airport, you have been asked to develop an environmental management system. First, what are the benefits of doing so? Second, how would you develop such a system?

2. A former FBO operator at your airport has left behind several underground storage tanks on their former leasehold. One was used for Avgas and one for Jet-A fuel. Now that the airport is planning to redevelop the area once occupied by this FBO, what must be done with these underground tanks? If problems are discovered (i.e., leaking tanks with contaminated soil), how should this be resolved? What if the former FBO operator can't be located or is bankrupt and no longer in business?

3. With a Part 150 study recently completed, it is obvious that several residential areas surrounding the airport are affected by noise (included in the 70 dB DNL contour). What options are available to the airport to minimize the impacted areas?

4. With the EPA's new technology-based effluent limitations guidelines and new source performance standards to control discharges of pollutants from airport deicing operations, you are tasked with minimizing the environmental impact of airfield pavement deicing at your airport. What are your options for ensuring compliance?

5. What options are available to you to reduce emissions at your airport? Consider emissions from aircraft APUs at the gate, ground support equipment, airport vehicles, public transit, etc.

References and Resources for Further Study

American Association of Airport Executives (AAAE). 2010. "Body of Knowledge Module 2. Planning, construction, and environmental." Washington, DC: AAAE.

————. 2011. "ACE Operations Module 4: Hazardous Materials, FOD, Wildlife, ARFF, Winter Operations, and Security." Alexandria, VA: AAAE.

Environmental Protection Agency (EPA). 2014. "Airport Deicing Effluent Guidelines." Retrieved from http://water.epa.gov/scitech/wastetech/guide/airport/index.cfm

Federal Aviation Administration (FAA). n.d. "Details on FAA Noise Levels, Stages, and Phaseouts." Retrieved from http://www.faa.gov/about/office_org/headquarters_offices/apl/noise_emissions/airport_aircraft_noise_issues/levels/

————. 1983. *Noise Control and Compatibility Planning for Airports*. AC 150/5020-1. Washington, DC: FAA.

————. 2002. *Estimated Airplane Noise Levels in A-weighted Decibels*. AC 36-3. Washington, DC: FAA.

————. 2007. *Environmental Management Systems for Airport Sponsors*. AC 150/5050-8. Washington, DC: FAA.

Massport. n.d. "Mitigating Airport Noise in the Community." Retrieved at http://www.massport.com/environment/environmental-reporting/noise-abatement/sound-insulation-program/

McCarron, M. 2011. Media Advisory, "SFO's Terminal 2 Certified LEED Gold." Retrieved from http://www.flysfo.com/web/page/about/news/pressrel/2011/sf1186.html

McGormley, R. W., J. A. Lengel, D. E. Seal, J. N. Foster, M. Kenney, P. K. Sanford, B. J. Siwinski, C. Lurie, E. Humblet. 2011. "ACRP Report 43: Guidebook of Practices for Improving Environmental Performance at Small Airports." Washington, DC: Transportation Research Board. Retrieved from http://onlinepubs.trb.org/onlinepubs/acrp/acrp_rpt_043.pdf

Roberts, D. and G. Evans. 2011. "Recycling: DEN's Sustainable Approach." Retrieved from http://www.aviationpros.com/article/10290507/recycling-dens-sustainable-approach?page=2

San Francisco International Airport. 2011. "SFO's Terminal 2 Certified LEED® Gold." News release. Retrieved from http://www.flysfo.com/media/press-releases/sfos-terminal-2-certified-leed%C2%AE-gold

Chapter 7

Operations

Objectives ↘

Upon completion of this chapter, you should understand:

- the airports to which 14 CFR Part 139 applies
- the classes of Part 139 airports
- the airport certification manual (ACM) and its typical contents
- each of the sections of 14 CFR Part 139 and the conditions to which certificated airports must adhere
- the purpose of a snow and ice control plan (SICP)
- the aircraft rescue and firefighting (ARFF) index, equipment and agents, and operational requirements
- the airport emergency plan (AEP)
- wildlife hazard management
- the NOTAM system
- airport communications
- the impacts of new generation aircraft

Key Terms ↘

active control
airport certification manual (ACM)
airport emergency plan (AEP)
Airport/Facility Directory (A/FD)
airport operating certificate (AOC)
ARFF Index
Class I
Class II
Class III
Class IV

habitat management
new large aircraft (NLA)
Notice to Airmen (NOTAM)
scheduled operation
snow and ice control plan (SICP)
turret
unscheduled operation
wildlife attractant
wildlife strike

In Chapter 7

FEATURES

Ronald Reagan Washington National Airport Emergency Exercise 297

A full-scale emergency exercise in compliance with 14 CFR §139.325

Orlando International Airport's Wildlife Hazard Management Program 310

Efforts to minimize wildlife hazards at Orlando International Airport have enhanced safety for airport users.

Introduction

Airports, by their nature, are operations-driven. It is the operation of aircraft that justifies the existence of an airport. Although airports across the United States vary in size and operational activity, airport operators must focus on providing safe airports that are properly maintained. This chapter discusses the operation of public-use airports in the United States (Figure 7-1).

Figure 7-1.
San Francisco International Airport, a public-use, publicly-owned Part 139 certificated airport.

(©iStock.com/StephanHoerold)

Title 14 CFR Part 139

The federal regulation that applies to the commercial service airports in the United States is 14 CFR Part 139, Certification of Airports. This regulation applies to all airports serving scheduled air carrier aircraft with more than 9 seats and unscheduled air carrier aircraft with more than 30 seats. Part 139 does not apply to:

- GA airports (meaning those airports not being served by air carriers)
- Airports serving scheduled air carrier operations only by reason of being designated as an alternate airport
- Airports operated by the United States
- Airports located in the State of Alaska that only serve scheduled operations of small air carrier aircraft and do not serve scheduled or unscheduled operations of large air carrier aircraft (small aircraft have a certificated maximum takeoff weight of 12,500 pounds or less)
- Airports located in the state of Alaska during periods of time when not serving operations of large air carrier aircraft
- Heliports
(FAA, 2004, p. 1)

Among those airports to which Part 139 does apply, four classes of airports exist. These classes are:

- **Class I**—Serve scheduled operations of large air carrier aircraft and unscheduled passenger operations of large air carrier aircraft and/or scheduled operations of small air carrier aircraft.
- **Class II**—Serve scheduled operations of small air carrier aircraft and unscheduled passenger operations of large air carrier aircraft.
- **Class III**—Serve scheduled operations of small air carrier aircraft.
- **Class IV**—Serve unscheduled passenger operations of large air carrier aircraft.

(FAA, 2004)

As of 2015, there were 393 Class I airports, 33 Class II airports, 31 Class III airports, and 82 Class IV airports, resulting in 544 certificated airports nationwide. As evident by these numbers, most of the certificated airports in the United States are capable of serving any type of operation and size of aircraft as may be necessary.

A **scheduled operation** is any common carriage passenger-carrying operation for compensation or hire conducted by an air carrier for which the air carrier or its representatives offer in advance the departure location, departure time, and arrival location. An **unscheduled operation** is any common carriage passenger-carrying operation for compensation or hire, using aircraft designed for at least 31 passenger seats, conducted by an air carrier for which the departure time, departure location, and arrival location are specifically negotiated with the customer or the customer's representative. Unscheduled operations include any passenger-carrying supplemental operation conducted under 14 CFR Part 121 and any passenger-carrying public charter operation conducted under 14 CFR Part 380. In simple terms, an unscheduled operation is typically a charter of some sort, whereas a scheduled operation occurs at the same time each week, allowing anyone to plan to take a scheduled flight (FAA, 2004).

For an airport to operate under Part 139, it must apply for and obtain an **airport operating certificate (AOC)** from the FAA. Obtaining an AOC requires developing an **airport certification manual (ACM)** that addresses each of the requirements in Part 139. The ACM provides specific local guidance unique to that airport and explains how the airport will comply with each of the requirements of Part 139. Since Part 139 is a regulation that applies to airports, large and small, the airport develops an ACM to notify the FAA how their specific airport will comply with the regulation. Thus, although there are similarities among various airports' ACMs, each ACM is unique to the airport for which it is developed.

It is a best practice to address each section of Part 139 Subpart D, in order, in the ACM. Many airports develop their ACM using the exact same numbering as the sections in Subpart D. The FAA likes an ACM that has the same structure as Subpart D, and this can easily be done by incorporating the same numbering system as the regulation. Typically, the ACM is prepared in a three-ring binder, allowing for subsequent revisions of specific pages without the need to revise the entire manual. Each page of the ACM is approved and signed by the FAA. A page control table at the front of the manual allows the airport and the FAA to make certain the manual is current, based on future page revisions. Once prepared, the ACM is submitted to the FAA for approval. Once approved, the ACM is updated regularly with any revised pages submitted to the FAA for approval.

A key point to remember when preparing an ACM is that it should be comprehensive, yet conservative. The ACM, once approved by the FAA, becomes an extension of the regulation and the airport will be held responsible for complying with this extension of the regulation. For instance, if Part 139 requires a self-inspection once each day, but the airport states in the ACM that three will be conducted each day, the airport will in fact be held to the three-per-day standard, even though it is contrary to the regulation. Part 139 contains minimum requirements, and the airport should meet these minimums. Exceeding these minimums is admirable, but formalizing in the ACM the specific manner by which the minimums will be exceeded is not recommended.

To be eligible for an AOC, airports must (a) provide written documentation that air carrier service will begin on a certain date, (b) submit an ACM, and (c) be found properly and adequately equipped and able to provide a safe airport operating environment in accordance with Part 139 and the ACM. It should be noted that not all airports are eligible to obtain an AOC, even if they prepare and submit an ACM. The FAA is only interested in providing an AOC to airports that will serve air carriers, whether scheduled or unscheduled. Once obtained, an AOC is effective until the airport surrenders it or the FAA suspends or revokes it. Although an AOC has no expiration date, certificated airports are required to ensure their ACM is current at all times. Each page of the ACM will have an approval date (typically in the form of a date block with the initials of the FAA certification inspector approving the page).

Each ACM is required to have certain elements that address each of the required areas of Part 139. Interestingly, Class I, Class II, and Class III airports are each required to include the same elements in their ACM. However, Class IV airports are not required to include seven of the elements that other Classes of Part 139 airports are required to include. See Table 7-1 for the required certification manual elements.

Subpart D of Part 139, entitled Operations, presents the specific requirements for certificated airports relating to daily airport operations. In essence, Subpart D presents the "real meat" of the regulation as it pertains to airports.

Table 7-1. Required elements in an airport certification manual.

Manual elements	Airport certificate class			
	Class I	Class II	Class III	Class IV
1. Lines of succession of airport operational responsibility	X	X	X	X
2. Each current exemption issued to the airport from the requirements of this part	X	X	X	X
3. Any limitations imposed by the Administrator	X	X	X	X
4. A grid map or other means of identifying locations and terrain features on and around the airport that are significant to emergency operations	X	X	X	X
5. The location of each obstruction required to be lighted or marked within the airport's area of authority	X	X	X	X
6. A description of each movement area available for air carriers and its safety areas, and each road described in §139.319(k) that serves it	X	X	X	X
7. Procedures for avoidance of interruption or failure during construction work of utilities serving facilities or NAVAIDS that support air carrier operations	X	X	X	
8. A description of the system for maintaining records, as required under §139.301	X	X	X	X
9. A description of personnel training, as required under §139.303	X	X	X	X
10. Procedures for maintaining the paved areas, as required under §139.305	X	X	X	X
11. Procedures for maintaining the unpaved areas, as required under §139.307	X	X	X	X
12. Procedures for maintaining the safety areas, as required under §139.309	X	X	X	X
13. A plan showing the runway and taxiway identification system, including the location and inscription of signs, runway markings, and holding position markings, as required under §139.311	X	X	X	X
14. A description of, and procedures for maintaining, the marking, signs, and lighting systems, as required under §139.311	X	X	X	X
15. A snow and ice control plan, as required under §139.313	X	X	X	
16. A description of the facilities, equipment, personnel, and procedures for meeting the aircraft rescue and firefighting requirements, in accordance with §§139.315, 139.317 and 139.319	X	X	X	X
17. A description of any approved exemption to aircraft rescue and firefighting requirements, as authorized under §139.111	X	X	X	X
18. Procedures for protecting persons and property during the storing, dispensing, and handling of fuel and other hazardous substances and materials, as required under §139.321	X	X	X	X

Table 7-1. *(continued)*

Manual elements	Airport certificate class			
	Class I	Class II	Class III	Class IV
19. A description of, and procedures for maintaining, the traffic and wind direction indicators, as required under §139.323	X	X	X	X
20. An emergency plan as required under §139.325	X	X	X	X
21. Procedures for conducting the self-inspection program, as required under §139.327	X	X	X	X
22. Procedures for controlling pedestrians and ground vehicles in movement areas and safety areas, as required under §139.329	X	X	X	X
23. Procedures for obstruction removal, marking, or lighting, as required under §139.331	X	X	X	X
24. Procedures for protection of NAVAIDS, as required under §139.333	X	X	X	
25. A description of public protection, as required under §139.335	X	X	X	
26. Procedures for wildlife hazard management, as required under §139.337	X	X	X	
27. Procedures for airport condition reporting, as required under §139.339	X	X	X	X
28. Procedures for identifying, marking, and lighting construction and other unserviceable areas, as required under §139.341	X	X	X	
29. Any other item that the Administrator finds is necessary to ensure safety in air transportation	X	X	X	X

RECORDS

First, §139.301, Records, requires airports to maintain personnel training records, as required by §§139.303 and 139.327, for 24 consecutive calendar months. Emergency personnel training records for aircraft rescue and firefighting and emergency medical service personnel, as required by §139.319, must be retained for 24 consecutive calendar months. Records of airport fueling agent inspections, as required by §139.321, must be maintained for 12 consecutive calendar months. Records of fueling personnel training, as required by §139.321, must be maintained for 12 consecutive calendar months.

Figure 7-2.
14 CFR Part 139 specifies requirements for records that must be maintained and furnished to the FAA upon request.

(Wikimedia Commons; see credit on page 624)

Records of self-inspections, as required by §139.327, must be maintained for 12 consecutive calendar months. Records of training given to pedestrians and ground vehicle operators with access to movement areas and safety areas, as required by §139.329, must be maintained for 24 consecutive calendar months. Records of each accident or incident in movement areas and safety areas involving an air carrier aircraft and/or ground vehicle, as required by §139.329, must be maintained for 12 consecutive calendar months. Records of airport condition information dissemination, as required by §139.339, must be maintained for 12 consecutive calendar months. Each of the records required to be maintained under §139.301 must be furnished to the FAA upon request, which usually occurs once annually during the annual certification inspection (Figure 7-2) (FAA, 2004).

PERSONNEL

14 CFR §139.303, Personnel, requires airports to provide sufficient and qualified personnel to comply with the requirements of the airport's ACM. Personnel who access movement areas and safety areas and perform duties in compliance with the ACM and Part 139 must be trained prior to the initial performance of duties and at least once every 12 consecutive calendar months thereafter in at least the following areas:

- Airport familiarization, including airport marking, lighting, and signs systems
- Procedures for access to, and operation in, movement areas and safety areas
- Airport communications, including radio communication between the air traffic control tower and personnel, use of the common traffic advisory frequency if there is no air traffic control tower or the tower is not in operation, and procedures for reporting unsafe airport conditions
- Duties required under the airport certification manual and the requirements of Part 139.
- Any additional subject areas required under §§139.319, 139.321, 139.327, 139.329, 139.337, and 139.339, as appropriate.

Airports must also equip these personnel with sufficient resources necessary to perform the functions required of them according to the ACM (Figure 7-3). Generally, new operations personnel spend three to six months receiving on-the-job training, including learning the layout of the airfield, the airport's inspection program, Security Identification Display Area (SIDA) and movement area training, and familiarization with the ACM, emergency response manual (ERM), etc.

Figure 7-3. Airport operations vehicle.

PAVED AREAS

Section 139.305, Paved Areas, requires airports to maintain and promptly repair the pavement of each runway, taxiway, loading ramp, and parking area on the airport that is available for air carrier use. Specifically, airports are required to maintain pavement as follows:

- The pavement edges must not exceed 3 inches difference in elevation between abutting pavement sections and between pavement and abutting areas.

- The pavement must have no hole exceeding 3 inches in depth nor any hole the slope of which from any point in the hole to the nearest point at the lip of the hole is 45 degrees or greater, as measured from the pavement surface plane, unless, in either case, the entire area of the hole can be covered by a 5-inch diameter circle (Figure 7-4).

- The pavement must be free of cracks and surface variations that could impair directional control of air carrier aircraft, including any pavement crack or surface deterioration that produces loose aggregate or other contaminants.

(FAA, 2004)

Figure 7-4. Tolerances not to be exceeded for paved areas.

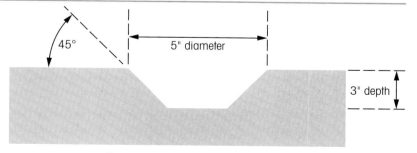

Pavement cross-section

Additionally, mud, dirt, sand, loose aggregate, debris, foreign objects, rubber deposits, chemicals, and other contaminants must be removed promptly and as completely as practical. Pavement must also be sufficiently drained and free of depressions to prevent ponding that obscures markings or impairs safe aircraft operations. Section 139.305 does not apply to the control of snow and ice accumulations. Paved areas are inspected daily and often generate the most work orders for repair. Whether flexible or rigid, pavement reaches the end of its useful life and starts deteriorating, requiring rehabilitation or repair (see Figure 7-5). It is often airport operations personnel who keep tabs on the pavement as part of the inspection program and initiate this repair as needed (FAA, 2004).

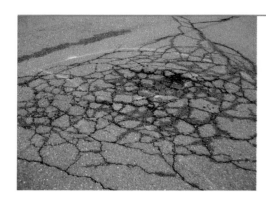

Figure 7-5.
Pavement in need of repair.

UNPAVED AREAS

14 CFR §139.307, Unpaved Areas, requires airports to maintain and promptly repair the surface of each gravel, turf, or other unpaved runway, taxiway, or loading ramp and parking area on the airport that is available for air carrier use (see Figure 7-6). Specifically, airports are required to maintain unpaved areas as follows:

- No slope from the edge of the full-strength surfaces downward to the existing terrain must be steeper than 2:1.
- The full-strength surfaces must have adequate crown or grade to assure sufficient drainage to prevent ponding.
- The full-strength surfaces must be adequately compacted and sufficiently stable to prevent rutting by aircraft or the loosening or build-up of surface material, which could impair directional control of aircraft or drainage.
- The full-strength surfaces must have no holes or depressions that exceed 3 inches in depth and are of a breadth capable of impairing directional control or causing damage to an aircraft.
- Debris and foreign objects must be promptly removed from the surface.
  (FAA, 2004)

Often, unpaved areas are not inspected as frequently as paved areas yet they are important nonetheless. A best practice involves walking these unpaved areas on a regular basis to detect any depressions or holes that could impair the directional control of aircraft.

Chemical methods involve material spreaders that disperse deice/anti-ice granules or liquid. Airports in snow-prone areas such as Salt Lake City, Denver, Milwaukee, and New York have millions of dollars invested in snow removal equipment.

ARFF: INDEX DETERMINATION

Part 139 also specifies aircraft rescue and firefighting (ARFF) requirements. Specifically, §139.315, Aircraft Rescue and Firefighting: Index Determination, states that certified airports must have an **ARFF Index** and includes the manner by which this index is determined. The index is determined by the length of air carrier aircraft and the average daily departures of air carrier aircraft. The ARFF Index specifies the required number of ARFF vehicles and required amount of extinguishing agents (see Table 7-2).

Table 7-2. ARFF Index determination.

The index is determined by a combination of: 1. The length of air carrier aircraft and   2. Average daily departures of air carrier aircraft.
For the purpose of Index determination, air carrier aircraft lengths are grouped as follows: 1. Index A includes aircraft less than 90 feet in length.   2. Index B includes aircraft at least 90 feet but less than 126 feet in length.   3. Index C includes aircraft at least 126 feet but less than 159 feet in length.   4. Index D includes aircraft at least 159 feet but less than 200 feet in length.   5. Index E includes aircraft at least 200 feet in length.

According to §139.315, if there are five or more average daily departures of air carrier aircraft in a single index group serving that airport, the longest aircraft with an average of five or more daily departures determines the index required for the airport. When there are fewer than five average daily departures of the longest air carrier aircraft serving the airport, the index required for the airport will be the next lower index group than the index group prescribed for the longest aircraft. For example, if there are three average daily departures of B-767 aircraft (Index D) and two average daily departures of B-717 aircraft (Index B), the ARFF Index for the airport would be Index C, even though the airport in this case is not served by any Index C aircraft. The minimum ARFF Index for certificated airports will be Index A. Additionally, Class III airports may comply with the ARFF Index requirements by providing a level of safety comparable to Index A that is approved by the FAA.

ARFF: EQUIPMENT AND AGENTS

Section 139.317, Aircraft Rescue and Firefighting: Equipment and Agents, specifies the response equipment and type and amount of extinguishing agents required for each index. There are several standard extinguishing agents in use at airports. First, a sufficient quantity of water is carried, which is the main reason ARFF trucks are so large. Water is generally not used by itself, but is mixed at the time of application with aqueous film forming foam (AFFF) (in 3% or 6% concentrate) to form a blanket of foam which starves a fire of

Unless otherwise authorized by the Administrator, the following rescue and firefighting equipment and agents are the minimum required for the Indexes referred to in §139.315:

(a) Index A. One vehicle carrying at least—

(1) 500 pounds of sodium-based dry chemical, halon 1211, or clean agent; or

(2) 450 pounds of potassium-based dry chemical and water with a commensurate quantity of AFFF to total 100 gallons for simultaneous dry chemical and AFFF application.

(b) Index B. Either of the following:

(1) One vehicle carrying at least 500 pounds of sodium-based dry chemical, halon 1211, or clean agent and 1,500 gallons of water and the commensurate quantity of AFFF for foam production.

(2) Two vehicles—

(i) One vehicle carrying the extinguishing agents as specified in paragraphs (a)(1) or (a)(2) of this section; and
(ii) One vehicle carrying an amount of water and the commensurate quantity of AFFF so the total quantity of water for foam production carried by both vehicles is at least 1,500 gallons.

(c) Index C. Either of the following:

(1) Three vehicles—

(i) One vehicle carrying the extinguishing agents as specified in paragraph (a) (1) or (a)(2) of this section; and

(ii) Two vehicles carrying an amount of water and the commensurate quantity of AFFF so the total quantity of water for foam production carried by all three vehicles is at least 3,000 gallons.

(2) Two vehicles—

(i) One vehicle carrying the extinguishing agents as specified in paragraph (b) (1) of this section; and
(ii) One vehicle carrying water and the commensurate quantity of AFFF so the total quantity of water for foam production carried by both vehicles is at least 3,000 gallons.

(d) Index D. Three vehicles—

(1) One vehicle carrying the extinguishing agents as specified in paragraphs (a)(1) or (a)(2) of this section; and

(2) Two vehicles carrying an amount of water and the commensurate quantity of AFFF so the total quantity of water for foam production carried by all three vehicles is at least 4,000 gallons.

(e) Index E. Three vehicles—

(1) One vehicle carrying the extinguishing agents as specified in paragraphs (a)(1) or (a)(2) of this section; and

(2) Two vehicles carrying an amount of water and the commensurate quantity of AFFF so the total quantity of water for foam production carried by all three vehicles is at least 6,000 gallons.

Figure 7-9.
ARFF equipment requirements.

(14 CFR §139.317)

oxygen, suppresses fuel vapors, and cools the fire. In essence, AFFF attacks all three sides of the fire triangle. Dry chemical, either sodium-based or potassium-based, is also used. Purple K is a common potassium-based dry chemical in use by ARFF. The requirements are presented in Figure 7-9.

In addition to specifying the equipment, §139.317 specifies the foam discharge capacity. First, each ARFF vehicle used to comply with Index B, C, D, or E requirements with a capacity of at least 500 gallons of water for foam production must be equipped with a **turret**.[1] Each vehicle with a water tank capacity of between 500 to 2,000 gallons must have a turret discharge rate between 500 and 1,000 gallons per minute. For vehicles with water tank capacities of at least 2,000 gallons, the turret discharge rate must be between 600 and 1,200 gallons per minute. For each ARFF vehicle required to carry dry chemical, halon 1211, or clean agent, the minimum discharge rates are 5 pounds per second for a hand line and 16 pounds per second for a turret. Lastly, for ARFF vehicles required to carry AFFF, a sufficient amount of AFFF must be carried to enable mixing with twice the water required to be carried by the vehicle (Figure 7-10) (FAA, 2004).

Figure 7-10. 3,000-gallon ARFF truck.

(Nan Phanitsuda Sophonpanasak, Denver International Airport)

ARFF: OPERATIONAL REQUIREMENTS

Operational requirements for ARFF are specified in §139.319, Aircraft Rescue and Firefighting: Operational Requirements. First, if there is an increase in the average daily departures or the length of air carrier aircraft to the extent that the airport's index changes, the airport must comply with the increased requirements. Also, this section allows an airport to reduce the ARFF level corresponding to the index group of the longest air carrier aircraft being operated, during those times when only air carrier aircraft shorter than the normal index are being operated. However, this is subject to specific procedures (including full recall of the ARFF capability) being included in the airport certification manual. Additionally, the reductions may not be implemented unless notification to air carriers is provided in the ***Airport/Facility Directory*** (**A/FD**) or via

---

[1] A device which allows for extinguishing agent to be dispersed from either a roof mount or bumper mount.

Notices to Airmen (NOTAMs), and by direct notification of local air carriers. The *Airport/Facility Directory*, which is updated every 56 days, is a government publication that is published per FAA region providing detailed information about public airports, seaplane bases, heliports, military facilities, and selected private-use airports in that region. NOTAMs are the official manner in which to convey airport condition information to pilots. NOTAMs may be issued by airport personnel or the FAA via Flight Service.

This section also requires each required ARFF vehicle to be equipped with two-way voice radio communications that allows for communication with all other required emergency vehicles, the ATCT, the CTAF when an ATCT is not in operation or there is no ATCT, and fire stations, as specified in the airport emergency plan. ARFF vehicles are required to be equipped with a flashing or rotating beacon and painted or marked in high-contrast colors. Additionally, vehicles must be maintained so as to be available and operationally capable during all air carrier operations. At airports located in geographical areas subject to prolonged temperatures below 33 degrees Fahrenheit, the vehicles must be provided with cover or other means to ensure equipment operation and discharge under freezing conditions. If any required vehicle becomes inoperative to the extent that it cannot perform as required, it must be replaced immediately with equipment having at least equal capabilities. If replacement equipment is not immediately available, the regional airports division manager and each air carrier using the airport must be notified. Also, if the required index level of capability is not restored within 48 hours, the airport operator (unless otherwise approved by the FAA) must limit air carrier operations to those compatible with the index corresponding to the remaining operative ARFF equipment (Figure 7-11).

14 CFR §139.319 also requires that ARFF equipment respond to an aircraft accident in a timely manner. Specifically, at least one required ARFF vehicle must reach the midpoint of the farthest runway serving air carrier aircraft from its assigned post within three minutes from the time of alarm. The ARFF vehicle must also begin application of extinguishing agent during this time.

Figure 7-11.
ARFF facility.

All other required vehicles must arrive and begin application of extinguishing agent within four minutes from the time of alarm. ARFF response time is tested annually by the FAA during the airport's Part 139 certification inspection.

Section 139.319 also requires ARFF personnel to be properly equipped and trained to perform the duties required of their position (see Figure 7-12). Training must take place prior to initial performance of duties and every 12 consecutive calendar months thereafter. The curriculum for this initial and recurrent training must include:

- Airport familiarization, including airport signs, marking, and lighting
- Aircraft familiarization
- Rescue and firefighting personnel safety
- Emergency communications systems on the airport, including fire alarms
- Use of the fire hoses, nozzles, turrets, and other appliances required for compliance with this part
- Application of the types of extinguishing agents required for compliance with this part
- Emergency aircraft evacuation assistance
- Firefighting operations
- Adapting and using structural rescue and firefighting equipment for aircraft rescue and firefighting
- Aircraft cargo hazards, including hazardous materials/dangerous goods incidents
- Familiarization with firefighters' duties under the airport emergency plan

Figure 7-12. Engine fire in an ARFF aircraft trainer being extinguished.

Additionally, §139.319 requires all ARFF personnel to participate in a live fire drill prior to initial performance of duties and every 12 consecutive calendar months thereafter (see Figure 7-13). There must also be at least one person available during air carrier operations who is trained and current in basic emergency medical care, including 40 hours of training covering:

- Bleeding
- Cardiopulmonary resuscitation
- Shock
- Primary patient survey
- Injuries to the skull, spine, chest, and extremities
- Internal injuries
- Moving patients
- Burns
- Triage

Figure 7-13.
Live ARFF burn training.

(Nan Phanitsuda Sophonpanasak, Denver International Airport)

Records of this training must be maintained for 24 consecutive calendar months after completion of training. In addition to having sufficient personnel on duty to comply with the requirements of Part 139, airports must have an alerting system in place to notify ARFF personnel of any existing or impending emergency requiring their assistance. Each ARFF vehicle is also required to carry (or have access to) the "North American Emergency Response Guidebook" published by the U.S. Department of Transportation (or similar). Lastly, §139.319 requires airports to provide and maintain emergency access roads that are capable of supporting ARFF vehicles.

Depending on the airport, ARFF personnel may be specific only to the ARFF function, may also serve a public safety function role as police officers, or may also serve as operations personnel. Typically, job specialization is more pronounced at larger airports, meaning that ARFF personnel would generally be responsible only for ARFF. Unlike snow removal equipment, all certificated airports must invest in ARFF equipment, with today's modern ARFF trucks costing over $1 million.

HANDLING AND STORING OF HAZARDOUS SUBSTANCES AND MATERIALS

Section 139.321, Handling and Storing of Hazardous Substances and Materials, is designed to address both hazardous cargo and fuel. If a certificated airport acts as a cargo handling agent, procedures for the protection of persons and property during the storing or handling of any hazardous material must be developed. Although it is uncommon for an airport to act as a cargo handling agent, if it does, it must provide for at least:

- Designated personnel to receive and handle hazardous substances and materials

- Assurance from the shipper that the cargo can be handled safely, including any special handling procedures required for safety

- Special areas for storage of hazardous materials while on the airport

It's much more likely for an airport to handle fuel. If so, standards must be developed to protect against fire and explosion in the storing, dispensing, and handling of fuel. Fueling agents on the airport must be held to these same standards, requiring regular surveillance of fueling activity to verify compliance. These standards must address:

- Bonding
- Public protection
- Control of access to storage areas
- Fire safety in fuel farm and storage areas
- Fire safety in mobile fuelers, fueling pits, and fueling cabinets
- Training of fueling personnel in fire safety
- The fire code of the public body having jurisdiction over the airport.

In addition, §139.321 requires airports to inspect the physical facilities of each airport tenant fueling agent at least once every 3 consecutive months, with records being maintained for at least 12 consecutive calendar months. Fire safety training must be given to at least one supervisor with each fueling agent prior to initial performance of duties and at least every 24 consecutive calendar months thereafter. Those employees who fuel aircraft, accept fuel shipments, or otherwise handle fuel are able to receive initial on-the-job training from their supervisor, as well as recurrent instruction every 24 consecutive calendar months. To verify that required training has taken place, each certificated airport must obtain a written confirmation of this training once every 12 consecutive calendar months. Airports are required to maintain this record for 12 consecutive calendar months.

TRAFFIC AND WIND DIRECTION INDICATORS

Section 139.323, Traffic and Wind Direction Indicators, requires certificated airports to maintain the following:

- A wind cone that visually provides surface wind direction information to pilots. For each runway available for air carrier use, a supplemental wind cone is required to be installed at the end of the runway or at least at one point visible to the pilot while on final approach and prior to take-off. For airports open for air carrier operations at night, the wind direction indicators and supplemental indicators must be lighted (see Figure 7-14).

Figure 7-14.
Lighted wind cone.

- A segmented circle, landing strip indicator, and a traffic pattern indicator must be installed around a wind cone for each runway with a right-hand traffic pattern at certificated airports if air carrier operations are conducted without a control tower in operation.

AIRPORT EMERGENCY PLAN

Section 139.325, Airport Emergency Plan, requires certificated airports to develop and maintain an **airport emergency plan (AEP)**. The AEP must include procedures (including a communications network) for prompt response to all emergencies, sufficient detail to provide adequate guidance to each person who must implement the AEP, and an emergency response for the largest air carrier aircraft in the airport's index group. Specifically, and in accordance with AC 150/5200-31, *Airport Emergency Plan*, the AEP must include instructions for responses to:

- Aircraft incidents and accidents;
- Terrorism incidents;
- Structural fires, and fires at fuel farms and fuel storage areas;
- Natural disasters, including hurricane, earthquake, tornado, volcano, flood;
- Hazardous materials incidents;
- Sabotage, hijack, and other unlawful interference with operations;
- Failure of power for movement area lighting;
- Water rescue situations; and
- Crowd control

The AEP must also include provisions for medical services; contact information and emergency capability of hospitals and medical facilities in the local community; contact information for rescue squads, ambulance services, military installations, and government agencies that have agreed to provide medical assistance and/or transportation; an inventory of surface vehicles and aircraft available to transport injured and deceased persons; a list of hangars or buildings that can be used to accommodate uninjured, injured, and deceased persons; and procedures for removing disabled aircraft.[2] Additionally, the AEP must provide for the marshalling, transportation, and care of ambulatory injured and uninjured accident survivors; the removal of disabled aircraft; emergency alarm or notification systems; coordination of airport and control tower functions relating to emergency actions; and the rescue of aircraft accident victims from significant bodies of water or marshlands adjacent to the airport that are crossed by the approach and departure paths of air carriers.

Once the AEP is developed, all certificated airports must:

- Coordinate the plan with law enforcement agencies, rescue and firefighting agencies, medical personnel and organizations, the principal tenants at the airport, and other persons who have responsibilities under the plan;

- Ensure that all airport personnel having duties and responsibilities under the plan are familiar with their assignments and are properly trained;

- At least once every 12 consecutive calendar months, review the plan with all of the parties with whom the plan is coordinated, to ensure that all parties know their responsibilities and that all of the information in the plan is current (often referred to as a tabletop exercise); and

- If a Class I certificated airport, hold a full-scale airport emergency plan exercise once every 36 consecutive calendar months.

Ronald Reagan Washington National Airport Emergency Exercise

A recent full-scale emergency exercise at Ronald Reagan Washington National Airport was held to meet the 14 CFR Part 139 requirement for Class I airports to exercise the airport emergency plan. A training aircraft was used at the southern end of the airport to simulate a crashed aircraft (Alert III). The exercise, which required months of planning and coordination across multiple jurisdictions and disciplines, consisted of more than 50 responding emergency vehicles, including mutual aid from 13 surrounding fire departments to transport victims to hospitals, nearly 150 volunteers who were moulaged to simulate injuries sustained in the accident, boats used as part of a river rescue, and helicopters for support and rapid transport to area hospitals.

(Metropolitan Washington Airports Authority, 2013)

---

[2] Refer to ACRP Synthesis 38, *Expediting Aircraft Recovery at Airports.*

Planning for a full-scale emergency exercise at a certificated airport requires months of preparation. Some airports begin planning for this exercise one year in advance. Not only must an accident scenario be developed, but an aircraft has to be arranged, volunteers need to be coordinated, a date must be set, and all interested parties must be invited to participate. On the day of the event, everyone responds to the accident site in response to a "simulated Alert III" just as if there were a real accident (see Figure 7-15). The exercise tests everyone's response. Afterward, a thorough debriefing is held to discuss what worked well and what didn't work well. Changes can then be made so that personnel are better prepared in the future.

Figure 7-15.
Full-scale emergency exercise.

(Jordan Biegler, Tampa International Airport)

SELF-INSPECTION PROGRAM

Section 139.327, Self-Inspection Program, presents the requirements for airports to self-inspect on a daily basis to ensure Part 139 compliance. Specifically, certificated airports are required to inspect:

- daily, except as otherwise required by the airport certification manual;
- when required by any unusual condition, such as construction activities or meteorological conditions, that may affect safe air carrier operations; and
- immediately after an accident or incident.

To meet these requirements, certificated airports must provide sufficient, qualified personnel; equipment to be used by these personnel in conducting inspections; procedures, facilities, and equipment to disseminate information to air carriers; and a reporting system to ensure prompt correction of unsafe airport conditions (including wildlife strikes) noted during an inspection. Personnel responsible for meeting the requirements of §139.327 must receive initial and recurrent training (every 12 consecutive calendar months) in at least the following topic areas:

- Airport familiarization, including airport signs, marking and lighting
- Airport emergency plan
- Notice to Airmen (NOTAM) notification procedures
- Procedures for pedestrians and ground vehicles in movement areas and safety areas
- Discrepancy reporting procedures

Additionally, §139.327 requires certificated airports to maintain a record of each inspection (showing the conditions found and all corrective actions taken) for a period of 12 consecutive calendar months. Airports must also maintain training records for 24 consecutive calendar months showing a description of the training and the date on which the training took place.

Of all the responsibilities of operations personnel, conducting self-inspections is the most significant. This is the manner by which airports ensure their compliance with Part 139 and maintain a safe airport. At larger Part 139 airports, a complete self-inspection may take two to three hours or more. Some airports, such as Los Angeles International Airport, actually have operations personnel assigned to the airfield for their entire shift. At the majority of certificated airports, however, once the self-inspection is complete, operations personnel respond to the airfield as needed throughout the shift.

PEDESTRIANS AND GROUND VEHICLES

Section 139.329, Pedestrians and Ground Vehicles, presents requirements necessary for certificated airports to provide protection for pedestrians and ground vehicles in the movement areas and safety areas. Specifically, certificated airports must:

- Limit access to movement areas and safety areas to those pedestrians and ground vehicles necessary for airport operations.
- Establish and implement procedures for the safe and orderly access to, and operation in, movement areas and safety areas by pedestrians and ground vehicles, including provisions identifying the consequences of noncompliance with the procedures by an employee, tenant, or contractor.
- When an air traffic control tower is in operation, ensure that each pedestrian and ground vehicle in movement areas or safety areas is controlled by one of the following:
  - › Two-way radio communications between each pedestrian or vehicle and the tower;
  - › An escort with two-way radio communications with the tower accompanying any pedestrian or vehicle without a radio; or

> › Measures authorized by the FAA Administrator for controlling pedestrians and vehicles, such as signs, signals, or guards, when it is not operationally practical to have two-way radio communications between the tower and the pedestrian, vehicle, or escort.

- When an air traffic control tower is not in operation, or there is no air traffic control tower, provide adequate procedures to control pedestrians and ground vehicles in movement areas or safety areas through two-way radio communications or prearranged signs or signals.

- Ensure that each employee, tenant, or contractor is trained on proper procedures (including consequences of noncompliance) prior to moving on foot, or operating a ground vehicle, in movement areas or safety areas (Figure 7-16).

Figure 7-16.
Contractor on the movement area.

(Lee Brown, Fort Lauderdale-Hollywood International Airport)

In compliance with §139.327, certified airports are required to maintain a record of training on each individual (including a description and date of training) for 24 consecutive calendar months after the termination of an individual's access to movement areas and safety areas. Additionally, certified airports are required to maintain a description and date of any accidents or incidents in the movement areas and safety areas involving air carrier aircraft, ground vehicles, or a pedestrian for 12 consecutive calendar months from the date of the accident/incident.

OBSTRUCTIONS

Section 139.331, Obstructions, requires certified airports to ensure that each object within its authority that has been found to be an obstruction to air navigation (as a result of a Part 77 analysis) be removed, marked, or lighted, unless determined to be unnecessary by the FAA. Lighted obstructions are checked by operations personnel during a self-inspection.

PROTECTION OF NAVAIDS

Section 139.333, Protection of NAVAIDs, requires certified airports to protect navigational aids from interference and other detrimental impacts (see Figure 7-17). Specifically, certified airports must:

- Prevent the construction of facilities on the airport that would adversely impact the operation of an electronic or visual NAVAID and air traffic control facilities on the airport;

- Protect all NAVAIDs located on the airport from vandalism and theft;

- Prevent, to the extent possible, interruption of visual and electronic signals of NAVAIDs.

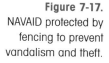

Figure 7-17. NAVAID protected by fencing to prevent vandalism and theft.

PUBLIC PROTECTION

Section 139.335, Public Protection, requires certified airports to protect the public from entering areas that are unsafe and from the effects of jet blast and propwash. Specifically, certified airports must install safeguards to prevent inadvertent entry to the movement area by unauthorized persons or vehicles and protect persons and property from aircraft blast (see Figure 7-18). Fencing that meets TSA and FAA regulations is considered a sufficient safeguard.

Figure 7-18.
Airport blast fence.

WILDLIFE HAZARD MANAGEMENT

Section 139.337, Wildlife Hazard Management, presents the requirements for certified airports to manage wildlife to prevent any dangerous aircraft strikes with wildlife. In addition to the requirement to take immediate action whenever wildlife hazards are discovered, certified airports are required to carry out a wildlife hazard assessment when any of the following events occur on or near the airport:

- An air carrier aircraft experiences multiple wildlife strikes;
- An air carrier aircraft experiences substantial damage that adversely affects the structural strength, performance, or flight characteristics of the aircraft as a result of striking wildlife;
- An air carrier aircraft experiences an engine ingestion of wildlife; or
- Wildlife of a size, or in numbers, capable of causing any of these events is observed to have access to any airport flight pattern or aircraft movement area (see Figure 7-19).

If required, the wildlife hazard assessment must be carried out by a wildlife damage management biologist who has professional training and/or experience in wildlife hazard management at airports. The wildlife hazard assessment will contain at least the following:

- An analysis of the events or circumstances that prompted the assessment.
- Identification of the wildlife species observed and their numbers, locations, local movements, and daily and seasonal occurrences.
- Identification and location of features on and near the airport that attract wildlife.
- A description of wildlife hazards to air carrier operations.
- Recommended actions for reducing identified wildlife hazards to air carrier operations.

Figure 7-19.
Airport wildlife.

(Lee Brown, Fort Lauderdale-Hollywood International Airport)

Once completed, the wildlife hazard assessment is submitted to the FAA for approval, as well as a determination of whether the airport needs a wildlife hazard management plan. In determining whether a wildlife hazard management plan is needed, the FAA will consider the wildlife hazard assessment, actions recommended in the assessment to reduce wildlife hazards, the aeronautical activity at the airport, views of the airport and users, and any other known factors. If the FAA determines that an airport needs a wildlife hazard management plan, a plan should be developed that provides measures to alleviate or eliminate wildlife hazards to air carriers, is approved by the FAA, and becomes part of the ACM.

Specifically, a wildlife hazard management plan must include:

- A list of the individuals having authority and responsibility for implementing each aspect of the plan.
- A list prioritizing the following actions identified in the wildlife hazard assessment and target dates for their initiation and completion:
  › Wildlife population management;
  › Habitat modification; and
  › Land use changes.
- Requirements for and, where applicable, copies of local, state, and federal wildlife control permits.
- Identification of resources that the certificate holder will provide to implement the plan.

- Procedures to be followed during air carrier operations that at a minimum include:
  › designation of personnel responsible for implementing the procedures;
  › provisions to conduct physical inspections of the aircraft movement areas and other areas critical to successfully manage known wildlife hazards before air carrier operations begin;
  › wildlife hazard control measures; and
  › ways to communicate effectively between personnel conducting wildlife control or observing wildlife hazards and the air traffic control tower.
- Procedures to review and evaluate the wildlife hazard management plan every 12 consecutive months or following an event previously described, including:
  › the plan's effectiveness in dealing with known wildlife hazards on and in the airport's vicinity, and
  › aspects of the wildlife hazards described in the wildlife hazard assessment that should be reevaluated.
- A training program conducted by a qualified wildlife damage management biologist to provide airport personnel with the knowledge and skills needed to successfully carry out the wildlife hazard management plan.

AIRPORT CONDITION REPORTING

Section 139.339, Airport Condition Reporting, requires certified airports to report airport conditions to air carriers. This requires airports to have in place a system of collecting and disseminating airport condition information, typically the NOTAM system. Specifically, airports are required to provide information on the following airport conditions:

- Construction or maintenance activity on movement areas, safety areas, or loading ramps and parking areas.
- Surface irregularities on movement areas, safety areas, or loading ramps and parking areas.
- Snow, ice, slush, or water on the movement area or loading ramps and parking areas.
- Snow piled or drifted on or near movement areas contrary to §139.313.
- Objects on the movement area or safety areas contrary to §139.309.
- Malfunction of any lighting system, holding position signs, or ILS critical area signs required by §139.311.
- Unresolved wildlife hazards as identified in accordance with §139.337.
- Non-availability of any rescue and firefighting capability required in §§139.317 or 139.319.
- Any other condition as specified in the airport certification manual or that may otherwise adversely affect the safe operations of air carriers.

Certificated airports are required to maintain records of each dissemination of airport condition information to air carriers for a period of 12 consecutive calendar months. Generally, operations personnel are responsible for issuing NOTAMs as needed. It is always better to err on the side of safety and issue a NOTAM to report unsafe conditions to pilots, rather than not issue a NOTAM.

IDENTIFYING, MARKING, AND LIGHTING CONSTRUCTION AND OTHER UNSERVICEABLE AREAS

Section 139.341—Identifying, Marking, and Lighting Construction and Other Unserviceable Areas—requires certificated airports to properly mark and light (if appropriate):

- each construction area and unserviceable area that is on or adjacent to any movement area or any other area of the airport on which air carrier aircraft may be operated (see Figure 7-20);
- each item of construction equipment and each construction roadway, which may affect the safe movement of aircraft on the airport; and
- any area adjacent to a NAVAID that, if traversed, could cause derogation of the signal or the failure of the NAVAID.

Additionally, certificated airports are required to develop procedures to prevent interruption of utilities (including cables, wires, conduits, pipelines, or other underground facilities) during any construction work on the airport. Procedures typically require a review of all appropriate utility plans prior to construction.

Figure 7-20. Low-profile barricades in use for an airport construction project.

NONCOMPLYING CONDITIONS

Section 139.343, Noncomplying Conditions, states that whenever Part 139 requirements cannot be met by a certificated airport to the extent that unsafe conditions exist on the airport, the airport must limit air carrier operations to those areas of the airport not rendered unsafe by those conditions. Note that this requirement (and all Part 139 requirements) refers to air carrier operations. Thus, it would be possible to allow GA operations in an area that does not meet Part 139 standards. In this case, however, the airport operator would still be certain not to allow any aircraft activity in areas that are considered unsafe. Indeed, the airport operator is responsible for maintaining a safe and secure airport; thus, if an area is under construction or has an unsafe condition, it is the responsibility of the airport operator to NOTAM that area closed to prevent inadvertent entry by aircraft (whether air carrier or GA) into an area that would cause damage to the aircraft or result in loss of directional control of the aircraft.

Airport Communications

Airports have often been characterized as "small cities." Indeed, many of the larger airports generate some of their own power; have their own police force, system of governance, and form of transportation; generate their own sources of revenue; are self-contained with food, beverage and retail establishments; etc. For a "small city" or airport to operate effectively, sufficient communication must be in place. In fact, one key to an efficiently run airport is a well-developed communication system.

On the surface, this would appear easy to accomplish. It is important to keep in mind, however, that an airport serves two types of customers. First, internal customers include all of the individuals employed by the entity that owns and operates the airport. If the airport is owned and operated by an airport authority, for instance, internal customers would be the employees of the airport authority. Although these employees are often thought of simply as employees, when airport leadership and employees in all departments view each other as internal customers, morale typically improves, efficiency is enhanced, and the airport is able to better meet the needs of the other customer group— the external customers.

To be sure, external customers are the ones typically thought of as customers, because they represent passengers and meeters and greeters, as well as employees of the various tenants on the airport (including airlines, FBOs, maintenance organizations, concessionaires, and others). It is important for an airport to effectively communicate with these external customers so that the airport is perceived not only as a well-managed and welcoming facility, but also as a great place to work and conduct business. Effectively communicating with external customers requires the airport to hold regular tenant meetings;

issue NOTAMs as appropriate; adopt a policy of transparency with regards to fees, rates, and charges; and regularly communicate priority issues via memos, meetings, and other forms of communication.

In addition to those external customers that airport personnel interact with daily, external customers also include citizens and businesses in the surrounding community, whether or not these groups ever visit the airport. It is important for the airport to consider local businesses in meeting the air transportation needs of the region. Local business leaders often play an important role in securing new or additional commercial air service. Also, as will be discussed in more detail in Chapter 11, communicating with the community is imperative if the airport wants to experience positive relations with the community. Often, negative community relations are not perceived as being detrimental until the public hearing phase of an airport project. Yet these relations may be so negative as to derail the entire project. Communicating with the community involves issuing press releases, inviting community groups to tour the airport and attend regular noise meetings, and being responsive to community needs and concerns.

When considering airport communications and their role in the operation of the airport, many airports (especially larger ones) have a dedicated airport communications center (see Figure 7-21). Although the airport communications center is referred to differently among airports (including the "Center," "Comm Center" or "Airport Command Center"), the role of the "Center" is much the same among airports. Typically, the Center serves as the central receiving point for all phone calls from the public (whether emergency or routine in nature). These phone calls include calls made by airport patrons within the terminal.

Additionally, the Center has a phone line used by ATCT to report emergencies (often referred to as the "netline" or "crash phone"). This netline is a direct line that allows ATCT to pick up the phone and report the details of an aircraft emergency (often referred to as "Alert I," "Alert II," and "Alert III") to the Center, as well as ARFF stations and possibly others including police, any mutual aid agencies, and operations. Often, however, the Center records the pertinent information (such as airline/operator, flight number, aircraft type,

Figure 7-21.
Airport communications center.

(Lee Brown, Fort Lauderdale-Hollywood International Airport)

fuel on board, souls on board, intended runway, and estimated time of arrival) and then relays this information to appropriate personnel (such as operations, police, maintenance, and senior airport leadership). At a minimum, however, each airport ARFF station must have landline access to enable ARFF personnel to receive the information as early as possible so that they can ensure a rapid response as first responders to the scene.

In addition to answering phone calls, the Center plays an important role in monitoring airport systems and facilities. Depending on the size of the airport, the Center may be staffed 24/7 with two to six operators (also known as "dispatchers"). These individuals typically sit at a computer with one or more monitors, located in a large room with a number of larger monitors (typically in the form of large, flat-panel screens). These allow the operators to monitor people movers (shuttles, monorails, trams, moving sidewalks, escalators, and elevators), fire alarm systems, access control systems, lightning warning systems, fuel systems, and more. Additionally, the operators have the ability to control hundreds of security cameras (many with full pan-tilt-zoom functionality) that enable them to observe terminal areas, gate areas, airfield areas, parking areas, etc. Airports typically have hundreds of cameras to record passenger activity, accidents, medical events, security breaches, and criminal activity such as thefts, assaults, etc. When a significant event occurs (such as a security breach), the operators are able to find the correct camera to bring up the event on the monitor. Often, for those personnel desiring more information, but not necessarily wanting to respond to the scene, they can visit the Center to observe the event in progress. During these events, a picture (or video image) truly is worth a thousand words.

With all of this capability, the Center plays an important role in logging all events that occur on the airport. Typically in the form of an incident log, the operator first receiving a phone call about an aircraft emergency or other incident begins an entry in the computer to record all details and actions related to the incident. Often, airport operations personnel relay information to the Center operator to make this entry more complete. Once the incident is resolved, this chronological log is useful for any debriefing sessions that might be held.

Wildlife Hazard Management

As spelled out earlier in this chapter, 14 CFR §139.337 details the requirements of certificated airports to properly manage wildlife and alleviate wildlife hazards to aircraft. According to the FAA, wildlife is defined as, "Any wild animal, including without limitation any wild mammal, bird, reptile, fish, amphibian, mollusk, crustacean, arthropod, coelenterate, or other invertebrate, including any part, product, egg, or offspring thereof, as well as feral animals and domestic animals out of the control of their owners" (FAA, 2007, p. 22). Hazardous wildlife is defined as, "Species of wildlife (birds, mammals, reptiles), including feral animals and domesticated animals not under control, that are associated with aircraft strike problems, are capable of causing structural damage to airport facilities, or act as attractants to other wildlife that pose a strike hazard." (See Figure 7-22) (FAA, 2007, p. 22).

In practical terms, wildlife hazards at airports are typically managed by airport operations personnel. Although many certified airports have developed wildlife hazard management plans, even those airports without such a plan are required by Part 139 to alleviate wildlife hazards whenever they are detected. FAA Advisory Circular (AC) 150/5200-33, *Hazardous Wildlife Attractants On or Near Airports*, contains guidance on the attractants at airports that can contribute to wildlife hazards. According to this advisory circular, a **wildlife attractant** is "Any human-made structure, land-use practice, or human-made or natural geographic feature that can attract or sustain hazardous wildlife within the landing or departure airspace or the airport's AOA. These attractants can include architectural features, landscaping, waste disposal sites, wastewater treatment facilities, agricultural or aquaculture activities, surface mining, or wetlands" (FAA, 2007, p. 22).

In general, airport wildlife management programs (whether formalized in a wildlife hazard management plan or not) are built upon two components: habitat management and active control. **Habitat management** is a planned activity that includes identifying the habitat, considering modifying or eliminating the habitat, and incorporating any changes into a long-term land-use management practice. This may include altering grass height; removing trees, ponds, building ledges, and other unnecessary perches or roosting areas; installing fencing at least 7 feet high (10–12 feet at airports with deer problems) with three-strand barbed wire; placing glycol storage basins and storm water ponds underground or providing netting or wires over them to keep birds out; draining all areas of standing water; designing ponds with a 4:1 slope; and using sweepers to remove worms from the airport's hard surfaces (see Figure 7-23).

Figure 7-22.
Airport wildlife.

Figure 7-23.
Habitat management technique showing the use of mylar tape across a wetland to prevent Canada geese nesting.

(Alaska DOT)

Orlando International Airport's Wildlife Hazard Management Program

Orlando International Airport (MCO), which is surrounded primarily by residential areas, industrial parks, major roadways, and commercial businesses, is known to have significant wildlife concerns. In addition to operations personnel who constantly monitor the airfield for wildlife activity, MCO has employed a wildlife biologist to manage the wildlife program at the airport since 1996. The airport has been reporting wildlife strikes to the FAA since 1990. Today, the wildlife biologist and a staff of two wildlife control specialists daily address wildlife hazards at the airport.

Passive wildlife management techniques include regular mowing, perimeter fence inspections and maintenance, daily foreign object debris (FOD) inspections, installing perching deterrents, proper disposal of dead animal remains, and maintaining ditch/pond vegetation. Active wildlife management techniques include harassing or dispersing of wildlife using vehicles, using pyrotechnics, and taking lethal control when necessary. Lethal control techniques also take place outside the airport perimeter fence when large mammals, such as deer and coyote, are observed near the fence line. Annually, the deer populations outside the perimeter fence on adjacent airport property are reduced. As expected at a Florida airport, birds are a significant wildlife hazard at MCO. The four most hazardous bird species within the AOA are cattle egrets, turkey vultures, ring-billed gulls, and sandhill cranes. The most frequently struck bird species, from 2003 to 2014, were tree swallows (73 strikes), cattle egrets (61 strikes), killdeer (59 strikes), barn swallows (55 strikes), mourning doves (41 strikes), and turkey vultures (36 strikes). The reason for the difference in these two metrics is because even though tree swallows are the most often struck species, they are not considered the most hazardous because of their small size. When struck, these small birds cause little to no damage to an aircraft. Regardless, wildlife control personnel at MCO must maintain constant vigilance and actively work to minimize wildlife hazards to aircraft on the AOA.

(Greater Orlando Aviation Authority, 2015)

AIRPORT MANAGEMENT

Active control includes harassing, scaring, dispersing, frightening, or trapping wildlife, or the use of lethal control. Specific techniques can include bird distress-call tapes, pyrotechnic devices, propane cannons, whistles, decoys, shotgun blasts with screamer shells, and high-pressure water from fire hoses. Chemicals can also be used to cause dispersal and movement of flocks. Lethal control or the killing of wildlife through the use of chemicals, firearms, or other mechanical means normally requires a depredation permit from a state or federal fish and wildlife service. Because birds and animals adapt to these various strategies, it is important for airports to implement both habitat modification and active control, while also varying the techniques used with each (see Figure 7-24).

Figure 7-24. Equipment used for active control of wildlife.

Even with the implementation of these various wildlife control techniques, a wildlife strike may still occur at an airport. According to FAA Advisory Circular 150/5200-32, *Reporting Wildlife Aircraft Strikes*, a **wildlife strike** has occurred when:

1. A pilot reports striking one or more birds or other wildlife.

2. Aircraft maintenance personnel identify aircraft damage as having been caused by a wildlife strike.

3. Personnel on the ground report seeing an aircraft strike one or more birds or other wildlife.

4. Bird or other wildlife remains, whether in whole or in part, are found within 200 feet of a runway centerline, unless another reason for the animal's death is identified.

5. An animal's presence on the airport had a significant negative effect on a flight (i.e., aborted takeoff, aborted landing, high-speed emergency stop, aircraft left pavement area to avoid collision with animal) (see Figure 7-25).

Pilots, airport operations personnel, aircraft maintenance personnel, or anyone else who has knowledge of a strike is encouraged to report it to the FAA. Wildlife strikes may be reported to the FAA using the paper FAA Form 5200-7, "Bird/Other Wildlife Strike Report," or electronically at the Airport Wildlife Hazard Mitigation web site: http://wildlife-mitigation.tc.faa.gov. All reported strikes are then edited and entered into the National Wildlife Aircraft Strike Database, which allows for trend analysis by species, airport, etc. Worldwide, wildlife strikes have cost the civil aviation industry an estimated $1.2 billion annually. Each year in the United States, wildlife strikes to U.S. civil aircraft cause about $500 million in aircraft damage and about 500,000 hours of civil aircraft downtime (FAA, 2004).

Figure 7-25.
Bird strikes can result in costly aircraft damage, as shown in the blades of this turbine engine, and downtime.

(Wikimedia Commons; see credit on page 624)

New Generation Aircraft

Airports are also being confronted with new generation aircraft, including **new large aircraft (NLA)**. Currently, the Airbus A380 and Boeing 747-8 are two aircraft that are considered NLA. Specifically, the A380-800 (which is built by Airbus Industries) is 239 feet long with a 261-foot wingspan, a maximum takeoff weight of 1,235,000 pounds, and capacity for 555 to 822 passengers (depending on seating configuration) (see Figure 7-26). The Boeing 747-8 (which is built by Boeing Corporation and is considered the largest commercial aircraft built in the United States) is 250 feet long with a 224-foot wingspan, a maximum takeoff weight of 975,000 pounds, and capacity for 467 to 581 passengers (depending on seating configuration). These two NLA contrast to the much smaller, narrow-body B737-600, for example, which is 102 feet long with a 117-foot wingspan, a maximum takeoff weight of 145,500 pounds, and capacity for 108 to 130 passengers (depending on seating configuration). Considering the A380 and 747-8, it is obvious that NLA require significant consideration

Review Questions ↘

1. To which airports does 14 CFR Part 139 not apply?

2. Explain the various classes of Part 139 airports.

3. Explain the airport certification manual, including its purpose and its role.

4. Which subpart of Part 139 presents most of the guidance regarding airport operations?

5. Explain the various recordkeeping requirements of Part 139.

6. In which areas must personnel who access movement areas and safety areas and perform duties in compliance with the airport certification manual be trained?

7. Explain the standards to which paved areas must be maintained at certificated airports.

8. What are the minimum markings that make up an airport marking system at certificated airports?

9. Explain how to determine the ARFF Index for a certificated airport.

10. List the required Part 139 training areas for ARFF personnel.

11. What fire fuel safety standards must be developed at certificated airports?

12. What is required of certificated airports in 14 CFR §139.327, Self-Inspection Program?

13. Under what circumstances are certificated airports required to conduct a wildlife hazard assessment?

14. List the components of a wildlife hazard management plan.

15. For what conditions are certificated airports required to report to air carriers, according to §139.339?

16. Explain the types of customers that an airport serves and the manner by which these customers should be served.

17. Explain the function of the airport communications center.

18. What is a wildlife attractant, according to the FAA?

19. Under what situations is a wildlife strike considered to have occurred, according to AC 150/5200-32?

1. As the manager of a small general aviation airport, you are being pressured by the city manager to pursue commercial airline service. Although your airport is located only 48 miles (by road) from a major commercial service airport, the city manager feels that your community of 100,000 can support commercial airline service to cities such as Atlanta and St. Louis. Remember, your airport is not currently able to accommodate commercial airline service because it is not Part 139 certificated. What must be done to obtain Part 139 certification? How do you relay these requirements (and associated costs) to the city manager?

2. As you prepare for your annual Part 139 certification inspection, you know you need to make sure every aspect of your airport is in compliance with the regulation and your ACM. Develop a "to-do" list for your staff to make certain that your airport is ready for this important annual inspection.

3. As the result of a recent Part 139 certification inspection by an FAA inspector, your aircraft received three discrepancies: (1) Hazardous ruts in the 36L safety area; (2) Inadequate response by ARFF in the timed response drill (first truck arriving in 3 minutes, 20 seconds, and all others within 4 minutes); and (3) Faded mandatory surface painted signs at the Taxiway B, C, D entrances to runway 36R. The FAA inspector is requesting an action plan from your airport to immediately correct these discrepancies. Develop this plan, as well as a longer-term plan to prevent similar discrepancies in the future.

4. Your airport received FAA approval of the newly developed Wildlife Hazard Management Plan 13 months ago. However, since the plan has been implemented, bird strikes at your airport are on the rise. What is your next step?

5. You are the director of operations at a small-hub, ARFF Index B airport. Your airport employs 8 operations personnel responsible for Part 139 compliance, a city-contracted ARFF crew, 23 airport police officers, and requisite maintenance and other personnel. Develop a training program to comply with 14 CFR §139.301 and §139.303. If any assumptions are made, please state those assumptions.

References and Resources for Further Study

American Association of Airport Executives. 2005. "Body of Knowledge Module 3: Airport Operations, Security, and Maintenance." Washington, DC: AAAE.

de Neufville, R. and A. Odoni. 2003. *Airport Systems: Planning Design and Management.* New York: McGraw Hill.

Federal Aviation Administration (FAA). 1997. *Measurement, Construction, and Maintenance of Skid-Resistant Airport Pavement Surfaces.* AC 150/5320-12C. Washington DC: FAA.

———. 2004. Title 14 Code of Federal Regulations, Part 139, Airport Certification. Washington, DC: FAA.

———. 2007. *Hazardous Wildlife Attractants On or Near Airports.* AC 150/5200-33B. Washington, DC: FAA.

———. 2009. National Plan of Integrated Airport Systems (NPIAS).

———. 2013. *Reporting Wildlife Aircraft Strikes.* AC 150/5200-32B. Washington, DC: FAA.

Greater Orlando Aviation Authority. 2015. "Wildlife Hazard Site Visit Report." Retrieved from http://www.orlandoairports.net/east_airfield/2015/Appendix_H.pdf.

Metropolitan Washington Airports Authority. 2013. "Full-Scale Emergency Preparedness Exercise at Reagan National Airport on Saturday, Sept. 21." News Release. Retrieved from http://www.metwashairports.com/6552.htm

Transportation Research Board. 2012. "ACRP Synthesis 38: Expediting Aircraft Recovery at Airports." Washington, DC: TRB. Retrieved from http://onlinepubs.trb.org/onlinepubs/acrp/acrp_syn_038.pdf

Chapter 8

Maintenance

Objectives ↘

Upon completion of this chapter, you should understand:

- inspections and preventive maintenance at airports
- the types of airside maintenance performed at airports
- the types of landside maintenance performed at airports
- the purpose of an airport pavement management program (PMP) and the general types of pavement distress
- the benefits of contracted maintenance services

Key Terms ↘

airport pavement management program (PMP)

continuous friction measuring equipment (CFME)

decelerometer (DEC)

heating, ventilation, and air conditioning (HVAC)

hot mix asphalt (HMA)

Portland cement concrete (PCC)

preventive maintenance (PM)

In Chapter 8

FEATURES

Texas DOT Routine Airport Maintenance Program 330

By funding matching grants at airports throughout Texas, pavement and airside maintenance are better ensured.

References and Resources for Further Study

American Association of Airport Executives. 2005. "Body of Knowledge Module 3: Airport Operations, Security, and Maintenance." Washington, DC: AAAE.

deNeufville, R. and A. Odoni. 2003. *Airport Systems: Planning Design and Management*. New York: McGraw Hill.

Federal Aviation Administration (FAA). 1997. *Measurement, Construction, and Maintenance of Skid-Resistant Airport Pavement Surfaces*. AC 150/5320-12C. Washington, DC: FAA.

————. 2004. *Airfield Pavement Surface Evaluation and Rating Manuals*. AC 150/5320-17. Washington, DC: FAA.

————. 2007. *Guidelines and Procedures for Maintenance of Airport Pavement*. AC 150/5380-6B. Washington, DC: FAA.

————. 2009. National Plan of Integrated Airport Systems (NPIAS).

————. 2014. *Airport Pavement Management Program*. AC 150/5380-7B. Washington, DC: FAA.

Grothaus, J., T. Helms, S. Germolus, D. Beaver, K. Carlson, T. Callister, R. Kunkel, and A. Johnson, 2009. "ACRP Report 16: Guidebook for Managing Small Airports." Washington, DC: Transportation Research Board.

Texas Department of Transportation. n.d. "2015 Routine Airport Maintenance Program (RAMP) Grants." Retrieved from http://ftp.dot.state.tx.us/pub/txdot-info/avn/ramp_grants.pdf

Transportation Research Board. 2011. "Current Airport Inspection Practices Regarding FOD." Washington, DC: TRB. Retrieved from http://onlinepubs.trb.org/onlinepubs/acrp/acrp_syn_026.pdf

Chapter 9

Safety and Security

Objectives ↘

Upon completion of this chapter, you should understand:

- the importance of safety at airports
- methods to provide public protection at airports
- methods to provide tenant, contractor, and employee protection at airports
- methods and documents related to ensuring operational safety on airports during construction
- the various classes of fires, fire hazards present during aircraft fueling, and the methods to ensure safety during aircraft fueling
- the unique considerations when driving on the movement area and methods and procedures to ensure safety during this activity
- the history of SMS and its purpose, as well as its role in ensuring safety at airports
- the importance of emergency preparedness at airports
- the role of the airport emergency plan and its unique characteristics
- the various types and levels of aircraft accidents and incidents
- the importance of media relations
- the characteristics of a precision lightning warning system
- the history of aviation security
- the agencies involved in ensuring aviation security
- the various regulations and methods related to security of airport operators and aircraft operators

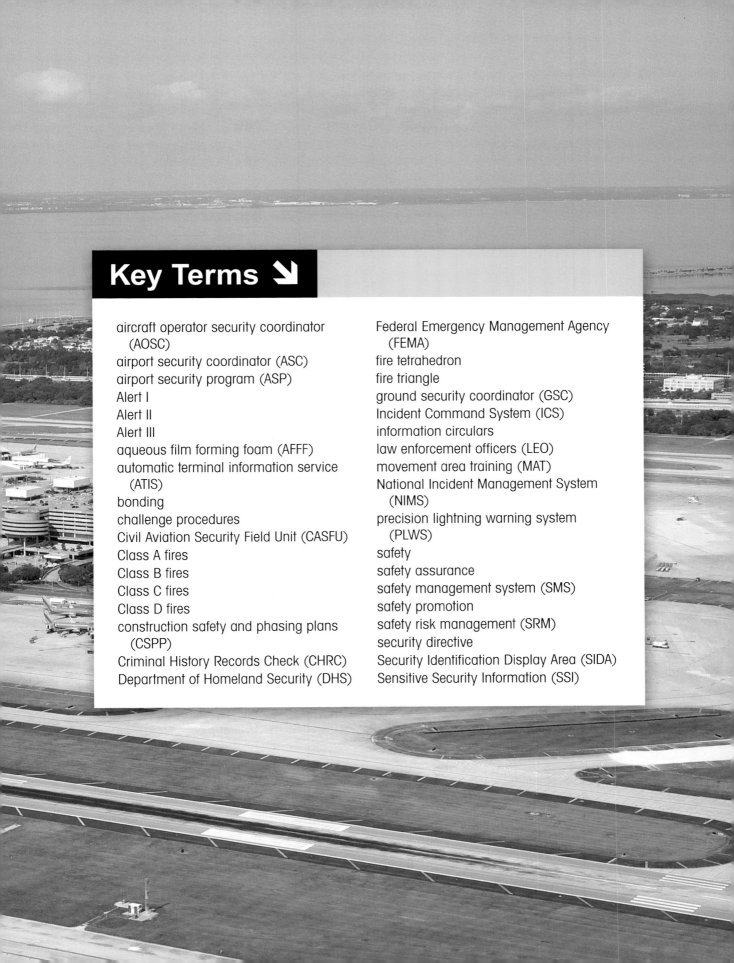

Key Terms ↘

aircraft operator security coordinator (AOSC)

airport security coordinator (ASC)

airport security program (ASP)

Alert I

Alert II

Alert III

aqueous film forming foam (AFFF)

automatic terminal information service (ATIS)

bonding

challenge procedures

Civil Aviation Security Field Unit (CASFU)

Class A fires

Class B fires

Class C fires

Class D fires

construction safety and phasing plans (CSPP)

Criminal History Records Check (CHRC)

Department of Homeland Security (DHS)

Federal Emergency Management Agency (FEMA)

fire tetrahedron

fire triangle

ground security coordinator (GSC)

Incident Command System (ICS)

information circulars

law enforcement officers (LEO)

movement area training (MAT)

National Incident Management System (NIMS)

precision lightning warning system (PLWS)

safety

safety assurance

safety management system (SMS)

safety promotion

safety risk management (SRM)

security directive

Security Identification Display Area (SIDA)

Sensitive Security Information (SSI)

In Chapter 9

FEATURES

Tampa International Airport's Precision Lightning Warning System 367

By installing a lightning warning system, employees at this airport are safer while working on the ramp.

of certain chemical fire extinguishers, such as carbon dioxide (which displaces oxygen). Although the fire triangle is appropriate for learning the components necessary to start a fire, the **fire tetrahedron** is necessary to learn how a fire continues to burn (see Figure 9-4). The fourth side is a chemical chain reaction. If uninterrupted, this chain reaction will maintain a fire. The chemical chain reaction can only be interrupted by application of certain extinguishing agents.

Aircraft fuel fires are not Class A fires, however. Class A fires are composed of ordinary combustibles (such as wood or paper). **Class B fires** are composed of flammable and combustible liquids (such as greases and gas). **Class C fires** are composed of energized electrical equipment. **Class D fires** are composed of combustible metals (magnesium and sodium). Water, which has a cooling effect, is most effective in extinguishing Class A fires. Carbon dioxide, which smothers the fire as it displaces oxygen, is effective on Class B or Class C fires. Dry chemical, which is a mixture of specially treated sodium bicarbonate, also deprives the fire of oxygen and is effective on Class B and C fires. For Class B fires (such as fuel fires), foam is most effective (see Table 9-1).

Figure 9-3.
Fire triangle.

Figure 9-4.
Fire tetrahedron.

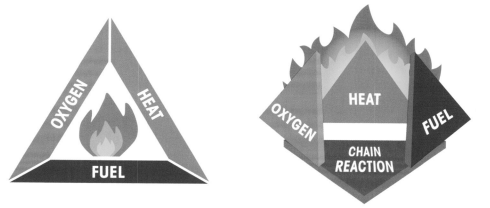

Also known as **aqueous film forming foam (AFFF)**, this extinguishing agent is a blend of bicarbonate of soda and aluminum sulfate. When applied, AFFF creates an aqueous film on the fuel surface that prevents evaporation and hence, reignition of the fuel once it has been extinguished by the foam (see Figure 9-5). Additionally, the film can self-heal and reseal areas that are disturbed by falling debris. AFFF effectively blankets a fire with a layer of foam, thus cooling the fire and starving it of oxygen. It is primarily used on Class B fires, such as on-airport fuel fires, but may also be effective on Class A fires. However, foam is not effective on vertical surfaces or pressure fires (such as broken fuel lines). AFFF is now in use on all U.S. Navy aircraft carriers and by major airports, refineries, and other areas where potentially catastrophic fuel fires can occur.

Halon is a liquefied gas which breaks the chemical reaction by interrupting the supply of oxygen. Due to the ability of Halon to degrade the ozone layer, a replacement, Halitron, has been invented that is more environmentally friendly

Table 9-1. Classes of combustibles.

Class of Fire		Type of Combustible	Example	Common Extinguishing Agents
A		Common combustibles	Wood, paper, cloth, etc.	Water; chemical foam; dry chemical*
B		Flammable liquids and gases	Gasoline, propane and solvents	Carbon dioxide (CO_2); halon**; dry chemical; aqueous film forming foam (AFFF)
C		Live electrical equipment	Computers, appliances	CO_2; halon; dry chemical
D		Combustible metals	Magnesium, lithium, titanium	Dry powder (suitable for the specific combustible metal involved)
K		Cooking media	Cooking oils and fats	Wet chemical (Potassium acetate based)

* Dry chemicals, CO_2 and halon can be used on Class A fires, but may not be effective on their own. They need to be supplemented with water.
** Halon extinguishers are no longer made but some may still be in use. Dangerous gases are formed when halon is used to extinguish fires. Wear proper respiratory equipment, particularly in enclosed spaces. After use, do not allow anyone to enter the area until it has been well ventilated.

Figure 9-5.
Aqueous film forming foam (AFFF).

(Jeff Price)

and very effective for aircraft engine fires and aircraft brake fires. For class D fires, only specialized agents such as METL-X and G-1 powder are effective.

Airports must ensure that training for all fuelers focuses on regularly minimizing the risk of fire (Figure 9-6). Liquid fuels, such as AvGas and Jet-A, emit vapors that can ignite when the flashpoint is reached. The flashpoint of AvGas is -50 degrees Fahrenheit, while Jet-A has a 100 degree Fahrenheit flashpoint. As a result, the vapors released from these two fuels will be at or above the flashpoint in almost every circumstance in which they'll be handled. All mobile fuelers should be equipped with air filter/flame arrestor equipment and a leak-free exhaust system which terminates into a standard baffle muffler at the front of the vehicle. Line service personnel should only wear clothing composed of 100 percent cotton. Fabrics such as silk, polyester, nylon, and wool generate static, which can produce a spark that may ignite fuel or fuel vapors. Additionally, refueling personnel should not carry any type of igniting device on their person or within 100 feet of any fuel tank or refueler. Only high-quality non-galvanized metal funnels should be used. **Bonding**, which grounds the fueler to the aircraft via a metal cable or wire, is imperative during fueling operations. Static can build up on an aircraft during flight and while fuel is flowing through a hose and nozzle. Thus, bonding is necessary to equalize these charges and prevent an errant spark. Personnel must also remain aware of additional ignition sources, including hot brakes, hot engine surfaces, jet engine exhaust, thunderstorms and lightning, portable electrical devices, fixed electrical equipment, and exposed light bulbs.

Even with adequate training and proper procedures, airports may experience a fuel spill (see Figure 9-7). Typically, fuel spills can occur if a fueler has been filled beyond its capacity at the fuel farm, an aircraft has vented a significant amount of fuel, or a fueler has been moved while connected to an aircraft or fuel farm. If a spill does occur, it is important to stop the flow of fuel. If possible, a fire extinguisher must be placed upwind of the spill. Next, a supervisor or the

Figure 9-6.
Aircraft fueling.

airport fire department must be notified. In addition, it's necessary to ensure that fueling vehicles are not moved and equipment is not started or turned off (due to a possible backfire). If trained and properly equipped, personnel may begin cleaning up the spill. Typically, a spill cart will need to be brought on scene to enable proper cleanup of the spill. It is important to have ARFF or fire extinguishers standing by, as the vapors may ignite (Prather, 2009).

Figure 9-7.
Fuel spill at the aircraft gate, with ARFF on scene, although not visible in the photograph.

DRIVING ON THE MOVEMENT AREA

Driving on the movement areas of the airfield presents a unique set of complex factors that require personnel authorized to drive on the AOA to be well-trained. In addition to SIDA training, 14 CFR §139.303 requires all personnel who access movement areas and safety areas and perform duties in compliance with the airport's ACM to be trained in at least the following areas:

- Airport familiarization, including airport marking, lighting, and signs system.
- Procedures for access to, and operation in, movement areas and safety areas.
- Airport communications, including radio communication between the air traffic control tower and personnel, use of the common traffic advisory frequency if there is no air traffic control tower or the tower is not in operation, and procedures for reporting unsafe airport conditions.
- Duties required under the airport certification manual and Part 139.
- Any additional areas as appropriate.

Often, those employees with access to the movement areas will include employees in the areas of operations, maintenance, ARFF, and police. Almost universally, the employees with access to the movement areas are employed by the airport operator. These employees must complete **movement area training (MAT)**. This training will produce employees who are knowledgeable of airfield markings, signage, lighting, and procedures to enable safe driving on the AOA. This will include the right-of-way that aircraft always maintain, communication procedures with ATCT, escort procedures, and the need to maintain constant situational awareness on the AOA. With vehicles operating on the movement areas, there is an increased risk of runway incursions. Thus, training will focus on making sure that all employees with access to the movement areas are very familiar with procedures necessary to avoid such an incursion. Indeed, ensuring safety on the airfield requires proper training of all personnel authorized to operate on the AOA, while restricting the number of personnel authorized to operate on the AOA (see Figure 9-8).

Figure 9-8.
Airport operations vehicle on the AOA.

SMS

On October 7, 2010, the FAA issued a notice of proposed rulemaking (NPRM) requiring a **safety management system (SMS)** for certificated airports. The rule would require certificated airports to establish an SMS for their entire airfield environment (including movement and non-movement areas) to improve safety at airports hosting air carrier operations. This proposal would require a certificate holder to submit an implementation plan and implement an SMS within certain timeframes. This NPRM stemmed from the November 2005 amendment to ICAO Annex 14, Volume I (Airport Design and Operations) that required member states (countries) to have certificated international airports establish an SMS. The United States is one such member state and the FAA is the U.S. regulatory agency responsible for enforcing this requirement. The NPRM allowed for public comment until January 5, 2011, which was then extended to July 5, 2011. More than 150 comments were submitted.

The FAA also funded two pilot studies to explore SMS at airports. In the first pilot study, 22 larger airports participated. Nine airports participated in the second pilot study, which focused on SMS at smaller airports. In these first two pilot studies, the consultants were generally retained by the airport to develop an SMS manual, but the airports were not required to implement the SMS. More recently, the FAA funded an Implementation Pilot Study which consisted of 14 airports that participated in either the first or the second pilot study and involved actually implementing the SMS that was already developed.

Even though the NPRM was issued in 2010, by May 2015, the FAA had not revised Part 139 to require SMS at certified airports, nor had the agency issued a final rule in response to the NPRM and the comments received. So airports remain in a holding pattern, so to speak. Airports have been issued some guidance on this topic, however. Specifically, in 2007 the FAA published Advisory Circular 150/5200-37, *Introduction to SMS for Airport Operators*. This AC was designed to introduce the concept of a SMS for airport operators. This was necessary, especially since the SMS concept requires a more proactive, top-down approach to safety, which is a relatively new concept to U.S. airports. Additionally, in June 2012, the FAA issued a draft advisory circular (150/5200-37A) entitled "Safety Management Systems for Airports." Comments were due to the FAA by August 31, 2012. As of May 2015, the FAA had not released this AC in its final form, nor issued any regulatory guidance for airports requiring the development and implementation of SMS. Readers are encouraged to visit the SMS section of the FAA website (www.faa.gov/about/initiatives/sms/) for the most current information regarding SMS efforts for airports.

What is SMS? According to AC 150/5200-37, an SMS is a formalized approach to managing safety by developing an organization-wide safety policy, developing formal methods of identifying hazards, analyzing and mitigating risk, developing methods for ensuring continuous safety improvement, and creating organization-wide safety promotion strategies. Specifically, an SMS consists of the following four elements (see Figure 9-9):

- Safety policy and objectives
- Safety risk management
- Safety assurance
- Safety promotion

Safety Policy and Objectives

The safety policy, which is a formal commitment to safety expressed by senior management, is the foundation of an effective SMS. If senior management has not formally expressed a commitment to safety, it will be difficult to obtain "buy-in" from employees on the front line. To establish specific safety objectives, an airport will typically appoint a safety manager to oversee the SMS and ensure accountability within the organization. With a solid foundation of the safety policy and objectives, an airport will better be able to develop a positive "safety culture." In positive safety cultures, there are clear reporting lines, clearly defined duties and well understood procedures. Personnel will fully understand their responsibilities and know what to report, to whom, and when (FAA, 2007).

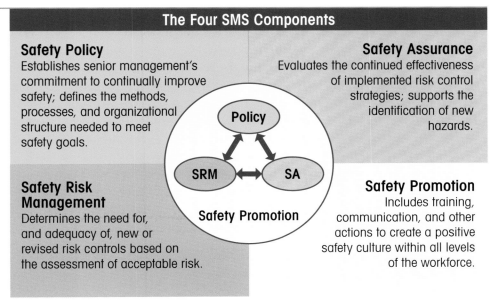

Figure 9-9. Elements of a safety management system (SMS).

(FAA)

Safety Risk Management

Safety risk management (SRM) is the main cornerstone of SMS. SRM requires a proactive approach to safety, rather than reacting after an accident or incident has occurred. The five phases in the SRM process are:

1. Describe the system.

2. Identify the hazards.

3. Determine the risk.

4. Assess and analyze the risk.

5. Treat the risk.

Phase 1, describing the system, requires consideration of the airport's current safety program as required by Part 139 and outlined in the ACM. Knowing the baseline safety status of the airport is important in knowing how much progress needs to be made to develop an SMS and a supportive safety culture (FAA, 2007).

Phase 2, identifying the hazards, requires an assessment of hazards of the system. Properly identifying hazards requires operational expertise, training in SMS, a simple hazard analysis tool, and adequate documentation of the process. In essence, the hazard identification stage considers all the possible sources of system failure (FAA, 2007).

Phase 3, determining the risk, requires each hazard to be identified to determine what risks exist that may be related to the hazards. In this phase, all potential risks associated with each hazard are identified and documented. There is no determination of the severity or potential of the risk occurring (FAA, 2007).

Phase 4, assessing and analyzing the risk, requires the airport operator to estimate the level of risk by using a predictive risk matrix. Risk is defined as the composite of the predicted severity and likelihood of the outcome or effect (harm) of the hazard in the worst credible system state. In order to assess the risk of an accident or incident occurring, severity and likelihood must be determined. Hazards are ranked according to the severity and the likelihood of their risk. The likelihood of an event is broken down into frequent, probable, remote, extremely remote, and extremely improbable. The severity of an event is broken down into no safety effect, minor, major, hazardous, and catastrophic. Depending on where an event/activity falls on the predictive risk matrix, various levels of risk may be possible (FAA, 2007).

Risk severity can be broken down into three levels. These levels of risk include high, medium, and low. A high risk activity is considered unacceptable. In this instance, the activity cannot be undertaken unless hazards are further mitigated so that risk is reduced to a medium or low level. A medium risk activity presents an acceptable level of risk. In this instance, the activity can continue, but tracking and management are required. Finally, a low risk activity presents the target level of risk. Low risk activities are acceptable without restriction or limitation, and the identified hazards are not required to be actively managed, but are documented (see Figure 9-10) (FAA, 2007).

Phase 5, treating the risk, requires the airport operator to develop options to mitigate the risk and alternative strategies for managing a hazard's risk(s). Generally, these strategies are designed to address medium-risk and high-risk hazards. Strategies may include avoidance, assumption, control, or transfer. Of course, risk mitigation may require a management decision to approve, fund, schedule, and implement one or more risk mitigation strategies. This phase is specifically designed for the airport operator to mitigate hazards (FAA, 2007).

An example of the SRM process at an airport could involve the construction of a new parallel taxiway at a two-runway airport. In identifying hazards,

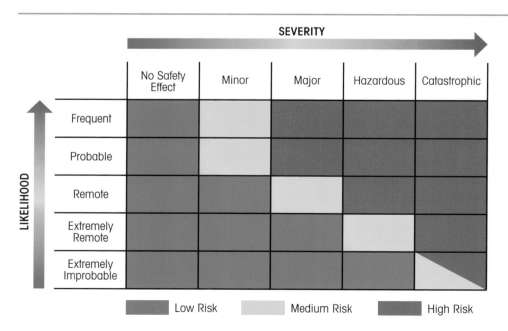

Figure 9-10.
Hazard risk matrix.

(From FAA AC 150/5200-37.)

AIRPORT MANAGEMENT

Figure 9-15.
Baggage screening.

Even with the implementation of the ATSA of 2001, threats to aviation security remain and have resulted in additional attacks and attempted attacks on the U.S. aviation system. On December 22, 2001, Richard Reid attempted unsuccessfully to ignite explosives concealed in his shoes while on an American Airlines flight from Paris to Miami. As a result of this incident, the TSA began requiring passengers to remove their shoes to be separately screened. On December 25, 2009, on a Northwest Airlines flight from Amsterdam to Detroit, Michigan, Umar Farouk Abdulmutallab attempted to detonate plastic explosives hidden in his underwear. As a result of this incident, the TSA began quickly deploying advanced imaging screening technology that could "see" through articles of clothing worn by passengers. Although this technology had first been deployed by the TSA in 2007, this 2009 attempted bombing created a sense of urgency for more widespread deployment of this technology. There are two types of advanced imaging technology—millimeter wave and backscatter. As of 2012, there were more than 640 imaging technology units in use at approximately 165 airports nationwide (Figure 9-16) (Price and Forrest, 2010; TSA, n.d.[a]).

Figure 9-16.
TSA screening checkpoint.

In order for the TSA to stay ahead of emerging security threats and prevent terrorist attacks that are either aimed at or utilize the aviation system, a multi-layered approach has been necessary. These layers have included Visible Intermodal Prevention and Response (VIPR), Travel Document Checker, behavior detection officers (BDO), Secure Flight, federal air marshals (FAMs), Federal Flight Deck Officer (FFDO) program, employee screening, and checkpoint screening technology. According to the TSA, the use of technology is an important component in this multi-layered approach. As of 2012, the TSA was using technology in the following forms:

1. Paperless boarding pass

2. Biometrics

3. Bottle liquids scanners

4. CastScope (for screening of casts and prosthetics)

5. Explosive detection system

6. Explosives trace detection

7. Threat image projection

8. Imaging technology
   (TSA, n.d.[c])

AGENCIES

There are several agencies involved with securing aviation. Prior to the TSA, the FAA was responsible for securing aviation and the airlines were responsible for screening passengers and carry-on baggage, often contracting this function out to private security firms. In the early days, the Federal Aviation Agency, which was created by the 1958 Federal Aviation Act, assumed the responsibilities of the Civil Aeronautics Authority. Although safety was the foundation of their responsibilities, aviation security soon became a responsibility, as well. Prior to the Federal Aviation Agency assuming responsibility for aviation security, however, the U.S. Immigration and Naturalization Service assumed this responsibility. Specifically, with the first U.S. aircraft hijackings in 1961, the federal government began using armed guards on civilian aircraft. These armed guards were actually border patrolmen recruited from the U.S. Immigration and Naturalization Service. That same year, President Kennedy signed an amendment to the Federal Aviation Act of 1958 making it a crime to hijack an aircraft, interfere with an active flight crew, or carry a dangerous weapon aboard an air carrier aircraft. To help enforce these revisions to the Act, and allow the Federal Aviation Agency to assume responsibility for aviation security, a special corps of FAA safety inspectors began training for duty aboard airline flights. In March 1962, the Federal Aviation Agency's first "peace officers" were sworn in as special U.S. deputy marshals. These men worked as safety inspectors for the FAA flight standards organization and carried out their role as armed marshals on flights only when specifically requested to do so (FAA, 2010a).

Figure 9-17.
Airport employee's
SIDA badge.

Figure 9-18.
Airport operations
conducting a SIDA
challenge to verify
this individual's
authorization to be in
the SIDA area.

identification media must be under escort by an authorized individual. Personnel must wear their SIDA badge at all times above waist level while in the secured area or SIDA (see Figure 9-18) (Price and Forrest, 2010).

A requirement of the Aviation and Transportation Security Act of 2001 was for personnel of all airport operators, aircraft operators, and foreign air carriers with access to the SIDA to undergo a fingerprint-based **Criminal History Records Check (CHRC)**. In fact, any individual who will have unescorted access to a SIDA or a sterile area, or who will have the authority to authorize others to have unescorted access, is required to undergo a fingerprint-based CHRC with a result that does not reveal any prior convictions or findings of not-guilty-by-reason-of-insanity of a disqualifying criminal offense. The 28 disqualifying offenses are:

1. Forgery of certificates, false marking of aircraft, and other aircraft registration violations
2. Interference with air navigation
3. Improper transportation of a hazardous material
4. Aircraft piracy
5. Interference with flight crewmembers or flight attendants
6. Commission of certain crimes aboard aircraft in flight
7. Carrying a weapon or explosive aboard an aircraft
8. Conveying false information and threats
9. Aircraft piracy outside the special aircraft jurisdiction of the United States
10. Lighting violations involving transporting controlled substances
11. Unlawful entry into an aircraft or airport area that serves air carriers or foreign air carriers contrary to established security requirements
12. Destruction of an aircraft or aircraft facility
13. Murder
14. Assault with intent to murder
15. Espionage
16. Sedition
17. Kidnapping or hostage taking
18. Treason
19. Rape or aggravated sexual abuse
20. Unlawful possession, use, sale, distribution, or manufacture of an explosive or weapon
21. Extortion
22. Armed or felony unarmed robbery
23. Distribution of, or intent to distribute, a controlled substance
24. Felony arson
25. Felony involving a threat
26. Felony involving willful destruction of property; importation or manufacture of a controlled substance; burglary; theft; dishonesty, fraud or misrepresentation; possession or distribution of stolen property; aggravated assault; bribery; or illegal possession of a controlled substance punishable by a maximum term of imprisonment of more than one year
27. Violence at international airports
28. Conspiracy or attempt to commit any of the criminal acts listed above

If the airport finds that the result of an applicant's CHRC indicates an arrest for a disqualifying criminal offense without disposition (guilty or not guilty), it is important to investigate further to determine whether the arrest resulted in a disqualifying offense. This must be determined before granting unescorted access authority. If there is no disposition or the disposition did not result in a finding of guilty or not guilty by reason of insanity, the applicant would not be disqualified from unescorted airport access (Price and Forrest, 2010).

Part 1542 also requires airports to provide **law enforcement officers (LEO)** to assist in carrying out the ASP and support the TSA at the passenger screening checkpoints. LEOs in use at airports must have arrest authority, be identifiable in uniform, be armed with and authorized to use a firearm, have completed a law enforcement officer training program, and be trained in the responsibilities of LEOs in carrying out the ASP (see Figure 9-19) (Price and Forrest, 2010).

The TSA typically communicates security information to the airport operator either in the form of a **security directive** or information circular. Security directives mandate measures with which airports must comply. Airport operators are required to acknowledge receipt of the security directive within the time prescribed and also to notify the TSA of the manner in which the airport will comply with the security directive. If unable to implement the measures required in the SD, the ASC must propose alternative measures to the TSA for approval within the time prescribed in the security directive. **Information circulars** contain advisory information and do not require implementation of any measures by the airport, other than possibly a heightened sense of security or awareness of specific threats highlighted in the information circular (Price and Forrest, 2010).

Figure 9-19.
Airport law enforcement officer.

Title 49 CFR Part 1544—Aircraft Operator Security

Similar to airport operators, aircraft operators are required to designate an **aircraft operator security coordinator (AOSC)** and this individual will be the main point of contact for the airline to the TSA. The AOSC is also responsible for developing the Aircraft Operator Standard Security Program (AOSSP) for the airline. The airline will also have a **ground security coordinator (GSC)** to oversee security for each passenger and cargo flight. The AOSSP will be designed to fit the needs of the airline, considering size of aircraft and number of passenger seats. An aircraft operator security program can be one of five types: full, partial, all-cargo, private charter, or twelve-five.

Full programs apply to aircraft operators with (a) seating configurations of 61 or more seats, or (b) seating configurations of 60 or fewer seats when operating to/from a sterile area. Indeed, full programs apply to most scheduled operators in the United States and require the aircraft operator to:

1. Screen individuals and carry-on bags.
2. Screen checked baggage.
3. Screen cargo.
4. Ensure that TSA has conducted screening of persons, carry-on and checked baggage, and cargo.
5. May use metal detectors to screen persons if part of the security program.
6. May use X-ray system for checked baggage if authorized by TSA.
7. Must use explosive detection system for checked baggage on international flights if authorized by the TSA.
8. Designate an aircraft operator security coordinator and a ground security coordinator for each flight.
9. Provide for law enforcement officer support.
10. Carry armed LEOs.
11. Carry prisoners.
12. Transport FAMs.
13. Prevent unauthorized access to exclusive area and the aircraft.
14. Conduct security inspection of the aircraft before placing in passenger operations.
15. Carry out provisions of the exclusive area agreement.
16. Conduct a security threat assessment for personnel with access to air cargo.
17. Conduct a search of the aircraft before departure.
18. Conduct CHRCs for those with unescorted access, screeners, and those with access to checked baggage or cargo.
19. Conduct CHRCs of flight crew members.
20. Use an airport-approved identification system.
21. Provide training for ground and in-flight security coordinator and crewmembers.

22. Provide training for individuals with security duties such as the ground security coordinator.

23. Restrict access to flight deck.

24. Have contingency plans.

25. Have bomb and air piracy threat procedures.

26. Comply with and protect security of SDs and ICs.

27. Use approved screeners and screening programs if not using TSA personnel. (Price and Forrest, 2010, pp. 120–122)

Partial programs apply to scheduled and public charter passenger operations with (a) seating configurations of 31 to 60 seats that do not enplane or deplane into a sterile area or (b) seating configurations of less than 60 seats to/from/outside the United States that do not enplane or deplane into a sterile area. Partial programs do not require the screening of persons and property. An airport operator may, however, require that passengers and property are screened prior to allowing passenger access to the airport's sterile area (Price and Forrest, 2010).

All-cargo operators are held to the all-cargo security program. A significant portion of this program involves the screening of cargo. Through the Implementing Recommendations of the 9/11 Commission Act of 2007, which was signed into law on August 3, 2007, TSA required cargo screening and as of October 2008, 100 percent of cargo being transported on narrow-body aircraft was being screened. Due to the significant amount of cargo being transported by air in the United States and the difficulty in screening this cargo, as of May 2012, 50 percent of air cargo on passenger carrying aircraft is screened, and 100 percent of the cargo on 96 percent of the flights originating in the United States is screened (TSA, n.d.[b]).

The Private Charter Standard Security Program (PCSSP) is an abbreviated program for private charter operators that requires screening of all passengers and accessible baggage prior to boarding the aircraft. Part 121 and 135 operators operating private charters with aircraft of a maximum certificated takeoff weight greater than 45,500 kg (100,309.3 pounds), or with at least 61 passenger seats, must ensure that all passengers and accessible baggage are screened prior to boarding the aircraft. However, to assist the private charter operator, this screening may be carried out by "non-TSA" screeners who have completed TSA-approved private charter screener training. These private charter operators must also develop a security program that includes use of metal detection devices, X-ray systems, security coordinators, law enforcement personnel, accessible weapons, CHRC, training for security coordinators and crewmembers, training for individuals with security-related duties, and training and procedures for bomb or air piracy threats (Price and Forrest, 2010).

For charter operators utilizing aircraft with a maximum certificated takeoff weight of more than 12,500 pounds, the "Twelve-Five rule" applies. The Aviation and Transportation Security Act of 2001 required the Under Secretary of Transportation for Security to implement a security program for charter air carriers with a maximum certificated takeoff weight of 12,500 pounds or more. A final rule was published in 2002 requiring certain aircraft operators using aircraft with a maximum certificated takeoff weight of 12,500 pounds or more to carry out security measures, including conducting CHRC on their flight crew members and restricting access to the flight deck. According to the final rule, "certain aircraft operators" were defined as those conducting operations in scheduled or charter service, carrying passengers or cargo or both. Aircraft operators falling under this rule are required to implement a Twelve-Five Standard Security Program (TFSSP).

Title 49 CFR Part 1546—Foreign Air Carrier Security

Part 1546 applies to security at foreign air carriers. Unless authorized by the TSA, foreign air carriers are not allowed access to SSI materials. Foreign air carriers also do not follow and are not allowed access to the domestic air carrier Aircraft Operator Standard Security Program (AOSSP). On the other hand, foreign air carriers are required to comply with a Model Security Program (MSP) (Price and Forrest, 2010).

Title 49 CFR Part 1548—Indirect Air Carrier Security

Indirect air carriers are those shippers that routinely ship cargo on air carriers either as part of their business or as their business. Indirect air carriers can be one of two types. First, direct shippers place the cargo on a truck and send it directly to the airport, where it is placed on an aircraft to be flown to its ultimate destination. Second, freight forwarders place the cargo on a truck, which delivers the cargo to a consolidation facility, and subsequently forwards that freight to an airport sorting center. These carriers must appoint security coordinators and have an approved Indirect Air Carrier Standard Security Program (IACSSP) (Price and Forrest, 2010).

GENERAL AVIATION AIRPORT SECURITY

The TSA does not regulate security at GA airports. However, in May 2004 the TSA issued Information Publication (IP) A-001, *Security Guidelines for General Aviation Airports*. Although GA airports are not obligated to utilize this IP, they are encouraged to do so by the TSA. The IP can actually be very helpful for the GA airport manager in not only determining the airport's current security posture, but also adopting tools and procedures to enhance this security posture (see Figure 9-20).

Specifically, the IP discusses the vulnerability of GA airports and the specific airport characteristics that affect an airport's risk to security threats. These characteristics include:

- 14 CFR §139.319 requires that ARFF personnel are trained in airport familiarization, aircraft familiarization, rescue and firefighting personnel safety, airport emergency communications systems, use of the fire hoses, nozzles, turrets, and other appliances, application of extinguishing agents required for compliance, emergency aircraft evacuation assistance, firefighting operations, use of structural rescue and firefighting equipment for aircraft rescue and firefighting, aircraft cargo hazards, and familiarization with firefighters' duties under the AEP.

- Alert I is used to indicate that an aircraft that is known or suspected to have an operational defect may or may not be landing at your airport. This is notification only. No response is required.

- Alert II is used to indicate an aircraft that is known or is suspected to have an operational defect that affects normal flight operations to the extent that there is danger of an accident (i.e., aircraft with a declared emergency is inbound to your airport).

- Alert III is used to indicate an aircraft incident/accident has occurred on or in the vicinity of the airport, requiring full response.

- Airports must be prepared to respond to media inquiries in a positive and proactive manner.

- A precision lightning warning system uses satellite lightning strike data and field mill sensors to measure voltage potential and provide some degree of likelihood for lightning strikes in the local area.

- The Aviation and Transportation Security Act (ATSA) was signed into law on November 19, 2001, creating the Transportation Security Administration and transferring all civil aviation security responsibilities to the TSA.

- As of 2012, the TSA was using technology for paperless boarding passes, biometrics, bottle liquids scanners, screening of casts and prosthetics, explosive detection system, explosives trace detection, threat image projection, and imaging technology.

- The Homeland Security Act, signed into law in 2002, created the Department of Homeland Security, which is the current home of the TSA.

- 49 CFR Part 1503 is titled Investigative and Enforcement Procedures.

- 49 CFR Part 1520 is titled Protection of Sensitive Security Information.

- 49 CFR Part 1540 is titled General Rules.

- 49 CFR Part 1542 is titled Airport Security. It requires an airport security coordinator, an airport security program, an access control system, personal identification media, challenge procedures, Criminal History Records Checks (CHRC) for personnel desiring unescorted access to the SIDA, and law enforcement officers.

- 49 CFR Part 1544, titled Aircraft Operator Security, requires aircraft operators to designate an aircraft operator security coordinator and a ground security coordinator, as well as an Aircraft Operator Standard Security Program.

- 49 CFR Part 1546 is titled Foreign Air Carrier Security.
- 49 CFR Part 1548 is titled Indirect Air Carrier Security.
- All-cargo operators are held to the all-cargo security program.
- Security at general aviation airports is not regulated by the TSA; however, TSA's Information Publication A-001, *Security Guidelines for General Aviation Airports*, addresses the vulnerability of GA airports and the specific airport characteristics that affect an airport's risk to security threats.

Review Questions ↘

1. Explain methods airports may use to protect the public from the hazards associated with the airport operating environment.

2. What are the vehicle and pedestrian requirements that should be included in construction safety and phasing plans at airports?

3. Explain the fire triangle.

4. What are Class A fires?

5. What are Class B fires?

6. What are Class C fires?

7. What are Class D fires?

8. Explain the purpose of bonding.

9. Explain the four elements of an SMS.

10. Explain the five phases of the safety risk management process.

11. Explain the National Incident Management System.

12. Explain the three levels of alert typically used at airports to convey information about aircraft emergencies.

13. Explain the purpose and function of a precision lightning warning system (PLWS).

14. What act created the Transportation Security Administration (TSA)?

15. What cabinet-level department in the executive branch was created by the Homeland Security Act of 2002?

16. What is an airport security coordinator responsible for?

17. Explain challenge procedures.

18. What capabilities must law enforcement officers at airports have?

19. Explain the Private Charter Standard Security Program (PCSSP).

20. What characteristics are addressed in TSA IP A-001, *Security Guidelines for General Aviation Airports*?

Scenarios ↘

1. As a newly-hired airport operations supervisor, you are asked to develop consequences for individuals that are found not in compliance with the airport's rules and regulations regarding access to and operation in movement areas and safety areas. Explain the program you would develop, to include various levels of noncompliance and the consequences associated with each level.

2. As a director of operations with a proactive safety mindset employed at a medium hub airport, you have decided to develop a safety management system. After speaking with other airports, you feel that this program can be developed in-house. How would you initiate such a project? Who would be mainly responsible for developing the SMS? Who would be involved in the process? What steps would you take?

3. As the airport security coordinator at a large hub airport, you are the sole individual responsible for ensuring compliance with TSA security directives. Consider the following SDs and specify how your airport would comply:

   a. All vehicles parking within 600 feet of the main terminal must be physically searched. (Your short-term parking garage has three levels equivalent to 1,500 spaces within 600 feet of the main terminal.)

   b. No baggage or items may be left unattended within the terminals.

   c. All employees, in addition to passengers with boarding passes, must be searched prior to entering the sterile area of the terminal.

   d. No metal knives may be present in the sterile area of the terminal.

4. Develop a fuel spill response plan for your airport, to include airport operations, police, ARFF, airline personnel, and the airport fueling company. Consider each of these stakeholders and the role they would be required to play if a fuel spill were to occur.

5. Utilizing the hazard risk matrix presented in this chapter, conduct an assessment for each of the following. In addition to the assessment, develop strategies to mitigate risk:

   a. Haul route across an active taxiway during an airfield construction project.

   b. Active taxiway crossing point due to the service road intersecting taxiways A and B.

   c. Airline mechanics taxiing aircraft from the ramp across an active runway to the maintenance hangar.

   d. Electrical maintenance performing lighting inspections three nights per week.

   e. Temporary tower erected during the annual airshow and fly-in.

   f. Closing a taxiway for three days for the upcoming AOPA Aviation Summit.

   g. Creating two new temporary helipads on taxiway T for the Super Bowl traffic.

   h. Aircraft taxiing to the new ground run-up enclosure adjacent to taxiway C.

References and Resources for Further Study

American Association of Airport Executives. 2005. "Body of Knowledge Module 3. Airport Operations, Security and Maintenance." Washington, DC: AAAE.

deNeufville, R. and A. Odoni. 2003. *Airport Systems: Planning Design and Management.* New York: McGraw Hill.

Federal Aviation Administration (FAA). 2002. *Ground Vehicle Operations on Airport.* AC 150/5210-5D.

————. 2007. *Introduction to Safety Management Systems (SMS) for Airport Operators.* AC 150/5200-37. Washington, DC: FAA.

————. 2009. *Airport Emergency Plan.* AC 150/5200-31C. Washington, DC: FAA.

————. 2010(a). "History." Retrieved April 18, 2012 from http://www.faa.gov/about/history/brief_history/

————. 2010(b). *Painting, Marking and Lighting Vehicles Used on Airport.* AC 150/5210-5D. Washington, DC: FAA.

————. 2011. *Operational Safety on Airports During Construction.* AC 150/5370-2. Washington, DC: FAA.

Federal Emergency Management Agency. 2015. "National Incident Management System." Retrieved from http://www.fema.gov/national-incident-management-system

Prather, C.D. 2009. *General Aviation Marketing and Management: Operating, Marketing, and Managing an FBO.* Malabar, FL: Krieger.

Price, J. and J. Forrest. 2010. "Airport operations, security, and maintenance." Washington, DC: AAAE.

Rumerman, J. n.d. "Aviation Security." U.S. Centennial of Flight Commission. Retrieved April 18, 2012 from http://www.centennialofflight.net/essay/Government_Role/security/POL18.htm

Transportation Security Administration (TSA). 2004. *Security Guidelines for General Aviation Airports.* Information Publication A-001. Retrieved April 22, 2012 from http://www.tsa.gov/assets/pdf/security_guidelines_for_general_aviation_airports.pdf

————. 2011. *Recommended Security Guidelines for Airport Planning, Design and Construction.*

————. n.d.(a) "Advanced imaging technology." Retrieved April 17, 2012 from http://www.tsa.gov/approach/tech/ait/index.shtm

————. n.d.(b) "Air Cargo." Retrieved April 21, 2012 from http://www.tsa.gov/stakeholders/air-cargo

————. n.d.(c) "Innovation and technology." Retrieved April 17, 2012 from http://www.tsa.gov/about-tsa/technology

————. n.d.(d). "What is TSA?" Retrieved April 18, 2012 from http://www.tsa.gov/about-tsa

"Vaisala Precision Lightning Warning System (PLWS)." n.d. Retrieved from Reference: http://app.tampaairport.com/about/media/PLWS-Summary.pdf

Chapter 10

Marketing

Objectives ↘

Upon completion of this chapter, you should:

- Understand the purpose of marketing.
- Understanding the basics of marketing.
- Understand the six steps involved in developing a marketing plan.
- Be able to discuss common marketing goals of commercial-service and GA airports.
- Be able to develop marketing goals and objectives.
- Be able to perform a SWOT analysis.
- Understand how to perform market segmentation.
- Understand how to select target markets.
- Understand the Five Ps of marketing.
- Understand the components of the promotional mix.
- Understand how to implement a marketing plan.
- Understand the controllable and uncontrollable variables affecting airport marketing.
- Be able to discuss the characteristics of an effective marketing plan.
- Understand the importance of air service development.
- Understand the steps in developing an effective ASD program.
- Understand the concessions airports may offer to air carriers.
- Understand allowable and non-allowable uses of airport revenue for ASD efforts.

Key Terms ↘

advertising
air service development (ASD)
communication
consumers
controllable variables
cost leadership goal
delegation
environmental scanning
Five Ps
goal
incentives
leakage
market expansion goal
market focus goal
market segmentation
marketing
marketing mix
marketing plan
mass marketing

motivation
multiple target market approach
networking
objective
press kit
promotional mix
public relations (PR)
quality goal
revenue diversion
single target market approach
Small Community Air Service
    Development Program
stakeholders
strategic business plan
subsidies
SWOT analysis
target markets
uncontrollable variables

In Chapter 10

FEATURES

This marketing plan was developed in an effort to increase airport business and revenues.

In an effort to increase tourism and business activity, LAWA was found to have diverted revenue from the airport to the city's convention and visitors bureau.

Purpose of Marketing

Marketing is defined as those sets of plans developed by a firm and the activities carried out based on these plans that are specifically designed to influence the behavior of consumers. The term "**consumers**" typically refers to those individuals making purchases, but may also refer to the firm's target audience. Indeed, some firms, including airports, may engage in marketing to generate goodwill or stimulate support. Marketing can prove beneficial even if the firm has nothing to sell. As Sean Mauger states, "Marketing is the art of identifying and understanding customer needs and creating solutions that deliver satisfaction to the customers, profits to the producers and benefits for the stakeholders." (Kramer et al., 2010, p. 2)

Essentially, customer satisfaction is the ultimate objective of the marketing process. And it will be challenging for a company to provide customer satisfaction if customer needs are not adequately understood. Firms rely on marketing to build stronger relationships with current customers and discover new target markets on which to capitalize. Most importantly, customers, not marketers, primarily determine what they need, want, and are willing to buy. Although savvy marketing can motivate impulse purchasing, generally the customer has certain needs and wants and the role of marketing is to both identify and satisfy those needs and wants (see Figure 10-1).

Unlike a retailer that focuses solely on attracting and retaining customers, airports must focus on the many stakeholders they serve. As a result, marketing approaches among airports can be quite different based on the stakeholders being targeted. Whether utilizing a comprehensive marketing strategy or simply placing an advertisement in the newspaper, all marketing approaches have commonalities among them. This chapter provides marketing concepts and practices that are common to airports of any size and any targeted audience.

Figure 10-1.
A satisfied customer—the ultimate objective of the marketing process.

(©iStock.com/Trish233)

Marketing Basics

In meeting customer needs and endeavoring to provide customer satisfaction, airports are in a unique situation to focus on tenants, airline passengers, and/or the community. In fact, airports can utilize marketing to reach a number of **stakeholders**, including the community, passengers, meeters and greeters, current and potential tenants (including airlines, fixed base operators, maintenance providers, corporate operators), and various business prospects. An airport's justification for marketing to these various groups is as follows:

- Community
  - › Generate goodwill and support for the airport.
  - › Generate awareness of the airport and its economic impacts on the economy.
- Passengers
  - › Convey the availability of airport services.
  - › Convey information about airport news and events.
  - › Attract more passengers.
- Meeters and greeters
  - › Convey information about parking services.
  - › Convey information about airport construction projects that may affect access and circulation of vehicles.
  - › Convey information about concessions that meeters and greeters may be able to utilize.
- Current tenants
  - › Generate support for airport capital development plans.
  - › Convey the financial basis for fees, rates, and charges.
  - › Motivate new services by tenants, including new routes, aircraft, and services by airlines.
  - › Retain current tenants.
- Potential tenants
  - › Motivate new services by tenants, including new airline service.
  - › Attract new tenants to the airport by conveying information about airport facilities, fees, services, and potential market for tenant products/services.
- Business prospects
  - › Generate investment in the airport.
  - › Motivate use of airport facilities and services.

  (Kramer et al., 2010)

Jackson County Airport's Marketing Plan

The Jackson County Airport—Reynolds Field, located in south central Michigan, developed an airport marketing plan in 2011. As a GA airport currently situated on over 700 acres providing air traffic control services, car rentals, a restaurant, aviation fuel and aircraft repair, flight training, and a variety of other airport-based businesses, the airport desired to overcome impacts of a sluggish economy, rising aviation fuel prices, and a poor business climate. The marketing plan was developed through the work of an advisory council, which included representatives from airport-based businesses. In addition to performing an issue analysis and SWOT analysis, the council collected 77 surveys from airport customers by placing surveys in the airport restaurant. Marketing strategies developed as part of this marketing plan included: (a) encourage and enhance partnerships and collaboration efforts; (b) encourage young people to get involved with airport events and aviation in general; (c) market the airport as a venue for special events and as a location for community meetings and gatherings; (d) initiate a "branding" study to create an airport brand; (e) research the feasibility of a modern electronic sign for the main airport entrance; and (f) encourage the availability of a based business that offers aircraft rentals and perhaps light sport aircraft sales and instruction. Although this plan is representative of a small, GA airport, even small airports need to be strategic about marketing their services and promoting the benefits of the airport to the community.

(Jackson County—Reynolds Field Airport. 2011)

Developing a Marketing Plan

Preparing an airport marketing plan takes significant focus and effort. If well designed, a properly developed airport marketing plan will answer the following questions:

- What are the marketing goals?
- Who are the target audiences?
- What is the message the airport intends to communicate?
- What methods of communication will the airport use to reach its audience?
- What staffing and financial resources will support the effort?
- How will the airport measure success?

  (Kramer et al., 2010, p. 6)

It's often said that if you fail to plan, you plan to fail. This pearl of wisdom could be applied to marketing. Without a plan, an airport will be "shooting in the dark" and likely waste valuable resources with ineffective marketing. In essence, a **marketing plan** is imperative if an airport wants to realize success in their marketing efforts. Although the process is not complex, preparing a marketing plan does involve six specific steps:

Step 1: Determine goals and objectives.

Step 2: Assess resources and perform a Strengths-Weaknesses-Opportunities-Threats (SWOT) analysis.

Step 3: Revise goals and objectives as necessary.

Step 4: Segment the market.

Step 5: Select target markets.

Step 6: Establish a unique marketing mix aimed at a particular audience.

    a. Product or service

    b. Price

    c. Channel of distribution (place)

    d. Promotion (advertising, sales promotion, personal selling, and publicity)

    e. Passion

(Prather, 2009; Kramer et al., 2010)

DETERMINE GOALS AND OBJECTIVES

Step 1 requires the airport to determine goals and objectives. A **goal** will generally encompass the "big picture" of the marketing effort, such as attracting an air carrier, increasing the number of based aircraft, increasing fuel sales, or minimizing vacancies in the airport business park. **Objectives**, on the other hand, are more specific and may include attracting an air carrier operating with non-stop capability to a specific hub airport, a specific aircraft type, or seating capacity. Although an airport may develop a long list of marketing goals, it is important to separate the various goals into distinct categories and develop a marketing plan with aspects focused on each of these categories. Without this, marketing efforts may prove confusing. For instance, marketing efforts to increase fuel sales will be quite different from marketing efforts to attract an air carrier, and the marketing plan should reflect this (Prather, 2009).

The most common marketing goals across all industries include: (a) market expansion, (b) market focus or segmentation, (c) cost leadership, and (d) quality. For commercial-service airports or those desiring to attract air carriers, a **market expansion goal** can refer to increasing enplanements, typically from other markets, and/or increasing air carriers or air service. For GA airports, a goal of market expansion may refer to increasing based aircraft or new tenants. A **market focus goal** refers to either focusing on a particular type of customer or specializing in a particular service. For airports, the focus may be on international passengers or attracting light sport aircraft. A **cost leadership goal** refers to the desire to have the lowest costs in an area. For airports, this may mean the lowest fuel prices, the lowest landing fees, or the lowest hangar rental fees. A **quality goal** can revolve around quality products or services, and for airports often refers to the goal of offering exceptional customer service. In fact, airports often pride themselves in the exceptional level of customer service they offer. A 2008 study of airports found the following marketing goals at commercial-service airports, in order of popularity:

1. Attract passengers.
2. Promote positive view of the airport in the community.
3. Improve air service.
4. Retain existing carriers.
5. Attract new businesses to the airport.
   (Kramer et al., 2010).

A 2008 study of GA airports found the following marketing goals, in order of popularity:

1. Attract new business to the airport.
2. Promote positive view of airport in the community.
3. Retain current airport tenants.
4. Attract more GA or business activity.
5. Promote airport to funding sources.
   (Kramer et al., 2010).

Although these lists show similarities in the marketing goals of commercial-service and GA airports, there clearly are differences as well. In airport marketing, the key factor for airports to consider is what they are hoping to achieve with their marketing efforts. It is also important for the goals and objectives to integrate with the airport's **strategic business plan**. Such a plan outlines the overall mission and vision of the airport, as well as its overall goals and objectives. Developing marketing goals and objectives that are at odds with the airport's mission would be a mistake. Although goals may not be, marketing objectives should be quantified and stated in understandable terms. For example, rather than simply desiring to attract an air carrier, it is helpful to express this in terms of desiring an air carrier that can provide a particular level of service with a certain number of seats by a certain date. A benefit of developing specific objectives is that the airport can measure the level of success of marketing efforts by determining to what degree the various objectives have been achieved. Vague objectives will leave airport personnel wondering whether or not (or to what degree) they were successful in their marketing efforts (Prather, 2009; Kramer et al., 2010).

It's important for airports to consider the stakeholders as they develop goals and objectives. As an airport begins thinking like a stakeholder, it is much easier to develop effective marketing goals and objectives. Statements that may stimulate the development of goals and objectives include:

- Our tenants think…
- Our customers think…
- The community thinks…
- Our airport is known for…
- We are proud of…
- We strive to…
- We want our customers to…
- This airport should…

ASSESS RESOURCES AND PERFORM A SWOT ANALYSIS

Step 2, although often seen as a time-consuming step that airports would rather avoid, requires airports to (a) assess the resources available for the marketing efforts and (b) perform a **SWOT analysis** (see Figure 10-2). An airport may perform step 2(a) simply by asking, "What's our budget?" but it is also helpful to examine the personnel and financial resources available to commit to the marketing plan. Step 2(b) requires a candid examination of the strengths and weaknesses of the airport, as well the opportunities and threats confronting the airport. This exercise can help an airport consider what they have to offer various stakeholders. Strengths and weaknesses are typically internal to the organization, while opportunities and threats refer to issues in the external environment. For instance, if a GA airport has an objective of attracting an air carrier, it will be beneficial to use the SWOT approach to evaluate the airport from the perspective of a potential air carrier. This exercise forces the airport to think like the air carrier to which they will be marketing, likely resulting in a more effective marketing plan. Strengths may include the airport's location, ILS availability, modern terminal building, support of air carrier service by the community, etc. Weaknesses may include lack of an ATC tower, lack of automobile parking, or lack of aircraft deicing services. Opportunities and threats

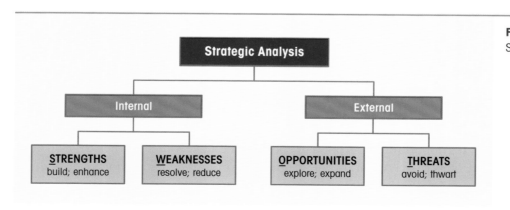

Figure 10-2.
SWOT analysis.

may apply more to the airport than the air carrier. Opportunities may include potential air carrier service and an FAA contract tower. Threats may include the close proximity of an airport with existing air carrier service (Prather, 2009; Kramer et al., 2010).

Although a SWOT analysis is usually completed as part of the airport's strategic business plan, it is beneficial to conduct such an analysis as part of the marketing plan. Additionally, although a SWOT analysis is often performed by airport personnel, it may be helpful to obtain customer feedback on the strengths and weaknesses of the airport. Without doing this, airport personnel will simply be guessing what stakeholders consider to be the strengths and weaknesses. This feedback can be obtained from customers via surveys, comments on social media, comment cards in the terminal, or random personal interviews in the terminal. Feedback can be obtained from tenants via surveys or tenant events (Kramer et al., 2010).

REVISE GOALS AND OBJECTIVES

In step 3, the airport has the opportunity to revise goals and objectives based on the results of the SWOT analysis. Oftentimes, the airport will uncover weaknesses or threats that will require a revision to the original marketing goals. If no revisions are necessary, the original goals and objectives may stand. However, this is the time to make revisions, not once thousands of dollars are spent on marketing efforts.

SEGMENT THE MARKET

In step 4, the airport further defines the market by segmenting it. **Market segmentation** is the process of breaking down the total market into smaller, more homogeneous groups with similar needs that the airport can satisfy. For instance, an airport desiring air carrier service can segment the market into major carriers and regional carriers. Regional carriers could be further segmented by the route structure, which will eventually allow the airport to focus on those carriers that would most likely be willing to add that airport to their existing route structure (Prather, 2009).

SELECT TARGET MARKETS

In step 5, **target markets** are selected. Although segmenting the market aids the airport in further defining the focus of its marketing efforts, selecting a target market allows the airport to pinpoint the object of the airport's marketing mix. This could take the form of a single target market approach or a multiple target market approach. A **single target market approach** requires the airport to select one primary market segment as the airport's target market. Although this approach allows the airport to narrow its focus, it also involves more financial risk than if the airport diversifies into multiple target markets. A **multiple target market approach** requires the airport to select two or more market segments, with each being treated as a separate target market. Although this approach allows for more diversification, each target market will also require a unique marketing mix. It is important to note that selecting a target market allows the airport to engage in targeted marketing rather than mass marketing. **Mass marketing** does not attempt to differentiate between the market segments, and instead aims toward all segments—a "shotgun" approach, which is effective in certain circumstances (Prather, 2009).

Examples of possible target markets for an airport include:

- Local passengers
- Destination passengers
- Airlines
- Local businesses
- Transient pilots
- Aircraft owners with registered aircraft in the region
- Flight schools in the area
- Affiliate service centers of the local FBO
- Aviation specialists (e.g., maintenance & repair, helicopters, offshore oil rig support, aircraft painting)
- Existing tenants
- Tenant leads
- Schools and colleges
- Government groups
- Congressional delegation
  (Kramer et al., 2010)

ESTABLISH A UNIQUE MARKETING MIX

In step 6, the final step, airports develop a unique marketing mix. The **marketing mix** refers to the set of controllable marketing variables that the airport uses to achieve marketing goals and objectives. This involves everything the airport does to influence the demand for its product or influence the behavior of the target market. Specifically, the marketing mix consists of the following "**Five Ps**":

1. Product or service
2. Price
3. Place (channel of distribution)
4. Promotion (public relations, advertising, and networking)
5. Passion

Product or Service

The first P represents *"product or service"*—the combination of benefits, physical features, and services designed to satisfy the needs or wants of the identified target market. In other words, what specifically is the airport marketing? In marketing to prospective air carriers, the airport will want to emphasize the demand that exists in the form of potential passengers.

Price

The second P, *price*, refers to the value of a good or service. Since customers perceive price as the sacrifice or cost they must pay, marketers must maintain the price level equal to or less than the amount customers are willing to pay to experience the perceived satisfaction provided by the product or service. This cost-benefit relationship plays a major role in pricing strategies. If an airport is marketing to prospective air carriers, these carriers must be convinced that airport fees, rates, and charges, as well as aircraft operating costs (also measured as costs per enplaned passenger), will be sufficiently less than the revenues they may realize on the routes to be established, based on load factors and ticket prices.

Place

The third P, *place*, refers to delivering the product and services to customers in a timely manner. In addition to a convenient airport location, the appropriate products and services must be available for each target market in the correct amount when customers need them. Obviously, a prospective air carrier will be interested in whether the geographic location of the airport integrates with the air carrier's existing routes structure.

Promotion

The fourth P, *promotion*, involves systematic decision making related to all aspects of the development and management of an airport's promotional effort. Promotion is any form of communication used to inform, persuade, or remind people about products, services, image, ideas, or community involvement. Promotion is the heart of marketing. Although an airport marketing plan may contain any or all of the components of the promotional mix (depending on the specific goals and objectives of the airport's marketing plan), the **promotional mix** available to airports consists of:

1. Public relations
2. Advertising
3. Networking

Public relations (PR) refers to the act of relating to the public. AOPA defines PR as "everything the airport is and does that addresses or affects the public interest." (Kramer et al., 2010, p. 69). In reality, PR involves the public opinion. Whether or not an airport engages in PR, the public likely already holds an opinion of the airport. Engaging in PR allows the airport the opportunity to proactively and positively influence that opinion. Tools available to influence the public opinion include:

- Earned media (includes press kits, press releases, interviews, public service announcements, featured articles and stories, and awards and special recognition)
- Public speaking (includes speaking at local community events and presentations at conferences or tradeshows)
- Other print communications (includes airshows, open houses, and educational programs)
- Events (includes contests and drawings, free services and amenities, giveaway items, reduction of rates and charges)
- Sponsorships and volunteering (includes sponsoring interns and students, board participation, supporting non-profit community events, and volunteering in the community)
- Other print materials (includes customer satisfaction surveys, print and electronic newsletters, economic impact studies, testimonials, and white papers)

A form of earned media that can be quite effective is a "**press kit**." A press kit is a tool for proactively utilizing the media for marketing and generating positive community support. In today's internet-driven culture, press kits are often in electronic form, a technological enhancement to the old stack of published materials. The internet allows anyone to access an airport's press kit on its website at any time, which also reduces or completely eliminates the expense associated with mailing press kits—a common practice in the days before the widespread use of the internet.

An airport press kit may include any or all of the following:

- A website or physical cover with the airport's brand (logo, key message, graphics, and colors)
- Information for media inquiries
  - › Office hours
  - › Phone numbers
  - › How to request an interview
  - › Parking and "live broadcast trucks"
  - › Airport access
- Fact sheet about the airport
- Image library (photos of the airport)
- Airport newsletter
- News releases
- Staff biographies

- Members of the airport governing group (airport commission or authority)
- Airport tenants and businesses
- Airport statistics
- Airport financial records
- Business cards and stationery that carry the airport's brand are used in the press kit

(Kramer et al., 2010)

Although developing a press kit takes time and possibly some contracted marketing expertise, it is an opportunity to distribute airport information and positive news in a proactive manner to those in the media that can provide free promotion of the airport. Press kits can equally benefit commercial-service and GA airports.

Yet another effective form of earned media is the press release. Press releases are free and can be quite effective at getting the word out about the airport. Effective press releases address who, what, when, where, and why. It requires skill to develop an effective press release. Important elements of a press release include a strong lead-in sentence, the use of quotes to give it a personal touch, and highlights that have human interest (see Figure 10-3).

The media, through their typically wide distribution (i.e., readership, viewership, or listenership) can generate positive and negative press for the airport. Therefore, it is important to fully utilize the media to ensure that all press about the airport is positive. Media contacts may include:

- News stations
- Television programs/features
- Public service announcements
- Radio programs
- Newswires
- Newspapers

Advertising tools are different than PR tools in that they are intentionally designed, paid for, and placed by the advertising sponsor. Advertising tools consist of:

- Internet and websites (includes airport websites, email distributions, and internet advertising)
- Print media (includes print ads in newspapers, magazines, and trade journals; direct mail; brochures; business cards and stationary; testimonials)
- Signage (includes billboards, posters, banners, and display signage)
- Multi-media tools (includes radio, television, and video)

Figure 10-3.
Sample press
release guidelines.

Airport Logo
NEWS RELEASE
Date: (The date the release is being distributed.)
FOR IMMEDIATE RELEASE
For more information, contact:
(Name, Department, Title)
(Phone Number)
(Email Address)—optional

SUBJECT: (A brief topic or event description, typically 5 words or less.)

The body of the press release is very basic; who, what, where, when and why. The first paragraph of the press release should contain in brief detail what the press release is about.

The second paragraph explains, in detail: who cares; why you should care; where one can find the event being promoted; and when the event will happen. The second paragraph also usually includes a quote that gives the release a personal touch. "Touchy-feelies" go a long way with journalists. Press releases and news stories are boring to journalists without a "human interest."

The third and generally final paragraph identifies department contact information and where the reader can get information, i.e., website, telephone numbers, etc.

The content of the press release should be typed in a clear, basic font (Times New Roman is preferred). The release should be about a page and generally no more than 400 to 500 words. If a press release exceeds one page, the second page should indicate "Page Two" in the upper right-hand corner, and "more" should appear at the bottom of the first page. Journalistic standards have set basic parameters to define the end of a press release: Three "#" symbols ("###") centered directly underneath the last line indicate the end of the release. Finally, verify your facts and check your spelling. Once a mistake is printed or reported in the media it is difficult to get it corrected.

###

(Kramer et al., 2010, p. 73)

Although multi-media tools can reach a wide audience, they can be quite expensive. An effective alternative is the internet and development of a website. Today, many potential customers conduct research and fact-finding on the internet, which makes this advertising tool very effective.

Networking comprises the third and final category of marketing tools. Networking refers to the process of building contacts and relationships through various means. This includes:

- Business, civic, and non-profit groups
- Professional organizations
- Tradeshows and conferences
- Strategic partnerships
- Lobbying

(Kramer et al., 2010)

Often, it is important for an airport manager to engage in networking with each of these groups. However, networking with local business, civic, and non-profit groups allows the airport to generate significant community goodwill. As stated by Kramer et al. (2010, p. 120), airports that engage in networking are able to:

- Continuously remind the community of the airport's value and role in the economic activity of the community.
- Create goodwill that makes it easier to resolve difficult airport–community issues.
- Build lasting relationships with organizations that have a vested interest in the airport's long-term vitality.
- Recruit champions, volunteers, marketers, and partners of the airport.
- Educate and excite the "next generation" of airport leaders and champions.

The specific promotional mix selected by an airport may be free or may cost a substantial amount of money. Although smaller, GA airports often operate on a tighter marketing budget than larger commercial-service airports, all airports must establish a marketing budget and strive to remain within that budget. Airports oftentimes fund their marketing budget with their retained earnings. However, there are alternative sources of funding for airport marketing, including grants, cash donations, in-kind contributions, and cost sharing. The most common grant source is the **Small Community Air Service Development Program** through the DOT. This program provides funding to airports in conducting air service development studies and funding marketing to attract new carriers or enhance existing air carrier service (Kramer et al., 2010).

Regardless of how funds are pooled to support an airport marketing plan, airports must develop and adhere to a marketing budget. Fortunately, many of the components of a promotional mix that can be quite successful to an airport's marketing efforts are inexpensive. The available components and their level of cost are as follows:

- Free/minimal cost
  - › Press releases
  - › Editorials
  - › Travel-related articles
  - › E-mail newsletter
  - › Chamber speeches
  - › Networking
  - › Testimonials
- Some cost
  - › Website
  - › Promotions
  - › Receptions
  - › Open house
  - › Social media
- More cost
  - › Radio
  - › Newspaper ads
  - › Billboards
- Most cost
  - › TV Ads

(Kramer et al., 2010)

Of all of the components available to an airport today, the internet allows for broad and often inexpensive exposure. A website may be designed to serve as a brochure, presenting various information about the airport (such as airlines, parking options, food and beverage choices, maps of the facilities, etc.). A website may also be more strategically designed as a marketing tool, with changing content (such as flight times, new airline services/routes, etc.) and links to the airport's presence on social networking sites such as Facebook and Twitter. Generally, a dynamic website that visitors can interact with will be more productive for the airport and successfully contribute to the airport's marketing efforts. Although an airport can utilize a website with little financial expense (other than domain registration, hosting, web design services, and staffing to maintain currency of the site), a myriad of advertising options are also available on the internet, although some of these can be quite expensive. Online advertising is typically based on the amount a firm will pay for each impression and/or click. Often, a fixed fee is charged for a certain number of impressions and another fee is charged if a visitor clicks on the ad.

In addition to a website, a relatively recent trend in promoting an airport involves the use of social media. Although websites are integral for getting information to customers and prospective customers, the various forms of social media (including Facebook, Twitter, and other platforms) allow airports the ability to interact with customers in real-time—holding contests, answering questions, posting photos and videos, and more. Social media has changed the manner in which companies are marketed and customers research products and services. The key in effectively using social media is to interact regularly (preferably daily) and make it fun for individuals to interact with the airport. To build a large fan base, the airport can pay for advertisements on Facebook, for example, and set a daily ad budget paying on a per-click basis.

In addition, airports may develop an application (app), allowing customers and prospective customers to install an airport-specific app on their smartphone. These apps may have flight information, parking information, maps of terminals, and more (see Figure 10-4).

Small airports most often rely on developing an airport website, generating newspaper articles, and issuing press releases to comprise their promotional mix. Commercial-service airports, on the other hand, most often develop an airport website, generate articles in newspapers and magazines, issue press releases, and produce radio ads. The use of billboards is also a popular marketing tool for commercial-service airports, especially when introducing new airline service (although the airline may assist with or completely handle billboard efforts).

Figure 10-4.
Airport app displaying an airport map.

Networking is also used by airports, although this often is among industry peers, rather than with customers the airports are trying to reach. In this case, airport personnel may attend events sponsored by agencies such as AAAE, Airports Council International (ACI) – North America (NA), and state airport associations. However, if trying to target potential passengers, an airport manager may network by speaking at a Rotary Club meeting or speaking with chamber of commerce members. If trying to reach potential air carriers, an airport manager may attend events such as Network USA and other events at which airline representatives would be present (Kramer et al., 2010).

Passion

The fifth of the "Five Ps" is *passion*, which is often intangible, but important nonetheless. When marketing the airport, it is important that passion about the airport and future potential is evident. If passion is lacking, it will be difficult to motivate stakeholders. How can an air carrier be motivated to begin service at an airport if the airport (or marketing) director lacks any passion about the airport or the air carrier? As an example, infomercials have historically been very effective at selling large numbers of products due in part to the passion exhibited by the presenter/host. Fortunately, those in aviation are generally quite passionate about the industry in which they work, which should benefit marketing efforts.

It is important for an airport to consider each of the Five Ps when developing a marketing plan. Potential customers will be considering each of the Five Ps (although maybe not explicitly), so it is imperative for the airport to do the same.

Variables

In any environment, there are variables that affect our level of success. Some of these variables can be controlled (such as our level of training, quality of running shoes, and clothing as we run in a marathon). Other variables are uncontrollable (such as the weather, the number of competing runners, etc.). This is also true of marketing. Although airports can control the money they dedicate toward marketing, the goals and objectives they adopt, and the marketing messages they choose (i.e., **controllable variables**), they must also contend with many **uncontrollable variables**.

The uncontrollable variables are those factors affecting the airport's performance that cannot be directed by marketing efforts. Any marketing plan, regardless of the expense involved, can fail if adversely influenced by uncontrollable variables. Therefore, it is important for an airport to regularly monitor the external environment and adjust the marketing plan as necessary. This process of continually acquiring information about trends occurring externally to the airport is referred to as **environmental scanning**. Typical uncontrollable variables include:

- Consumer demographics
- Competition
- Government regulations
- The economy
- Technology
- Media
- Public interest groups

First, although a firm has control over the selection of a target market, it cannot control the characteristics of the population. As demographics (such as age, income levels, marital status, occupation, race, education, and place and type of residence) change, airports can only react to these changes. It is important to anticipate changes in demographics and react as necessary.

Second, competitors can affect the success of any marketing effort. Especially among airports, potential passengers from a market area may drive to another airport (leakage) for lower-priced flights or better service. Competition can be experienced in one of three forms:

1. Direct competition between companies offering similar products and services.

2. Competition between companies that offer products or services that can be substituted for one another.

3. Competition for limited financial resources.

Third, governmental regulation can impact marketing success. In addition to the federal laws involving antitrust, discriminatory pricing, unfair trade practices, and occupational health and safety, the aviation industry must comply with numerous regulations promulgated by the Federal Aviation Administration. Occasionally, these laws change. In addition to federal laws, state and local governments have their own political climates that may adversely affect airport marketing efforts.

Fourth, the current state of the economy can greatly affect marketing efforts. For instance, if an airport is endeavoring to increase enplanements, but the country is enduring a recession, many individuals may choose not to fly because they cannot afford to. Indeed, an economic recession, high unemployment, and the rising cost of credit all affect purchasing power. On the other hand, if the country is enjoying a high rate of economic growth, marketing will likely be more successful.

Fifth, technological innovation can affect marketing success. The aviation industry has always been on the leading edge of technological change. Many technological advances are beyond the control of individual firms, especially smaller ones. However, unless they keep pace with improved technology, they will no longer remain competitive.

Sixth, the media can influence marketing success. In particular, the media can influence the behavior of consumers. The media can also provide positive or negative coverage of a company or an industry. Airports can, on the other hand, capitalize on the media's power by sharing positive news (as previously discussed).

Lastly, public interest groups can affect marketing success. The number of public interest groups has increased significantly during the past two decades. Hundreds of other consumer interest groups—private and governmental—operate at the national, state, and local levels. Some airports have been confronted with environmental groups opposing an airport expansion, so the existence, power, and influence of public interest groups is a real threat.

Implementing the Plan

Regardless of how much time and effort was required to develop the marketing plan, success will be not be realized if customers don't purchase goods and services, new airlines don't begin service, or fuel sales do not increase (depending on the specific marketing objectives). Therefore, once a plan is developed, it must be implemented—or put into action. Implementation of marketing plans requires three phases:

1. Delegation
2. Communication
3. Motivation

Delegation is necessary because it will be difficult for one person to do it all. Delegation is carried out both formally through organizational structure and informally through the daily assignment and sharing of tasks. In addition to determining appropriate duties, delegation requires matching the capabilities and preferences of employees to those duties. In other words, delegation is only successful when the duties to be performed have been clearly specified, and appropriate personnel have been assigned to perform those duties. For instance, one employee in the marketing department may be skilled at developing websites and utilizing social media, while another may be a skilled and passionate presenter and negotiator (Prather, 2011).

The implementation of a marketing plan also requires proper **communication**. Some in the organization may not be aware of the new marketing goals or the plans implemented to achieve those goals. Through proper communication, the firm can create shared understanding among individuals. Rather than solely the upper-level management sharing ideas, it is beneficial if information flows across the organizational hierarchy (among departments, for instance). As an example, the airport operations department should be informed if an air carrier is considering starting service with a larger aircraft, as it may impact the airport's ARFF Index or require a modification to standards based on the airport's airport reference code. Marketing plans are best implemented in a work environment that fosters a complete and open flow of information. Methods to improve communications include:

- *Information Dissemination*: Up-to-date organizational charts, telephone directories, a company newsletter, an in-house library of industry material, and a policy for releasing information as quickly as possible to avoid rumor.

- *Instruction*: Training programs, formal performance appraisals, sessions with supervisors, and financial assistance for educational pursuits.

- *Interaction*: Informal company gatherings and interdepartmental committees.

Even so, delegating and communicating will not necessarily lead to marketing success. **Motivation** is also key. It is important that efforts are undertaken to motivate employees to perform the tasks expected of them and buy in to the marketing goals and objectives. Employees can actually contribute to marketing success—or alternatively, if they do not believe in the marketing goals and objectives, they may hinder marketing efforts. Obtaining buy-in is important, not only to the success of the airport, but also to the success of the marketing efforts. Allowing employees to provide input into the marketing plan will likely enhance buy-in. The key is to design motivation efforts that assist employees in carrying out the marketing objectives of the airport.

Additionally, once implemented, it is important to determine the success of marketing efforts. Measuring success requires regular monitoring and evaluation of the plan. This requires an airport to stay abreast of the promotional mix in place, as well as the progress being made toward the marketing goals and objectives. For example, if a goal was to increase fuel sales, the airport will want to maintain a daily, weekly, and monthly total in gallons of fuel sold and the amount of gross sales. More specifically, the airport may want to track gallons of fuel sold to each customer, whether based or transient. By regularly monitoring the plan and the progress toward goals and objectives, mid-course corrections can be made to enhance marketing success.

Characteristics of an Effective Marketing Plan

Although marketing plans are as diverse as the airports that develop them, there are common characteristics of effective plans. These characteristics include:

- *Customer and service centered.* The main focus of the plan must be on meeting the demand(s) of its target audience(s).

- *Differentiates itself from competitors.* If possible, the airport should differentiate itself from its competitors and spell out unique reasons why users should select this airport over rivals.

- *Easily communicated.* The plan needs to be simple and clear to target audiences and also to airport staff so they can easily understand and talk about it.

- *Motivating.* A successful plan will be adopted enthusiastically by airport stakeholders.

- *Flexible.* The plan should be sufficiently broad to embrace a variety of marketing activities and to allow for mid-course corrections and unforeseen changes in the marketplace.

(Kramer et al., 2010, p. 53)

The main determinant of the success of any marketing plan is the degree to which the plan achieves the goals and objectives developed. Hence the need for specific and measurable objectives, as previously discussed.

Air Service Development

Although marketing plans can be designed to achieve a number of objectives, one of the most common objectives for airports with commercial air service—as well as those desiring to attract commercial air service—involves **air service development (ASD)**. This term comprises all activities that are designed to enhance commercial passenger service at an airport. Airports with existing airline service focus on maintaining the service presently in place, as well as increasing flights and carriers. Airports without existing airline service focus on attracting air carrier service. Airports desiring air service or additional air service know the benefits that air service can bring to the community, including the economic impacts (such as investment and employment).

The key to developing an effective ASD program is understanding how carriers make decisions as to which airports they will serve. Air carriers are profit-driven. Thus, airport costs (fees, rates, and charges) and potential revenues (passenger numbers the market will bear) are critical to an airline's decision. For example, regardless of how much a community is driven to attract airline service, if the numbers don't add up for the airline, ASD efforts may be unsuccessful. Many carriers today actually expect concessions (in the form of discounted or waived landing fees, low terminal rental rates, etc.) when initiating new service to an airport not currently served by the carrier. The air carriers see these concessions as a form of "risk sharing" between the airport and the airline. Thus, airports desiring initial air carrier service must use caution in having revenues as the sole impetus. It likely will take some time before these revenues are realized, based on the airline concessions granted and the success of the airline service.

When attempting to attract air carrier service, airports study the amount of "leakage" present. **Leakage** refers to the number of passengers that leave the local area to patronize another commercial-service airport to board a flight. Even well-developed airports with significant levels of airline service typically encounter some amount of leakage. Most leakage is due to other airports offering more choices, including nonstop flights, convenient departure and arrival times, and more frequent flights. However, some leakage may occur due to seemingly insignificant items such as long-term parking fees. Small airports in particular face several major challenges, including:

- Proximity to airports with service by major air carriers
- Proximity to airports with low-cost air carrier service
- Small isolated populations with little demand
- Fragmentation of the local passenger traffic base among competing nearby airports
- Predominantly inbound markets that rely on tourism

  (Martin, 2009)

and given by a knowledgeable and passionate airport professional (typically the director of marketing or director of air service development). Airports are encouraged not to bring local elected officials, as they often do not add any objective substance to the presentation and may actually introduce political bias that could hinder efforts (Martin, 2009).

Concluding Thoughts

Airports must engage in effective marketing programs to proactively attract airlines, maintain satisfied customers, and enhance public perception. This requires a multi-pronged effort, often requiring a dedicated marketing professional and/or marketing department. Even with the implementation of a marketing plan, it is important for airports to measure progress toward the achievement of marketing objectives. Changes to the plan can then be made to more effectively reach target markets and maintain highly satisfied customers.

Chapter Summary

- Marketing is the art of identifying and understanding customer needs and creating solutions that deliver satisfaction to the customers, profits to the producers, and benefits for the stakeholders.
- Customer satisfaction is the ultimate objective of the marketing process.
- Developing a marketing plan requires determining goals and objectives; assessing resources and performing a SWOT analysis; revising goals and objectives; segmenting the market; selecting target markets; and establishing a unique marketing mix.
- The most common marketing goals include market expansion; market focus or segmentation; cost leadership; and quality.
- A SWOT analysis requires assessing the airport's strengths, weaknesses, opportunities, and threats.
- Market segmentation is the process of breaking down the total market into smaller, more homogenous groups with similar needs that the airport can satisfy.
- Although segmenting the market aids the airport in further defining the focus of its marketing efforts, selecting a target market allows the airport to pinpoint the object of the airport's marketing mix.
- The five Ps consist of (1) product or service, (2) price, (3) place, (4) promotion, and (5) passion.

- The promotional mix consists of public relations, advertising, and networking.
- Tools available to influence the public opinion include earned media, public speaking, other print communications, events, sponsorships and volunteering, and other print materials.
- Advertising tools include internet and websites; print media; signage; and multi-media tools.
- Networking is the process of building contacts and relationships through various means, which can include business, civic, and non-profit groups; professional organizations; tradeshows and conferences; strategic partnerships; and lobbying.
- Typical uncontrollable variables include consumer demographics, competition, government regulations, the economy, technology, media, and public interest groups.
- Implementation of a marketing plan requires delegation, communication, and motivation.
- Effective marketing plans are customer and service centered; differentiating from competitors; easily communicated; motivating; and flexible.
- One of the most common objectives for airports with commercial air service, as well as those desiring to attract commercial air service, involves air service development (ASD).
- The key to developing an effective ASD program is understanding that air carriers are profit-driven and make decisions based on potential revenues.
- The Essential Air Service (EAS) program provides federal subsidies to air carriers to serve smaller underserved communities.
- An effective ASD program is based on identifying deficiencies; identifying major stakeholders; identifying available resources; establishing and validating goals; selecting ASD strategy and techniques; presenting a compelling case to the airlines; and evaluating efforts.
- Airline concessions may include minimum airline revenue guarantees; guaranteed ticket purchases; cost subsidies; marketing and advertising; non-financial contributions; and hiring an ASD consultant.
- Revenue diversion is prohibited by the FAA at federally-obligated airports.
- The FAA allows air carrier incentives, but prohibits subsidies.

Review Questions ⬇

1. What is marketing?

2. What is the ultimate objective of marketing?

3. What questions would a well-developed marketing plan answer?

4. Explain the six steps required to develop a marketing plan.

5. What is the difference between a goal and an objective?

6. Explain the SWOT analysis.

7. What are the five Ps?

8. What is the purpose of an airport press kit?

9. What advertising tools are available to airports?

10. What networking tools are available to airports?

11. What is the purpose of the Small Community Air Service Development Program?

12. Which components of the promotional mix are the least expensive?

13. Explain the three phases required to implement a marketing plan.

14. What are some characteristics of effective marketing plans?

15. Explain some challenges faced by small airports.

16. What steps are necessary in developing an effective air service development program?

17. What are allowable uses of revenues in developing an incentive program for air carriers?

18. What is the difference between incentives and subsidies?

19. What air carrier incentives are not acceptable to the FAA?

20. What are some considerations when preparing a presentation to an air carrier to secure air service?

Scenarios ↘

1. As the director of marketing at a small hub airport, you have been asked by the airport director to develop a marketing plan to secure scheduled airline service by an additional air carrier. Currently, one carrier has 100 percent of the market share at your airport. Develop this marketing plan, using the guidance in this chapter.

2. Currently, you serve as the airport manager of a small GA airport. The city manager recently asked you to do your best to make the airport financially self-sufficient. As it stands now, the airport operates at a $100,000 per year deficit, requiring financial support by the city. The airport does own and operate the FBO (with fueling, parking, and other line services as well as flight training services) and has twenty T-hangars that are 70 percent occupied. Develop a marketing plan with the aim of making the airport financially self-sufficient.

3. Visit a local airport, study their services, and perform a SWOT analysis from the perspective of a potential air carrier.

4. As director of community relations, you have been asked by the airport director to issue a press release announcing new non-stop service by an incumbent carrier, Twice Air, to Honolulu. Write this press release.

5. As director of marketing, you have been busy attempting to recruit an air carrier at your Part 139-certificated airport since the only air carrier serving the airport eliminated service three years ago. Develop an air service development plan, including concessions that you would be willing to make available to an air carrier that begins service.

References and Resources for Further Study

Department of Transportation. n.d. "Essential Air Service." Retrieved from http://www.dot.gov/policy/aviation-policy/small-community-rural-air-service/essential-air-service

Federal Aviation Administration (FAA). 2010. *Air Carrier Incentive Program Guidebook: A Reference for Airport Sponsors*. Retrieved from http://www.faa.gov/airports/airport_compliance/media/air-carrier-incentive-2010.pdf Washington, DC: FAA.

———. 2014. Grant Assurances Airport Sponsors. Retrieved from http://www.faa.gov/airports/aip/grant_assurances/media/airport-sponsor-assurances-aip.pdf

Jackson County—Reynolds Field Airport. 2011. "Marketing Plan 2011." Retrieved from http://www.co.jackson.mi.us/Agencies/airport/docs/Marketing_Plan_Jackson_County_Airport.pdf

Kramer, L., P. Fowler, R. Hazel, M. Ureksoy, and G. Harig. 2010. "Marketing Guidebook for Small Airports." ACRP Report 28. Washington, DC: Transportation Research Board.

Martin, S. 2009. "Passenger Air Service Development Techniques." ACRP Report 18. Washington, DC: Transportation Research Board.

Prather, C. D. 2009. *General Aviation Marketing & Management: Operating, Marketing, and Managing an FBO*. Malabar, FL: Krieger.

Weikel, Dan. 2009. "L.A. to return $21.2 million to LAX's operator." Los Angeles Times, December 17. Retrieved from http://articles.latimes.com/2009/dec/17/local/la-me-airport-money17-2009dec17

Chapter 11

Governmental, Legal, and Public Relations

Objectives ↘

Upon completion of this chapter, you should understand:

- the role of governmental relations in airport management
- the national level of government with which airport managers interact
- the state level of government with which airport managers interact
- the local level of government with which airport managers interact
- the State Block Grant Program
- the manner in which airport managers interact with airport boards and municipal officials
- Robert's Rules of Order
- the purpose of the notice of proposed rulemaking process
- the role of FAA orders
- the role of FAA advisory circulars, including those ACs important for airport operations personnel
- available airport law resources
- the regulatory agencies in the aviation industry
- the aviation industry trade associations
- the role of public relations in airport management

Key Terms ↘

adjournment
advisory circular
Aerospace Industries Association (AIA)
agenda
Aircraft Owners and Pilots Association
  (AOPA)
Airlines for America (A4A)
Airports Council International (ACI)
Airports Council International—North
  America (ACI-NA)
amendment
American Association of Airport Executives
  (AAAE)
Customs and Border Protection (CBP)
Experimental Aircraft Association (EAA)
FAA Order
Federal Aviation Administration (FAA)
Federal Register
Flight Standards District Office (FSDO)
General Aviation Manufacturers
  Association (GAMA)

Go Team
International Air Transport Association
  (IATA)
International Civil Aviation Organization
  (ICAO)
minutes
motion
National Air Transportation Association
  (NATA)
National Business Aviation Association
  (NBAA)
new business
notice of proposed rulemaking (NPRM)
Occupational Safety and Health
  Administration (OSHA)
old business
Regional Airline Association (RAA)
Robert's Rules of Order
vote

In Chapter 11

FEATURES

New Hampshire Airport Block Grants 428

New Hampshire, through the state's Department of Transportation Bureau of Aeronautics, provides airport improvement grants to qualifying airports throughout the state.

Governmental Relations

Public-use airports in the United States are typically owned and operated by governmental entities (generally municipalities). Therefore, by the very nature of the airports they manage, airport directors and senior airport personnel are usually very politically aware. Whether their airport is large or small, commercial-service or GA, these personnel are aware of the need for positive and proactive governmental relations.

NATIONAL, STATE, AND LOCAL RELATIONS

Although public-use airports are generally owned and operated by local municipalities, some are owned and operated by the state in which they are located. In the past, the federal government also owned and operated some public-use, commercial-service airports. For example, the FAA owned and operated Ronald Reagan Washington National Airport and Washington Dulles International Airport prior to 1987, at which time the airports were transferred to the Metropolitan Washington Airports Authority under a 50-year lease authorized by the Metropolitan Washington Airports Act of 1986. Regardless of the entity owning and operating an airport, it is crucial for the airport director to communicate with and recognize the role of other governmental units.

National

At the national level, the FAA handles all aspects of the nation's aviation system. In fact, the mission of the FAA is to provide the safest, most efficient aerospace system in the world. The FAA carries out this mission through the following departments at its headquarters in Washington, DC:

- Airports
- Air Traffic Organization
- Aviation Safety
- Chief Counsel
- Civil Rights
- Commercial Space Transportation
- Communications
- Financial Services
- Government and Industry Affairs
- Human Resources Management
- Information Services
- NextGen
- Policy, International Affairs and Environment

- Regions & Center Operations
- Security and Hazardous Materials

(FAA, 2012)

Additionally, the FAA is comprised of the following field and regional offices:

- Aircraft Certification Offices (ACO)
- Airports Regional Offices
- Flight Standards District Offices (FSDO)
- Manufacturing & Inspection District Offices (MIDO)
- Aircraft Evaluation Groups (AEG)
- International Field Offices and Units (IFO) (IFU)
- Certificate Management Offices (CMO)
- Regional Offices
- Security and Hazardous Materials Offices
- Mike Monroney Aeronautical Center
- FAA Academy
- Center for Management and Executive Leadership
- Logistics Center
- William J. Hughes Technical Center

(FAA, 2012)

Although the FAA is headquartered in the nation's capital, it is directly involved with airports at the local level through various departments and offices. For instance, the Airports office has responsibility for all programs related to airport safety and inspections, and standards for airport design, construction, and operation (including international harmonization of airport standards). Additionally, the Airports office is responsible for national airport planning and environmental and social requirements, and establishes policies related to airport rates and charges, compliance with grant assurances, and airport privatization.

State

Each state typically has a state aviation department or aeronautics agency (see Figure 11-1). The role of this department/agency is to promulgate statewide rules and regulations governing aviation and airports in the state, administer federal- and state-aid funds for public-use airports, play a role in the design of airport construction and maintenance projects, and ensure the continued and integrated growth of airports in the state. States also typically facilitate safety inspection efforts at all non-certificated public airports and some private airports. Many state aviation agencies have the following departments (although some may be combined):

- *Planning*—Initiates, compiles and monitors activities of the agency; initiates, develops, monitors and maintains statewide airport capital improvement projects; and ensures each airport maintains approved long range planning and environmental documents for sustainable airport facilities throughout the state.

- *Finance and Grant Management*—Maintains, releases and approves grants and loans. If the state is one of ten states nationwide that is a block grant state, the state aviation agency will also handle all AIP grants and funding to airports in the state (see below).

- *Engineering*—Works with airports and their consultants on maintenance and construction projects, and assists with securing equipment.

- *Air Service*—Carries out projects dedicated to the improvement and promotion of air service in the state.

- *Flight Operations*—Responsible for state-owned aircraft, providing flight services for the governor and other state personnel on state business.

Figure 11-1.
State aviation headquarters, Tennessee.

It should be noted that if a state participates in the State Block Grant Program, the state aviation agency is responsible for administering Airport Improvement Program grants at nonprimary commercial service, reliever, and general aviation airports throughout the state. Rather than the FAA distributing federal AIP funds to individual airports, a lump sum (block grant) is provided to the state, with funds then provided to the state's individual airports based on project needs and priority. As of 2015, the following ten states were members of the State Block Grant Program:

- Georgia
- Illinois
- Michigan
- Missouri
- New Hampshire
- North Carolina
- Pennsylvania
- Tennessee
- Texas
- Wisconsin

Local

Public-use airports are typically owned and operated at the local level. Whether a city, county, city/county, parish, authority, or some other form of municipal entity, the local level is the level at which ownership and daily operation of public-use airports typically occurs. This is as it should be, as the local municipalities have the most vested interest in maintaining a local airport. Indeed, the local community receives the most significant benefits (economic and otherwise) from the airport.

That being said, the local airport manager plays an important role, which revolves around governmental and public relations. Governmental relations is integral for the airport manager. As discussed, officials in the federal government,

 New Hampshire Airport Block Grants

As one of ten states in the FAA State Block Grant Program, New Hampshire, through the New Hampshire Department of Transportation Bureau of Aeronautics, serves as the FAA-equivalent airport grant funding agency for airports in the state. A member of the FAA's State Block Grant Program since FY2008, the Bureau "has a better understanding of local issues and needs that are used to help determine project and funding priorities. By giving the state the funding assistance, the FAA gives the Bureau the flexibility to redistribute these funds for non-primary airport improvements based, in part, on local needs" (NHDOT, 2009). Just as in non-block grant states, all airports receiving funding through the block grant must be included in the NPIAS for eligibility. During FY2014, New Hampshire provided $3.1 million in block grants to eight airports throughout the state. Funded projects included installation of perimeter fencing, land acquisition, equipment acquisition, master plan update, PAPI installation, obstruction analysis, and obstruction removal/lighting. The state also utilized $140,000 to update the state Airport Information Management System.

Table 11-1. FAA advisory circulars in the Part 150–Airports series.

Although all ACs in the Part 150 series are important, the ACs most pertinent to those involved in airport operations are indicated in bold type and highlighted yellow.

AC Number	AC Title
150/5220-21	Aircraft Boarding Equipment
150/5390-2	Heliport Design
150/5200-36	Qualifications for Wildlife Biologist Conducting Wildlife Hazard Assessments and Training Curriculums for Airport Personnel Involved in Controlling Wildlife Hazards on Airports
150/5220-26	Airport Ground Vehicle Automatic Dependent Surveillance-Broadcast (ADS-B) Out Squitter Equipment
150/5300-17	Standards for Using Remote Sensing Technologies in Airport Surveys
150/5370-10	Standards for Specifying Construction of Airports
150/5370-11	Use of Nondestructive Testing in the Evaluation of Airport Pavements
150/5370-15	Airside Applications for Artificial Turf
150/5340-30	Design and Installation Details for Airport Visual Aids
150/5345-28	Precision Approach Path Indicator (PAPI) Systems
150/5345-56	Specification for L-890 Airport Lighting Control and Monitoring System (ALCMS)
150/5370-2	**Operational Safety on Airports During Construction**
150/5345-39	Specification for L-853, Runway and Taxiway Retroreflective Markers
150/5100-13	Development of State Standards for Nonprimary Airports
150/5335-5	Standardized Method of Reporting Airport Pavement Strength–PCN
150/5345-47	Specification for Series to Series Isolation Transformers for Airport Lighting Systems
150/5100-19	Guide for Airport Financial Reports Filed by Airport Sponsors
150/5220-10	Guide Specification for Aircraft Rescue and Fire Fighting (ARFF) Vehicles
150/5220-16	Automated Weather Observing Systems (AWOS) for Non-Federal Applications
150/5370-17	Airside Use of Heated Pavement Systems
150/5220-25	Airport Avian Radar Systems
150/5210-23	ARFF Vehicle and High Reach Extendable Turret (HRET) Operation, Training and Qualifications
150/5210-24	**Airport Foreign Object Debris (FOD) Management**
150/5220-17	Aircraft Rescue and Fire Fighting (ARFF) Training Facilities
150/5000-16	Announcement of Availability of the Guide for Private Flyers U.S. International Airports
150/5210-13	Airport Water Rescue Plans and Equipment
150/5345-3	Specification for L-821, Panels for the Control of Airport Lighting
150/5345-10	Specification for Constant Current Regulators and Regulator Monitors
150/5345-44	Specification for Runway and Taxiway Signs
150/5345-12	Specification for Airport and Heliport Beacons
150/5200-35	Submitting the Airport Master Record in Order to Activate a New Airport

Table 11-1. *(continued)*

AC Number	AC Title
150/5345-51	Specification for Discharge-Type Flashing Light Equipment
150/5340-1	**Standards for Airport Markings**
150/5340-18	**Standards for Airport Sign Systems**
150/5000-15	Announcement of Availability of Airport-Related Research and Development Products
150/5210-5	Painting, Marking, and Lighting of Vehicles Used on an Airport
150/5220-24	**Foreign Object Debris Detection Equipment**
150/5300-9	Predesign, Prebid, and Preconstruction Conferences for Airport Grant Projects
150/5320-6	Airport Pavement Design and Evaluation
150/5340-26	Maintenance of Airport Visual Aid Facilities
150/5345-54	Specification for L-884, Power and Control Unit for Land and Hold Short Lighting Systems
150/5380-9	Guidelines and Procedures for Measuring Airfield Pavement Roughness
150/5200-12	**First Responders Responsibility for Protecting Evidence at the Scene of an Aircraft Accident/Incident**
150/5210-17	Programs for Training of Aircraft Rescue and Firefighting Personnel
150/5200-31	**Airport Emergency Plan (Consolidated AC includes Change 2)**
150/5210-19	Driver's Enhanced Vision System (DEVS)
150/5300-18	General Guidance and Specifications for Submission of Aeronautical Surveys to NGS: Field Data Collection and Geographic Information System (GIS) Standards
150/5345-46	Specification for Runway and Taxiway Light Fixtures
150/5220-23	Frangible Connections
150/5200-30	**Airport Winter Safety And Operations**
150/5210-14	Aircraft Rescue Fire Fighting Equipment, Tools and Clothing
150/5300-15	Use Of Value Engineering For Engineering And Design Of Airport Grant Projects
150/5345-26	FAA Specification For L-823 Plug And Receptacle, Cable Connectors
150/5210-18	Systems for Interactive Training Of Airport Personnel
150/5370-6	Construction Progress and Inspection Report—Airport Improvement Program (AIP)
150/5360-12	Airport Signing and Graphics
150/5210-15	Aircraft Rescue and Firefighting Station Building Design
150/5320-15	Management Of Airport Industrial Waste
150/5000-13	Announcement Of Availability: RTCA Inc., Document RTCA-221
150/5210-7	Aircraft Rescue and Fire Fighting Communications
150/5300-14	Design of Aircraft Deicing Facilities
150/5200-28	**Notices to Airmen (NOTAMS) for Airport Operators**
150/5370-12	Quality Control of Construction for Airport Grant Projects

Table 11-1. *(continued)*

AC Number	AC Title
150/5370-16	Rapid Construction of Rigid (Portland Cement Concrete) Airfield Pavements
150/5380-6	**Guidelines and Procedures for Maintenance of Airport Pavements**
150/5050-8	Environmental Management Systems for Airport Sponsors
150/5345-13	Specification for L-841 Auxiliary Relay Cabinet Assembly for Pilot Control of Airport Lighting Circuits
150/5345-50	Specification for Portable Runway and Taxiway Lights
150/5300-16	General Guidance and Specifications for Aeronautical Surveys: Establishment of Geodetic Control and Submission to the National Geodetic Survey
150/5220-18	Buildings for Storage and Maintenance of Airport Snow and Ice Control Equipment and Materials
150/5340-5	Segmented Circle Airport Marker System
150/5345-52	Generic Visual Glideslope Indicators (GVGI)
150/5200-33	**Hazardous Wildlife Attractants On or Near Airports**
150/5345-49	Specification L-854, Radio Control Equipment
150/5345-55	Specification for L-893, Lighted Visual Aid to Indicate Temporary Runway Closure
150/5200-29	Announcement Of Availability Of Airport Self-Inspection DVD
150/5070-6	**Airport Master Plans**
150/5345-45	Low-Impact Resistant (LIR) Structures
150/5200-37	**Introduction to Safety Management Systems (SMS) for Airport Operators**
150/5190-6	Exclusive Rights at Federally Obligated Airports
150/5220-9	Aircraft Arresting Systems
150/535-42	Specification for Airport Light Bases, Transformer Housings, Junction Boxes, and Accessories
150/5320-5	Surface Drainage Design
150/5370-13	Off-Peak Construction of Airport Pavements Using Hot-Mix Asphalt
150/5345-5	Circuit Selector Switch
150/5345-43	Specification for Obstruction Lighting Equipment
150/5380-7	**Airport Pavement Management Program**
150/5190-7	**Minimum Standards for Commercial Aeronautical Activities**
150/5200-34	Construction or Establishment of Landfills near Public Airports
150/5100-17	Land Acquisition and Relocation Assistance for Airport Improvement Program Assisted Projects
150/5100-14	Architectural, Engineering, and Planning Consultant Services for Airport Grant Projects
150/5220-22	Engineered Materials Arresting Systems (EMAS) for Aircraft Overruns
150/5345-53	Airport Lighting Equipment Certification Program
150/5325-4	Runway Length Requirements for Airport Design
150/5200-32	**Reporting Wildlife Aircraft Strikes**

Table 11-1. *(continued)*

AC Number	AC Title
150/5070-7	The Airport System Planning Process
150/5020-2	Guidance on the Balanced Approach to Noise Management
150/5320-17	**Airfield Pavement Surface Evaluation and Rating Manuals**
150/5210-6	Aircraft Fire and Rescue Facilities and Extinguishing Agents
150/5230-4	**Aircraft Fuel Storage, Handling, and Dispensing on Airports**
150/5345-27	Specification for Wind Cone Assemblies
150/5210-22	**Airport Certification Manual (ACM)**
150/5200-18	**Airport Safety Self-Inspection**
150/5210-21	Announcement of Availability: Airport Surface Safety Training Programs for Mechanics and Ramp Personnel
150/5210-20	**Ground Vehicle Operations on Airports**
150/5345-7	Specification for L-824 Underground Electrical Cable for Airport Lighting Circuits
150/5370-14	Hot Mix Asphalt Paving Handbook
150/5360-14	Access to Airports By Individuals With Disabilities
150/5320-12	Measurement, Construction, and Maintenance of Skid Resistant Airport Pavement Surfaces
150/5395-1	Seaplane Bases
150/5000-9	Announcement of Availability Report No. DOT/FAA/PP/92-5, Guidelines for the Sound Insulation of Residences Exposed to Aircraft Operations
150/5220-20	**Airport Snow and Ice Control Equipment**
150/5300-13	**Airport Design**
150/5360-13	Planning and Design Guidelines for Airport Terminal Facilities
150/5190-4	A Model Zoning Ordinance to Limit Height of Objects Around Airports
150/5150-2	Federal Surplus Personal Property for Public Airport Purposes
150/5060-5	**Airport Capacity And Delay**
150/5020-1	**Noise Control and Compatibility Planning for Airports**
150/5360-9	Planning and Design of Airport Terminal Facilities at Non-Hub Locations
150/5050-4	Citizen Participation in Airport Planning
150/5300-7	FAA Policy on Facility Relocations Occasioned by Airport Improvements or Changes

AIRPORT LAW RESOURCES

Due to the significant pieces of legislation, regulations, and other guidance at the federal, state, and even local level, it is imperative for the airport manager to maintain an awareness of issues affecting the airport on the legislative front. Larger airports may employ an individual in a Legal Counsel role to handle legal affairs, and/or an individual in a legislative affairs role to ensure the airport is aware of any pending or existing legislation that would affect the airport.

cause. Field investigations result in a factual report, from which the investigator recommends a probable cause determination to the Board. The Board then reviews field investigation reports and votes to adopt, reject or modify the probable cause determination recommended by a field investigator. With major accident investigations led by NTSB Go Teams, each group chairman prepares a report and submits it to the Investigator-In-Charge. The Investigator-In-Charge then prepares a draft NTSB report and submits it to the Board for review. The Board may conduct public hearings to gain more insight into the cause of the accident. The Board then meets and determines probable cause, resulting in a published final report.

DHS and TSA

In addition to aviation safety, the federal government is involved with securing the aviation system. The events of September 11, 2001, forever changed the landscape of aviation security in the United States. As a result of those events, Congress passed the Aviation and Transportation Security Act on November 19, 2001. This Act established the Transportation Security Administration (TSA) and gave it three major mandates:

- Secure all modes of transportation;
- Recruit, assess, hire, train, and deploy Security Officers for 450 commercial airports from Guam to Alaska in 12 months; and,
- Provide 100 percent screening of all checked luggage for explosives by December 31, 2002.

Prior to this, the airlines were responsible for passenger and baggage screening. However, as a result of the events of September 11, Congress felt that the airlines were doing an inadequate job. In reality, the screening functions had been contracted out to numerous security companies of varying capabilities that often paid minimum wages and offered minimal training to screeners. Further concentrating national security efforts, the Department of Homeland Security was created on November 25, 2002, by the Homeland Security Act of 2002. As part of this Act, the TSA was moved from the DOT to the new Department of Homeland Security (DHS) in March 2003.

As of 2015, the TSA employed 50,000 transportation security officers that screen 2 million passengers each day at more than 450 airports nationwide (see Figure 11-3). The TSA also deployed approximately 2,800 behavior detection officers at airports across the country, utilized more than 400 TSA explosives specialists, deployed thousands of federal air marshals on domestic and international flights each day, and both trained and deployed approximately 800 explosives detection canine teams to airports and mass transit systems across the nation (TSA, n.d.[b]; TSA, n.d.[c]).

Prior to the creation of the TSA, airport managers dealt with the FAA and typically the FAA Civil Aviation Security Field Unit (CASFU) locally regarding airport security matters. Today, however, airport personnel interact regularly

Figure 11-3.
Transportation Security Administration (TSA) screening checkpoint.

(Wikimedia Commons; see credit on page 624)

with the TSA regarding airport and airline security. Locally, the Federal Security Director (FSD) is the ranking TSA authority responsible for leadership and coordination of TSA security activities. The Assistant Federal Security Director—Regulatory Inspection serves as the principal advisor to the Federal Security Director on all matters concerning enforcement and compliance with security directives pertaining to airport and aviation security for Category X and Large Category I and II Airports. This Assistant FSD—Regulatory Inspection manages an inspection program for compliance by airlines, vendors, and other airport tenants and business interests with airport and aviation security policies and requirements. The Assistant Federal Security Director—Screening has responsibility for passenger security screening, managing a staff of security screeners, checkpoint supervisors, and screening managers who conduct screening, manage screening operations, and administer laws, regulations, and policies pertaining to TSA's aviation security program (TSA, n.d.[a]).

ICAO

The International Civil Aviation Organization (ICAO) is a specialized agency of the United Nations, and was established on December 7, 1944, via the Chicago Convention (also known as the Convention on International Civil Aviation). The purpose of ICAO is to promote the safe and orderly development of international civil aviation throughout the world through the creation of standards and regulations necessary for aviation safety, security, efficiency and regularity, as well as for aviation environmental protection. The ICAO is comprised of 191 member states, including the United States.

Although the ICAO operates on an international scale, and an airport manager will interact almost universally with the FAA and TSA, it is helpful to be aware of the role of ICAO and standards and recommended practices that are generated by ICAO. Often, the activities of the FAA can be traced back to

ICAO recommendations or requirements. Consider safety management systems (SMS) as an example. The ICAO first required SMS for the management of safety risk in air operations, maintenance, air traffic services and aerodromes in Annexes 1, 6, 8, 11, and 14 beginning in 2001. The FAA SMS rulemaking process then stemmed from this ICAO requirement.

CBP

In addition to the TSA, **Customs and Border Protection (CBP)** plays an important role in securing the borders and protecting the United States from threats. The CBP represents the largest law enforcement agency within the Department of Homeland Security with more than 58,000 employees serving both nationwide and overseas. The primary mission of the CBP is to prevent terrorists and terrorist weapons from entering the United States, while allowing legitimate travel and trade. This involves apprehending individuals attempting to enter the United States illegally; minimizing the flow of illegal drugs and other contraband; protecting agricultural and economic interests from harmful pests and diseases; protecting American businesses from theft of intellectual property; and regulating and facilitating international trade, collecting import duties, and enforcing U.S. trade laws (U.S. Customs and Border Protection, 2010).

Airport managers and personnel will likely interact with the CBP during the processing of passengers and crew on inbound international flights. The CBP has very strict access requirements for airport personnel needing access to the Federal Inspection Station (FIS) area, generally requiring airport personnel to undergo additional background checks and receive a special FIS access clearance. Airports are required to maintain areas where inbound international passengers can be screened separately by CBP and remain segregated from domestic passengers until after being allowed access to the United States. This is typically in the form of separate international arrivals terminals or in the basement (or ramp level) of an existing terminal building.

OSHA

Lastly, the **Occupational Safety and Health Administration (OSHA)** was established by the Occupational Safety and Health Act of 1970. The role of OSHA is to assure safe and healthful working conditions for workers by setting and enforcing standards and by providing training, outreach, education, and assistance. As part of the Department of Labor, OSHA is most concerned with protecting workers and ensuring a safe working environment. As a result, airports are required to provide personal protective equipment (PPE) to workers, material safety data sheets (MSDS) for personnel handling various chemicals, etc.

Industry Relations

In addition to interacting with governmental entities (both at the federal, state, and local levels), airport managers and personnel may also join various industry associations. Industry associations generally support their members by providing representation in Washington, DC, information on issues affecting members, and networking opportunities with other members. In essence, industry trade associations serve their members by ensuring effective industry relations.

INDUSTRY TRADE ASSOCIATIONS

AAAE

The **American Association of Airport Executives (AAAE)** was established in 1928 and currently represents nearly 5,000 individual members, including 3,000 airport professionals representing nearly 850 different airports. AAAE has evolved into a multi-functioning organization that not only represents airports' interests to those on Capitol Hill, but also provides a number of services to airports and individual members.

First, AAAE has an active legislative affairs team referred to as the Airport Legislative Alliance. The role of the Legislative Alliance is to represent airports nationwide by petitioning Congress for increased AIP funds and increased PFCs, as well as keeping the membership informed of changes in the political landscape, including newly elected officials and proposed and approved legislation. The role of the Legislative Alliance is a very typical role for industry associations that are based in the Washington, DC, area. Similar to the Legislative Alliance, AAAE also has a Regulatory Affairs Department, which is focused on representing airports before key executive agencies, including the Department of Transportation, the Federal Aviation Administration, and the Environmental Protection Agency.

AAAE's Transportation Security Policy team represents airports before key federal leaders in aviation security and homeland security. The team also keeps airports informed on the most recent issues affecting aviation security. This team created the Transportation Security Clearinghouse (TSC), which is a non-profit arm of AAAE that operates in partnership with the TSA to ensure security threat assessments (STA) and Criminal History Record Checks (CHRC) are accomplished for aviation workers who require access to the secure areas of airports. According to AAAE, the TSC is the nation's largest civilian clearinghouse, processing over 1.3 million TSA-mandated security threat assessments and more than half a million biometrically based Criminal History Records Checks annually (AAAE, n.d.).

One of AAAE's strengths lies in the hundreds of meetings, conferences and training events the association holds each year. Whether in the form of their annual conference, regional conferences, Basic or Advanced Airport Safety and Operations Specialist (ASOS) Schools, or Certified Member or Airport

Certified Employee (ACE) training, AAAE provides plenty of opportunities each year for members to enhance their knowledge of the industry or specific topics and network with other airport professionals.

AAAE also has additional tools that are helpful in training airport professionals, such as Interactive Employee Training (IET) and Airport News and Training Network (ANTN) Digicast. These industry training tools are widely utilized by airports. IET is an airport-specific, on-site training program that an airport contracts with AAAE to develop. However, ANTN is a web-based training platform that any airport can gain access to by paying a subscription fee. In addition, AAAE's publications such as *Airport Report Today*, *Airport Magazine*, and *Aviation News Today* are all extremely beneficial for airport professionals.

ACI and ACI-NA

In addition to AAAE, the **Airports Council International (ACI)** exists to represent airports on a global scale. According to ACI, they are the only global trade representative of the world's airports. ACI was established in 1991 and represents the world's airports to governments and international organizations such as ICAO. Prior to the formation of ACI in 1991, the world's airports were represented by the Airport Associations Coordinating Council (AACC). ACI also develops standards, policies and recommended practices for airports, and provides information and training opportunities for airport personnel. To better represent North American airports, ACI created **ACI-North America (ACI-NA)**. It was formed in 1948 as the Airport Operators Council (AOC). The purpose of ACI-NA is to represent airports throughout North America to federal decision makers in Washington, DC, keep airports up-to-date on issues affecting them, conduct research for the benefit of airports, and provide networking, training, and educational opportunities.

AOPA

The main industry association representing GA pilots and GA aircraft owners is the **Aircraft Owners and Pilots Association (AOPA)**. The AOPA has a membership of more than 400,000 pilots and aviation enthusiasts in the United States. According to AOPA, the organization is the largest, most influential aviation association in the world. AOPA supports GA by advocating on behalf of members; educating pilots, nonpilots, and policy makers; supporting activities that ensure the long-term health of general aviation; fighting to keep general aviation accessible to all; and securing sufficient resources to ensure success. AOPA also provides member services such as legal services, advice, and other assistance; insurance; aircraft buying assistance; aircraft financing; and networking and educational opportunities. This is often the first organization that student pilots join.

EAA

The **Experimental Aircraft Association (EAA)** also represents pilots and owners of aircraft. The EAA was initially founded in 1953 by a group of individuals who were interested in building their own airplanes. Today, however, the EAA membership includes pilots and owners of antiques, classics, warbirds, aerobatic aircraft, ultralights, helicopters, and contemporary manufactured aircraft. Less of a lobbying organization, the EAA is designed to develop camaraderie among those who fly, build, and restore recreational aircraft. Various local chapters often host monthly fly-ins, pancake breakfasts, and Young Eagle flights. Most popular with those who are 8 to 17 years old, the Young Eagle program provides free flights in a GA aircraft by EAA volunteers which are designed to introduce children to aviation.

NBAA

The **National Business Aviation Association (NBAA)** represents businesses that own and operate aircraft used for business purposes. Founded in 1947 and based in Washington, DC, the NBAA is the leading organization for companies that rely on general aviation aircraft to help make their businesses more efficient, productive and successful. NBAA represents more than 10,000 companies and provides more than 100 products and services to the business aviation community, including the NBAA Business Aviation Convention and Exhibition, the world's largest civil aviation trade show.

A4A

Airlines for America (A4A), formerly known as the Air Transport Association (ATA), is an industry association representing U.S. airlines. Founded by a group of 14 airlines in 1936, A4A endeavors to promote a business and regulatory environment that ensures safe and secure air transportation in the United States. The organization is designed to enable U.S. airlines to flourish, stimulating economic growth locally, nationally and internationally. In the past, this organization has been at odds with AAAE on important economic issues, such as raising the cap on PFCs. Generally, AAAE supports lifting or raising the cap, while A4A is against this.

IATA

The **International Air Transport Association (IATA)** is an international trade body created over 60 years ago by a group of airlines. Today, IATA represents some 240 airlines comprising 84 percent of total air traffic. To some degree, it could be argued that the IATA is the international arm of A4A, although they are not related.

NATA

The **National Air Transportation Association (NATA)** represents aviation service businesses such as fixed base operators, charter providers, aircraft management companies (including those supporting fractional shareholders), maintenance and repair organizations, flight training providers, and airline service companies. NATA was established in 1940 and promotes safety and the success of aviation service businesses through its advocacy efforts before government, the media and the public. It also provides various programs for the benefit of members, such as the NATA Safety First program—a line service safety training program.

RAA

The **Regional Airline Association (RAA)** is an industry association that represents smaller, regional airlines. The RAA also represents manufacturers of products and services supporting the regional airline industry to Congress, the DOT, the FAA and other federal agencies. It could be said that in effect the RAA is the regional arm of A4A, although they are not related. With more than 13,000 regional airline flights every day, regional airlines operate more than 50 percent of the nation's commercial service.

AIA

The **Aerospace Industries Association (AIA)** represents manufacturers and suppliers of civil, military, and business aircraft, helicopters, unmanned aircraft systems, space systems, aircraft engines, missiles, material and related components, equipment, services, and information technology. Although the AIA may not be an association that an airport manager would be acquainted with, it is one of the oldest associations in the aviation industry, having been established in 1919.

GAMA

Established in 1970, the **General Aviation Manufacturers Association (GAMA)** represents over 70 of the world's leading manufacturers of fixed-wing general aviation airplanes, engines, avionics, and components. The purpose of GAMA is to foster and advance the general welfare, safety, interests and activities of general aviation. This includes promoting a better understanding of general aviation and the important role it plays in economic growth and in serving the transportation needs of communities, companies and individuals worldwide.

GRASSROOTS EFFORTS

Most important to the future of general aviation are efforts at the grassroots level by many of the various industry trade associations to make aviation more attractive. Consider "GA Serves America" by AOPA. This site is designed to educate visitors about the benefits of GA and the many ways in which GA is used to serve America. AOPA also developed the "Be a Pilot" program, designed to increase the number of student pilots. EAA developed "Reach for the Sky," a brochure designed to generate interest in flying. Various associations have also developed teacher's modules for grades K–12 designed to provide teachers with curriculum to introduce students to aviation. These efforts have experienced varying levels of success. What is important to note is that the industry has taken responsibility for promoting general aviation, rather than relying on the FAA to handle this.

Public Relations

In addition to relating to the government and industry, airport managers must also relate to the public. In fact, public relations is integral to the success of an airport in the eyes of the community. Regardless of the number of non-stop airline flights or available automobile parking spots, if the community does not have a positive image of the airport, it can be quite detrimental to the airport. Indeed, a public relations disaster is not the goal of any airport manager.

COMMUNITY RELATIONS

First, the airport must be relatable to the community. Especially for GA airports, the at-large community often has no interest in the airport and sees the airport as only supporting the hobby of the rich. Worse, if the airport is not financially self-sufficient, the community may have a very negative view of it as a drain of community resources. Therefore, it is important, for the airport manager and other senior airport personnel to be present in the community, proactively delivering a positive message of the value of the airport and its benefits to the community. This may include presentations at the Chamber of Commerce, Rotary Club, schools, and other community groups. It should involve an overview of the services provided by the airport, including air ambulance, aircraft firefighting, and flight training. If the airport has conducted an economic impact study, it is important to present these positive findings as well. In short, community relations involves educating the community. To do this effectively, the airport manager must remain proactive.

Role and Value of Interest Groups

An interest group is defined as any voluntary association that seeks to publicly promote and create advantages for its cause. Interest groups may include corporations, charitable organizations, civil rights groups, neighborhood associations, and professional and trade associations. Fortunately, an interest group may be very supportive of an airport, such as the Cattaraugus County-Olean Airport Support Group in Ischua, New York:

"The purpose of the Cattaraugus County-Olean Airport Support Group, formed in 2005, is to act as a driving, unified and proactive advisory force to ensure promotion of the airport as a key area resource, the upgrade of general facilities maintenance and execution of an ongoing capital improvement program. Specific areas of focus include:

- Acting as a facilitator between the county, the city, airport users and airport supporters, providing continuous open channels of communication.
- Aggressively educating the county, city and public at large, providing accurate and factual information regarding the importance of the airport to the entire area.
- Providing technical support to the city and airport staff in selection and prioritization of general facilities maintenance, equipment upgrades and capital improvements.
- Providing technical assistance to the city in acquisition of federal, state, county and private funding.
- Advising and assisting the city, jointly with the Greater Olean Area Chamber of Commerce (GOACC), with promotional advertising and organizing airport promotional events—air shows, fly-ins, open houses, tourism literature, Web site design, etc."

(Cattaraugus County Olean Airport, n.d.)

Another example of a supportive airport interest group is the Grove Airport Support Group in Grove, Oklahoma:

"The mission of the Grove Airport Support Organization is to promote our airport to the community at large by executing annual events such as the Fly-In Breakfast and Fly-by-the-Pound, Promote Aviation Safety through seminars and identifying areas of potential facility improvements for the Grove, OK aviation and business community."

(Grove Airport Support Group, n.d.).

Much to the dismay of airport managers, however, interest groups can also show negative support for the airport. Perhaps the most unified national voice against aircraft and airport noise is Stop the Noise. A non-profit origination based in Harvard, Massachusetts, the organization works to "restore quiet to the skies above our communities by causing FAA to enforce existing regulations regarding aerobatic flight and by working to bring about changes in the FAA regulations and in the FAA culture" (Stop the Noise, 2008). There are also numerous anti-airport organizations at the local level. Citizens Against Airport

Pollution, in San Jose, California, is "dedicated to protecting and restoring the environmental quality of the Santa Clara Valley. We focus on noise, air and water quality, as well as other critical environmental issues to keep our neighborhoods clean and quiet" (Citizens Against Airport Pollution, 2012). They have filed lawsuits against the City of San Jose to prevent airport expansion, claiming a lack environmental review, significant noise, and detrimental impacts on wildlife. A sampling of other interest groups that oppose airport expansion and noise include Residents Against Airport Expansion in Delco (Delaware County, Pennsylvania); Concerned Residents Against Airport Pollution in Santa Monica, California; and the New Jersey Coalition Against Aircraft Noise.

Clearly, interest groups that support an airport are much easier for an airport manager to work with. Interest groups that oppose an airport can generate substantial negative press and create considerable difficulties for the airport manager. As a result, the airport manager must make efforts to reach out to these groups and endeavor to find common ground. Ignoring their efforts will likely create a major public relations issue for the airport.

MEDIA RELATIONS

Airport managers must recognize the power of the media. Even in small communities with one GA airport, the local media has a significant impact on the community and can greatly affect the community's perception of the airport, either in a positive or negative sense. It is important to utilize the media for the benefit of the airport in a proactive way, rather than attempting to respond to negative media publicity after the fact. Some ways to do this include press releases, inviting the media to the airport for a tour, contacting the media with "stories" that are newsworthy, and developing a relationship with transportation reporters. All of these are proactive efforts on the part of the airport manager. In other words, it is best not to sit and hope that news coverage will be positive. Rather, the airport manager can actually generate positive press by feeding positive stories and news to the right person in the media (see Figure 11-4).

Figure 11-4.
Media relations.

(auremar/Shutterstock.com)

CUSTOMER SERVICE

Customer service is one area which has suffered neglect in recent years. Consider the phone call to a national cable network, insurance company, or satellite provider. Inevitably, the caller will be greeted by an automated voice and presented with a dizzying array of menu choices from which to select. Eventually, and with enough patience, the caller may be granted an opportunity to speak with an actual person. Almost universally, callers feel this is poor customer service. However, companies have transitioned to automated phone systems to increase efficiency and more effectively direct calls to the correct person. It is important, therefore, for companies (including airports) to balance efficiency with the need for positive customer service.

Excellent airport customer service has been defined as "the synergy created when an airport's ability to exceed its customers' needs and expectations consistently matches its customers' perception that their needs and expectations are well met" (Paternoster, 2007, p. 218). It is important for airports to adopt a practice of exceeding customer expectations. For a period of time, Tampa International Airport's motto was "Going above and beyond." By adopting this slogan, the airport made it clear to passengers, tenants, and the community that customer service was a top priority and all efforts would be taken to exceed customer expectations.

Although there is a great deal of guidance available on customer service, the ten rules below perhaps best summarize what airports should be endeavoring to do on the customer service front:

- Understand the customer.
- Be a good listener.
- Identify and anticipate needs.
- Make customers feel important and appreciated.
- Help customers understand your methods and procedures.
- Learn how to say "Yes."
- Know how to apologize.
- Give more than expected.
- Get regular feedback.
- Treat internal customers (employees) well.

Although these rules may seem obvious, points such as regarding employees as internal customers may not be as obvious. Airports often focus on passengers and tenants, but may forget that internal employees are also customers. It is important to treat fellow coworkers with the same level of respect, understanding, and appreciation as you would treat your customers. After all, if employees aren't happy and morale is low, they in turn will not treat customers well, which will lead to lost revenues, lost customers, and lost opportunities for providing exceptional customer service.

EVENTS

Events are yet another way to generate publicity for an airport. Typically, these events are in the form of an airshow, open house, fly-in, or grand opening of a terminal or other facility. They can also be in the form of banquets, holiday parties, or conferences. By holding an event and inviting the general public, the airport is able to enhance the public perception of the airport and give something back to the community. Events can be expensive, so a careful analysis of costs and benefits will be necessary, but airports are often willing to incur the expenses associated with such events due to the positive publicity they produce.

SOCIAL MEDIA

The most recent form of public relations involves online media in the form of social interaction. In fact, a large percentage of the U.S. population utilizes various forms of social media (with Facebook being the most popular). Other services such as Twitter, LinkedIn, and Pinterest are also popular and being used by some airports. In essence, if current and potential customers are online, why shouldn't airports meet these customers online? Social media has allowed airports to effectively interact with current and potential customers in real-time.

Airports can effectively utilize social media by creating a Facebook page and keeping it current with new information. Contests and other giveaways will generate interest and allow the page to increase in popularity. Some airports effectively utilizing social media such as Facebook have a staff person dedicated to maintaining the page and can even post status updates on parking garage availability, security screening wait times, and food and beverage specials. Other airports have developed applications (apps) that allow customers to check on flight times/status, parking availability, maps of terminals, etc.

Concluding Thoughts

It is important for airport leadership to be politically aware both internally and externally. In other words, airport professionals should not only be able to interact and develop mutually beneficial relationships at the federal, state, and local levels, as well as with industry trade associations, but also be aware of the media and current and prospective customers/passengers. This requires airport professionals to be politically aware and in tune with the external environment.

Review Questions ↘

1. Explain the typical role of state aviation agencies.

2. Explain the State Block Grant Program (including listing participating states).

3. Explain the role of an airport advisory board.

4. Explain Robert's Rules of Order (including the most important Rules to remember).

5. Explain the purpose of a "notice of proposed rulemaking."

6. Explain the purpose of advisory circulars (ACs).

7. In what ways does the National Transportation Safety Board promote transportation safety?

8. Under what circumstances would the NTSB delegate accident investigation authority to a Flight Standards District Office?

9. What were the three original mandates for the Transportation Security Admiration (TSA)?

10. Which individuals would an airport manager most likely interact with regarding passenger screening at an airport?

11. Explain the role of the International Civil Aviation Organization (ICAO).

12. Explain the role of the Occupational Safety and Health Administration (OSHA).

13. Explain the purpose of the American Association of Airport Executives (AAAE).

14. Explain the purpose of the National Business Aviation Association (NBAA).

15. Explain the purpose of Airlines for America (A4A).

16. Explain the role and value of interest groups.

17. Explain how an airport manager can ensure effective media relations.

18. Explain how an airport manager can ensure positive customer service.

19. Explain the role of events in generating publicity for an airport.

20. Explain how an airport can effectively use social media in offering positive customer service.

1. As the airport manager of a small, GA airport, you are preparing for the monthly airport board meeting. The meeting topics will include old business (approval of minutes from past meeting), and new business (issuing an RFP for a new FBO operator; pay raise of 3 percent for staff, which total 5 employees not including yourself; a review of the number of noise complaints received during the past quarter; and an update on the new terminal construction project). Prepare an agenda for this meeting, and talk through the actions to be held during the meeting using Robert's Rules of Order.

2. As the airport manager of a city-owned and operated airport, you must present your budget request to the city manager and city council each year just as other city department heads must do. To ensure your airport gets a fair share of funds, what are some "selling points" you can bring forth during your presentation to the city manager and city council?

3. As an airport manager of a small, GA airport, which industry trade associations would you be a member of as an individual, and which would your airport be a member of as an organization, and why?

4. As an airport manager of a large, commercial-service airport, which industry trade associations would you be an individual member of, and which would your airport be an organization member of, and why?

5. You are the newly appointed airport manager of a small, GA airport that has been neglected by the community. In fact, the community has been pressuring the mayor to close the airport and turn it into a city park. What approach would you take to change this public perception? Prepare a detailed public relations strategy.

References and Resources for Further Study

American Association of Airport Executives. n.d. "Transportation Security Clearinghouse." Retrieved from http://www.aaae.org/federal_affairs/transportation_security_policy/tsc.cfm

Cattaraugus County Olean Airport. n.d. "Support Group." Retrieved from http://oleanairport.org/support/

Citizens Against Airport Pollution. 2012. "Mission Statement." Retrieved from http://www.caap.org/

Federal Aviation Administration (FAA). 2012. "Offices." Retrieved from http://www.faa.gov/about/office_org/

Grove Airport Support Group. n.d. "Grove, OK Municipal Airport." Retrieved from https://sites.google.com/site/groveokmunicipalairport/

New Hampshire Department of Transportation (NHDOT). 2009. "Block Grant Program." Retrieved from http://www.nh.gov/dot/org/aerorailtransit/aeronautics/programs/blockgrants.htm

Paternoster, J. 2007. "Excellent airport customer service meets successful branding strategy." *Airport Management* 2 (3): 218–226.

Preston, E. n.d. The Federal Aviation Administration and Its Predecessor Agencies. Retrieved from http://www.centennialofflight.net/essay/Government_Role/FAA_History/POL8.htm

Stop the Noise. 2008. "Who we are." Retrieved from http://stopthenoise.org/

Transportation Security Administration (TSA). n.d.(a) "Airport Security Careers." Retrieved from http://www.tsa.gov/careers/airport-security-careers

———. n.d.(b) "TSA by the numbers." Retrieved from http://www.tsa.gov/sites/default/files/publications/pdf/tsabythenumbers_final.pdf

———. n.d.(c) "What is TSA?" Retrieved from http://www.tsa.gov/about-tsa

U.S. Customs and Border Protection. 2010. "We are CBP!" Retrieved from http://www.cbp.gov/xp/cgov/careers/customs_careers/we_are_cbp.xml

Chapter 12

Properties, Contracts, and Commercial Development

Objectives ↘

Upon completion of this chapter, you should understand:

- the role of agreements in airport management
- the purpose and meaning of aeronautical lease agreements
- airline operating agreements
- the difference between signatory and non-signatory airlines
- the purpose of majority-in-interest provisions
- airline lease agreements
- residual-cost and compensatory rate-making methodologies
- the role of concessionaires and the manner by which airports earn revenues from concessionaires
- FBO agreements
- the purpose and role of minimum standards
- land leases
- MOUs and LOAs
- the terms and conditions of agreements
- rules of regulations
- self-fueling
- through-the-fence operations
- exclusive rights
- how to effectively interact with tenants
- the aeronautical and non-aeronautical commercial development of airports
- Disadvantaged Business Enterprise

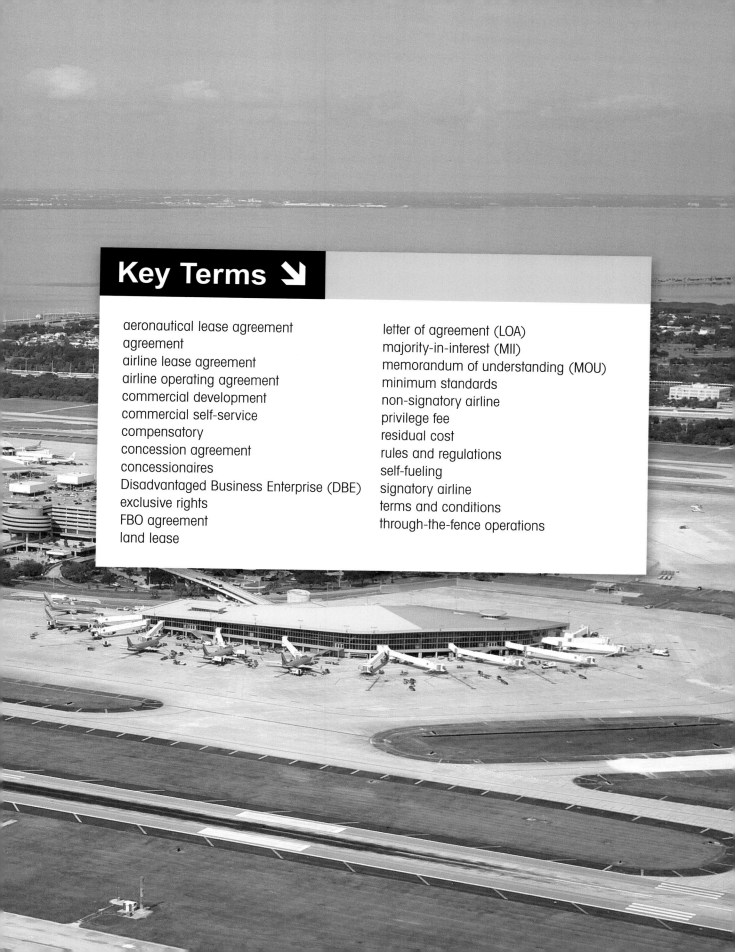

Key Terms ↘

aeronautical lease agreement
agreement
airline lease agreement
airline operating agreement
commercial development
commercial self-service
compensatory
concession agreement
concessionaires
Disadvantaged Business Enterprise (DBE)
exclusive rights
FBO agreement
land lease

letter of agreement (LOA)
majority-in-interest (MII)
memorandum of understanding (MOU)
minimum standards
non-signatory airline
privilege fee
residual cost
rules and regulations
self-fueling
signatory airline
terms and conditions
through-the-fence operations

In Chapter 12

FEATURES

New airline lease agreements provide guarantees to the airport as well as the airlines.

By developing an airport business park, this airport has generated additional revenues from airport land.

Agreements

Airports often own hundreds of acres of land and accommodate dozens of tenants that provide a number of different services. Since these vendors operate on land owned by the airport and airports recover revenue as a result of this, airports enter into **agreements** to clearly spell out the expectations, liabilities, lease rates, and other terms and conditions related to tenants being on airport property. In the world of business, including airport business, verbal agreements and understandings are not sufficient. Written agreements are the formal practice used to specify agreements and understandings between two or more parties. Although agreements with airport-based vendors, tenants, and others are quite common, airports may also enter into agreements with entities off-airport, such as nearby military bases or community organizations. In essence, lease agreements and operating agreements exist to protect the airport from uses that are detrimental to its operation and development, and arrange for revenues to be recovered from those operating on airport property.

Each agreement is specific to the tenant/vendor and the unique purpose of the agreement. **Aeronautical lease agreements** are generally designed for two types of airport users: commercial operators/tenants and non-commercial operators/tenants. In essence, commercial operators/tenants are individuals or entities that provide goods or services for a profit. Non-commercial tenants, on the other hand, are individuals or entities not using the airport in a for-profit manner. In practice, agreements can be very simple, perhaps totaling no more than one page. More commonly, however, agreements are rather complex, numbering 10–20 pages or more in length. Regardless of their length and purpose, agreements generally contain some common elements:

- Specific information about the property the tenant is allowed to use
- Responsibilities for utilities and other costs
- Language allowing property inspections for lease compliance
- Conditions under which the lease may be terminated
- Financial terms of the agreement
- Expiration dates for the agreement
- Escalation clause allowing rates to be revisited and adjusted over time or in the event of a significant change

AIRLINE AGREEMENTS

One of the most common agreements at commercial-service airports is the airline agreement. Airlines generally will be party to two agreements at an airport: an operating agreement and lease agreement.

First, the airline will enter into an **airline operating agreement** to obtain the authorization to land at the airport. This agreement will specify any landing fees, passenger facility charges to be collected, the process and deadlines by which revenues must be submitted, use of the airport, etc. In an effort to differentiate between airlines that may operate only one or two flights per week or seasonally and those that operate on a daily basis, airports have developed the terms signatory and non-signatory.

Signatory airlines enter into a fixed term agreement with the airport, and as a result, gain benefits such as lower landing fees (Figure 12-1). At Orlando International Airport, for example, to be categorized as a signatory airline, the airline must lease at least one preferential gate and other space in the terminal that is deemed sufficient by the executive director and totals at least 5,000 square feet. **Non-signatory airlines** operate limited or seasonal service and generally do not enter into a signatory agreement, so they are required to pay slightly higher landing fees and per-use fees for their use of the airport facilities. Non-signatory airlines at Orlando International Airport include airlines providing scheduled service to the airport, airlines operating from the airport's common facilities, airlines operating from the facilities of a fixed base operator (FBO), and cargo carriers using facilities other than the terminal facilities generally on a per-use basis.

Figure 12-1.
Signatory air carrier.

Majority-in-interest (MII) provisions refer to the degree of control given by the airport to the signatory airlines allowing these airlines to approve or disapprove capital expenditures and possibly even provide input into the budget, including fees, rates, and charges. MII provisions are more common at residual-cost airports than those with compensatory approaches (discussed later in this chapter). Signatory airlines generally have majority-in-interest.

Typical components of an airline operating agreement include:

- Definitions
- Term
- Rights of airline

- Maintenance, operation, use and condition of airport
- Airline rates and charges
- Other fees and charges
- Rules and regulations
- Indemnity and insurance
- Assignment and sub-use
- Taxes
- Default and cancellation
- Prohibited uses
- Federal grants and non-discrimination
- Miscellaneous

Second, airlines generally enter into an **airline lease agreement** (for land and/or facilities) occupied by the airline. A land lease is used for a maintenance hangar, reservations call center, or other facility that occupies airport land. An airport will generally never sell any land to a tenant, so if a tenant needs to have a facility on-airport, a land lease is entered into for the purpose of specifying the exact terms and conditions associated with the airline occupying airport-owned land. Land leases are usually on a per-acre or per-thousand-square-feet basis (depending on the amount of land being occupied). A facility lease is used for baggage claim space, a baggage claim office, ticket counter space, gate space, operations offices, and airline offices that occupy space in an airport-owned building, typically a terminal. Facility leases are generally on a per-square-foot

The Columbus Regional Airport Authority Signs New Airline Lease Agreements

In 2009, the Columbus Regional Airport Authority, owner and operator of Port Columbus International Airport, signed a new five-year airline lease agreement with the ten signatory airlines serving Port Columbus, which include Air Canada Jazz, AirTran, American, Chautauqua, Continental, Delta, Midwest, Southwest, United, and US Airways. The new lease agreement expanded revenue sharing with the airlines while holding down rent, landing fees and other airline charges. Specifically, the new agreement required the airport authority to share 75 percent of its annual net operating income after debt service and capital fund requirements with the airlines. The revenue sharing was to be paid to the airlines in the form of rent credits. In this way, the cost of doing business at the airport for airlines would be offset, while providing an incentive for airlines to maintain and expand service. In essence, higher airline activity would result in greater revenue sharing and, therefore, reduced airport charges. The former airline lease agreement included a fixed, pre-negotiated credit regardless of net revenues to the airport, which did not incentivize greater airline activity. The new agreement allows for a larger sum to be provided to the airlines tied to activity levels.

(Columbus Regional Airport Authority, 2009)

basis, with the monthly lease rate being based upon the price per square foot and the amount of square feet the airline occupies.

Additionally, airports must choose one of two general rate-making methodologies. Airline agreements and the rates and charges that airlines are assessed can be developed on a residual-cost basis or compensatory basis. These two methodologies differ in the manner in which airlines accept responsibility, possess authority over capital projects and budgets, and are assessed rates and charges (such as landing fees). Although the specific methodology in use at an airport is closely tied to revenues (addressed in chapter 13), the methodology also has an effect on airline agreements. Specifically, the **residual cost** approach requires airlines to collectively assume significant financial risk by agreeing to pay any costs of running the airport that are not allocated to other users or covered by nonairline sources of revenue. In essence, the airport measures revenues from all sources other than the airlines, and the amount necessary to then "break-even" is charged to the airlines in the form of landing (or other) fees. The residual cost approach is popular among smaller, less busy airports that often don't have significant sources of nonairline revenues, such as food and beverage concessions, auto parking, etc. With this approach, the airport is always assured of breaking even, but at the same time, the airport gives up some control over capital development to the airlines. In essence, the airlines have veto power over any expenditures that will result in higher landing fees to them.

The **compensatory** approach, on the other hand, requires the airport to assume the major financial risk of running the airport, with the airlines charged fees and rental rates based on the actual costs of the facilities and services that they use. With this approach, the airport is not guaranteed to break even, but on the other hand, it can generate substantial revenues. Thus, this approach is more popular at larger airports with significant sources of nonairline revenues.

CONCESSION AGREEMENTS

Airports also have tenants that offer food, beverages, or products (such as books, retail goods, etc.). These tenants are considered **concessionaires** (see Figure 12-2). Due to these concessionaires both occupying space within an airport-owned facility (such as a terminal building) and earning revenues on airport-owned property, a **concession agreement** is entered into. This agreement will specify the area that may be occupied by the concessionaire, and the percentage of revenues and any minimum privilege fee that will be payable to the airport, including the process and deadlines by which these payments must be submitted. A **privilege fee** is often paid to the airport by the concessionaire for the privilege of conducting business at the airport. Even if the concessionaire doesn't earn any revenues, the airport will still be paid a privilege fee and lease rate for the space occupied by the concessionaire.

Figure 12-2.
Airport concessions.

Although concession agreements vary in length and scope, the typical components of an agreement include:

- Premises
- Term
- Rent, fees, reporting, records, and audits
- Permissible uses
- Standard of operation
- Disadvantaged Business Enterprise
- Construction and capital investment
- Maintenance, utilities, and repairs
- Cash deposit and surety bond
- Insurance and indemnification
- Termination without cause
- Default and remedies
- Assignment and sublease
- General provisions

FBO AGREEMENTS

If an airport has a fixed base operator on site, the airport will enter into an agreement with this tenant. The FBO will not only occupy either an airport-owned or (more often) an FBO-owned building on airport property, but will also earn revenues and engage in services such as flight instruction, aircraft sales, aircraft charter, aircraft maintenance, line service, etc. (Figure 12-3). The

Figure 12-3.
Fixed base operator
(FBO).

FBO agreement must address the facility use and land use of the FBO, as well as the commercial aeronautical services offered by the FBO. Whereas each airline will generally have two agreements in effect with an airport (operating agreement and land or facility lease), airports often combine the facility/land lease and the operating agreement into one agreement with an FBO. This agreement will specify the facility or land occupied by the FBO and the lease rate for that space; the services to be offered by the FBO; and any other revenues the airport will collect from the FBO (usually a fuel flowage fee per gallon of aviation fuel sold by the FBO—to be discussed in chapter 13).

Components of an FBO agreement may include:

- Property description
- Building construction
- Term
- Rent and user fees
- Insurance
- Lessee Rights
- Maintenance of buildings
- Right to inspect
- Lease transfer
- Laws and regulations
- Hold harmless
- Quiet enjoyment
- Signs
- Obstruction lights
- Fair and nondiscriminatory services
- Nonexclusive rights

- Affirmative action
- Aircraft service by owner or operator
- Hours of operation
- Airport closings
- Snow removal
- Taxes
- Airport development
- Lessor's rights
- Obstructions
- Subordination of provision
- Performance bonds
- Financial disclosure
- Default
- Rights after termination
- Arbitration

One unique aspect of FBOs operating on an airport is the development of **minimum standards** to which an FBO must adhere. Not only will minimum standards set minimum service and quality levels, but these standards will also aid in preventing economic discrimination and the granting of an exclusive right to conduct aeronautical activities at the airport, both of which are violations of federal and state grant obligations. Airports are encouraged by the FAA to ensure providers of aeronautical services (such as FBOs) meet certain standards. It is in the airport's best interest to hold all aeronautical operators/ providers on the airport to a high level of quality, which will reflect positively on the airport and ensure top-quality services for users. Beyond simply hoping that this occurs, however, airports develop minimum standards, incorporate these standards into the agreement they enter into with the provider, and regularly audit or inspect the provider to make certain these standards are being met.

Although the development of minimum standards is optional, the FAA strongly recommends that airports hold FBOs to certain standards, and thus has developed Advisory Circular 150/5190-7, *Minimum Standards for Commercial Aeronautical Activities* (FAA, 2006). According to the FAA, minimum standards are meant to ensure a safe, efficient and adequate level of operation and services to the public. However, these standards must be reasonable and not unjustly discriminatory.

Specifically, 150/5190-7 states that minimum standards should be developed to "promote safety in all airport activities, protect airport users from unlicensed and unauthorized products and services, maintain and enhance the availability of adequate services for all airport users, promote the orderly development of airport land, and ensure efficiency of operations" (FAA, 2006, p. 3). When developing minimum standards, it is important to consider each aeronautical activity and the operating environment at the airport. In essence, minimum standards should be tailored to each specific aeronautical activity at the airport. For the FAA to support an airport's minimum standards, the airport must:

1. Apply standards to all providers of aeronautical services, from full service FBOs to single service providers;

2. Impose conditions that ensure safe and efficient operation of the airport in accordance with FAA rules, regulations, and guidance;

3. Ensure standards are reasonable, not unjustly discriminatory, attainable, uniformly applied and reasonably protect the investment of providers of aeronautical services to meet minimum standards from competition not making a similar investment;

4. Ensure standards are relevant to the activity to which they apply; and

5. Ensure standards provide the opportunity for newcomers who meet the minimum standards to offer their aeronautical services within the market demand for such services.

(FAA, 2006, p. 4)

The advisory circular contains specific questions to be answered in developing minimum standards. These questions address fuel sales; personnel requirements; airport and passenger services; flight training activities; aircraft engine/accessory repair and maintenance; skydiving; ultralight vehicles and light sport aviation; and fractional aircraft ownership. Clearly, not all of these activities may be present on an airport; thus, airports will need to develop minimum standards unique to their own activities (Figure 12-4) (FAA, 2006).

Items to consider in developing minimum standards are shown in Table 12-1.

Figure 12-4.
On-airport business.

Table 12-1. Considerations for developing minimum standards.

Category	Considerations
Fuel sales	Fuel tank locations and access Use of fuel trucks Fuel capacity and types of fuel for various aircraft Fuel supply Liability insurance for fueling operator
Personnel requirements	Number of trained and qualified personnel Training and qualifications of personnel
Flight training activities	Type of flight training offered Office space the school is required to maintain Full- or part-time training Type of aircraft Aircraft storage and maintenance provisions Coordination and contact with Flight Standards District Office
Aircraft engine accessory repair and maintenance	Types of services offered to the public Repair station ratings Qualifications of repair station employees Space requirements Standard parts storage space Lighting and ventilation requirements Safe spray painting, cleaning, or machining space
Skydiving, ultralight or sport aviation	These aeronautical activities must be accommodated at federally-obligated airports; however, airports may prohibit or limit these activities based on the operational safety of the airport, subject to FAA approval.

(Center for Transportation Studies, 2007, p. 2)

LAND LEASE

General **land leases** are utilized for any organization/entity that uses land on an airport. If this use is on a long-term, daily basis, the land lease may be incorporated into another agreement, such as an FBO agreement. However, if an organization, such as the Experimental Aircraft Association (EAA), only needs to utilize a specific portion of airport land for a one-week period (such as for an airshow), a land lease is created and entered into to specify liabilities, expectations, and other terms and conditions.

Generally, a land lease for short-term use will include:

- Leasehold
- Terms and conditions
- Lease payments
- Insurance
- Use of premises
- Utilities

- Repairs, maintenance, and appearance
- Alterations and improvements
- Waiver
- Time is of the essence
- Default
- Termination of use
- Mortgaging of leasehold
- Indemnity

MEMORANDUMS OF UNDERSTANDING AND LETTERS OF AGREEMENT

Although not as extensive as leases and other formal agreements, a **memorandum of understanding (MOU)** or **letter of agreement (LOA)** may be developed to specify terms of understanding or agreement between two parties. An MOU is generally less formal and can even be used for internal terms of understanding. For instance, an MOU may be developed to specify areas of agreement between an airport and union employees (such as police officers), or an airport and its community advisory group. An LOA may be more formal and is usually between the airport and an external organization—such as, for example, the FAA for an informal runway use program, or the EAA for an airshow/fly-in.

All MOUs and LOAs have common elements, such as the initial foundation, phrased in terms of "Whereas" statements. The action items are phrased as "Therefore" statements. In essence, an MOU or LOA simply states areas of agreement, cooperation, or understanding between both parties signing the document. It may have a defined term (such as one year) or an indefinite term.

CONSIDERATIONS

In developing use, lease, and operating agreements, airport staff must consider a number of items. These considerations are integral to ensuring a fair agreement that cannot be challenged and would be upheld by the FAA. In fact, airlines have challenged airports in the past by filing complaints with the FAA. Tenants other than airlines have also filed complaints. Informal complaints are filed under 14 CFR Part 13 (investigated by FAA regional staff), while formal complaints are filed under 14 CFR Part 16 (investigated by FAA headquarters). Parties filing under Part 16 must be substantially affected by the alleged noncompliance. Occasionally, these complaints have resulted in an FAA determination that the airport was not in compliance with grant assurances or federal regulations. Therefore, in developing an agreement, it is crucial to address specific considerations.

AERONAUTICAL

Aeronautical development of the airport includes facilities and services that benefit airport users (owners and operators of aircraft). The most common form of aeronautical development includes an FBO. An airport may only have one FBO, which is not considered an exclusive right if there is only enough activity (demand) on the airport for one FBO to be successful. However, many airports have more than one FBO. In any event, having an FBO on airport is an aeronautical form of commercial development that will benefit both the airport in the form of revenues and users in the form of desired aeronautical services.

In addition to FBOs, other aeronautical forms of commercial development may be considered. This may include aircraft maintenance facilities, aircraft paint shops, avionics shops, aircraft hangars, flight schools, etc. In reality, an airport should consider any businesses or use of airport property compatible with airport operations that will benefit airport users.

NON-AERONAUTICAL

An airport may also consider development with non-aeronautical forms of commercial activity—that is, businesses and activity that are not directly aeronautical, but still produce benefits. However, a balance is required between aeronautical and non-aeronautical use of the airport. Specifically, non-aeronautical use must not interfere with the aviation use of the airport. Airports must ensure that the use of the property does not jeopardize future airport development, and does not create or contribute to a flight hazard.

Although it may seem that an airport is no place for non-aeronautical activity, many airports have non-aeronautical forms of activity and realize substantial revenues from this activity. Consider that many airports have prime real estate that may be in demand by various businesses and developers, even without need for use of the airport. For instance, food, beverage, and retail concessionaires are very common at airports and represent forms of non-aeronautical activity. Consider a restaurant that just happens to be located in the airport terminal. This restaurant is no more involved in aeronautical activity than that same restaurant located in the downtown area of the community. It just happens that one is located on an airport. Consider shoeshine vendors, massage parlors, toy stores, and postal facilities located on airport property. These are all forms of non-aeronautical activity, and yet they have a very real place on an airport.

These examples of non-aeronautical activity are located within an airport terminal; generally, uses of airport property outside of the terminal buildings will be aeronautical in nature. However, there are airports with a golf course, a regional postal sort facility, a go-cart track, or a home improvement store on their property. One of the most common non-aeronautical uses of airport property is agricultural activity. Although this activity can generate revenues for the airport, there are some factors to consider:

- *Location and height of crops*—Agreements should specify that crops be of low height so as not to interfere with Part 77 surfaces, or visual NAVAIDs.

- *Wildlife attractant*—Generally, grain crops (including corn) can attract wildlife that can be hazardous to aircraft. It is helpful to require agricultural operators to submit crop plans to the airport for approval to prevent hazardous wildlife attractants from being planted and grown on airport property.

- *Equipment*—Equipment used in agricultural activities should also be addressed in the agreement. Specifically, the agreement should address routes to and from the leased area, as well as security requirements (clearances, closing and securing airport gates, etc.), parking, and storage of equipment.

- *Damages*—Lease agreements should require an agricultural operator to prevent damages to airport property, to include ruts, depressions, and the creation of foreign object debris. On the other hand, the airport should not provide for damages to the agricultural operator if crops are damaged or destroyed for reasons such as airport maintenance, operational, or development purposes.

- *Lease rates and terms*—In determining the lease rate for the ground on which agricultural activity will take place, it is important to charge fair market value. In other words, the airport should charge rates similar to those charged for other farmland in the area. Short-term leases for agricultural activities are beneficial, possibly numbering less than five years, with two- to three-year terms preferred. Again, it is important to include an escape clause that will allow the airport to terminate the lease in case the land is needed for other (such as aeronautical) purposes.

(Wisconsin Department of Transportation, 2011)

Often, the following non-aeronautical forms of commercial development can result in substantial revenues for the airport. The more innovative the use, often the higher are the profits for the airport.

- Blueberry farm—Georgia's largest blueberry farm is located on an airport.

- Solar panels—San Francisco, Long Beach, Denver and other airports are allowing for solar "farms" to be built on airport property. These may provide electricity for the airport or the land can be made available to the local utility company with revenues returning to the airport.

- Wind turbines—Boston Logan International Airport has 20 six-foot tall wind turbines on airport property.

- Golf course—Dallas Fort Worth International Airport has two 18-hole championship golf courses on airport property. Other airports with golf courses on airport property include Oakland International Airport (California), Huntsville International Airport (Alabama), and Los Angeles International Airport (California).

References and Resources for Further Study

Briggs, J. 2012. "How Airports Make Money and What's New in Compliance." Retrieved from http://www.faa.gov/airports/northwest_mountain/ airports_news_events/annual_conference/2012/media/how_airports_make_money_ and_whats_new_in_compliance.pdf

Center for Transportation Studies. 2007, Summer. "Navigating airport leases and agreements." *AirTap Briefings*. Minneapolis, MN: University of Minnesota.

Columbus Regional Airport Authority. 2009. "Expanded Revenue Sharing a Unique Feature of 5-Year Port Columbus-Airline Lease Agreement." News release, December 7. Retrieved from http://columbusairports.com/files/ press-releases/20091207_expanded_revenue_sharing_a_unique_feature_of_5_year_ port_columbus_airline_lease_agreement.pdf

Federal Aviation Administration (FAA). 2006. *Minimum Standards for Commercial Aeronautical Activities*. AC 150/5190-7. Washington, DC: FAA.

———. 2007. *Exclusive Rights at Federally-Obligated Airports*. AC 150/5190-6. Washington, DC: FAA. Retrieved from http://www.faa.gov/documentLibrary/ media/advisory_circular/150-5190-6/150_5190_6.pdf

———. 2011. "FAA issues residential through-the-fence policy." Retrieved from http://www.faa.gov/news/updates/?newsId=62676&omniRss=news_updatesAoc

———. 2012. "Grant Assurances Airport Sponsors." Retrieved from http://www.faa. gov/airports/aip/grant_assurances/media/airport-sponsor-assurances-aip.pdf

———. 2013. Compliance Guidance Letter 2013-01, FAA Review of Existing and Proposed Residential Through-the-Fence Access Agreements. Retrieved from http:// www.faa.gov/airports/airport_compliance/residential_through_the_fence/media/ cgl2013_1RTTF.pdf

Hillsborough County Aviation Authority. 2011. "Rules and Regulations for Tampa International Airport." Retrieved from http://m.www.tampaairport.com/about/ general_aviation/policies/r330.pdf

Prather, C. D. 2009. "The Right to Self-Fuel." *Legal Research Digest* 8: Retrieved from http://ntl.bts.gov/lib/43000/43800/43861/acrp_lrd_008.pdf

Smyrna-Rutherford County Airport, n.d. "Business Site Opportunities." Retrieved from http://www.smyrnaairport.com/business_sites

Wisconsin Department of Transportation. 2011. "Airport leases: An airport owner and management reference document."

Chapter 13

Financial Management

Upon completion of this chapter, you should understand:

- the budgeting process
- the operating budget and capital budget
- budget monitoring
- budget preparation
- the various budgeting techniques
- the income statement
- the balance sheet
- the statement of cash flows
- the annual report
- how to calculate the financial ratios
- aeronautical revenues
- non-aeronautical revenues
- innovative revenue sources
- O&M and capital expenses
- fees, rates, and charges
- risk management, including the various types of insurance policies

Key Terms ↘

activity-based budgeting
aeronautical revenues
annual report
assets
balance sheet
budget
budget monitoring
capital budgeting
capital expenditures
capital improvement plan (CIP)
consolidated rental car facilities
   (CONRAC)
cost of sales
current assets
current liabilities
current ratio
debt service safety margin
debt-to-asset ratio
depreciation
dividends
expenses
fees, rates, and charges
financial plan
financial ratios
financial statements
financing activities
fiscal year
fixed assets
fixed expenses
food and beverage (F&B) concession
fuel flowage fees
gross profit
hydrant fuel system fee
income statement
income tax

indemnification
insurance
interest expense
interest income
investing activities
landing fees
liabilities
line-item budgeting
long-term liabilities
lump sum budgeting
net profit
net take-down ratio
non-aeronautical revenues
noncurrent assets
non-operating revenues
operating activities
operating budget
operating expenses
operating ratio
operations and maintenance (O&M)
owner's (or shareholder's) equity
performance-based budgeting
program plan budgeting
retail concessions
return on assets ratio
revenue/cost-centered budgeting
revenues
risk management
statement of cash flows
statement of changes in equity
target-based budgeting
traditional budgeting
variable expenses
variance report
zero-based budgeting

In Chapter 13

FEATURES

Self-Sustained Enterprise Fund at Boise Airport 494

Dallas Fort Worth International Airport Gas Exploration 508

Budgeting Overview

Airports are financial enterprises. In reality, they serve as financial engines for the communities in which they operate. Just as an aircraft engine needs specific amounts of fuel, requiring the pilot to pre-plan for this required fuel, the airport financial engine requires financing as well as planning for this financing. This planning occurs in the form of a **budget**. Just as individuals develop budgets to manage personal finances, airports develop budgets to manage their finances. This is even more imperative with revenues and expenditures amounting to tens of millions of dollars, as is the case for many airports nationwide. An airport budget is intended to guide the airport in projecting revenues and expenditures for the year, while also keeping track of monthly progress in light of the budget to prevent the airport from spending more than projected revenues will allow.

Simply, a budget utilizes accounting data to plan for future operational and capital expenditures (as well as revenues). This **financial plan** becomes a fundamental tool used by management in making decisions that will have an impact on the airport's finances. Without a budget, the airport is likely to spend too much and run out of money prior to the end of the year. It goes without saying that a well-developed budget is a very effective tool for airport managers.

Budget Development

Prior to developing a budget, the airport establishes a **fiscal year**. The fiscal year is the 12-month year used for accounting purposes, which may or may not coincide with the calendar year. Once established, the dates coinciding with the fiscal year will not change. Although the fiscal year may be identical to the calendar year (January 1 to December 31), it typically is not (July 1 to June 30, or October 1 to September 30 are popular fiscal year dates). The purpose in having an alternate fiscal year is to enable the airport to close out the year and accounting statements at a time other than the end of the calendar year (which coincides with holidays). The FAA has a fiscal year of October 1 to September 30.

The development of a budget begins months prior to the start of a new fiscal year. Often, each department director is involved and tasked with developing funding requests, both of an operational and a capital nature. Department requests are generally higher than what may actually be included in the approved budget, but as the various airport departments submit their "wish lists," their needs and wants are made known to management. Clearly, all requested expenditures must be in line with projected revenues for the next year.

OPERATING BUDGET

The **operating budget** focuses on expenses and revenues associated with ongoing operations of the airport. The operating budget may include both revenues and expenditures or only expenditures. The functional areas generally included in the operating budget consist of airfield, terminal, landside, and general/administrative. To determine expenditures in each of these areas, employees may be asked to keep track of hours spent on various tasks, as well as supplies used. Salaries/wages may be included in a departmental operating budget, or this may be included in the airport's overall operating budget.

The operating budget is key to making sure each airport department spends within their means, especially for day-to-day operations. In fact, when departmental budgets are discussed, the operating budget is most often referred to. By definition, some airport departments such as maintenance and operations may have very large operating budgets. Other departments, such as finance or human resources, may have smaller operating budgets. Although the airport will have an overall operating budget, the unique operating budget developed for each department is more detailed and specific to the particular department. In fact, departmental budgets are essential; otherwise, each department's expenditures are likely to get lost in the airport's overall operating budget.

According to AAAE (2010, p. 112), in developing an operating budget, airport management must:

- Plan for the operational needs of the organization.
- Obtain resources from the airport's operating environment.
- Distribute those resources throughout the organization.
- Track the resource expenditures to ensure they are used effectively and efficiently.

Self-Sustained Enterprise Fund at Boise Airport

The City of Boise owns and operates Boise Airport, located in Boise, Idaho. The airport's website explains that the airport is a self-sustained enterprise fund department of the City of Boise. As such, no local tax funding contributes to the airport. Airport revenues are generated by fees and charges, as well as federal grant funding. Additionally, as a non-profit entity, all revenues above expenses are reinvested into the city's aviation operations.

In addition to revenue generated by airport fees and charges, Boise Airport is also the beneficiary of FAA grants. Since 1952, those grants have totaled more than $136 million and have funded projects such as runway and terminal improvements, land acquisition, noise abatement, security enhancements, baggage system upgrades, fire equipment, and basic infrastructure investment.

(Boise Airport, n.d.)

In practice, this requires airport management not only to prioritize operating expenditures in developing the operating budget, possibly deferring expenditures into future years, but also to track month-to-month expenditures once the operating budget is approved. Remember, airlines serving the airport are most concerned about their costs (often characterized as costs per enplaned passenger—CPE), and as a result, airport management must be conservative in developing operating budgets.

CAPITAL BUDGET

Unlike operating budgeting, **capital budgeting** focuses only on capital projects. These are long-term expenditures such as terminals, parking garages, new runways/taxiways, ARFF trucks, etc. Capital budgeting involves an examination of long-term capital needs and a prioritization of those needs based on realistic costs, resulting in a yearly capital budget (often for 3 to 5 years into the future). The multi-year plan becomes the airport's **capital improvement plan (CIP)**, which then integrates with state and national plans, such as the National Plan of Integrated Airport Systems (NPIAS).

Although the operating budget is used daily by a department director to track expenditures and make certain the department stays within budget, the capital budget is used less frequently and only to track big ticket items that are purchased much less frequently—maybe once per year. Even so, if only $1 million was budgeted for an ARFF truck, for example, it is important that no more than $1 million is spent on this piece of equipment. The capital budget will reveal this.

BUDGET PROCESS AND MONITORING

Once a budget is prepared, is must be continually monitored. Just as individuals prepare personal budgets and don't wait until the end of the year to check on their progress toward the budget, airports don't wait until the end of the year to check on progress toward their budgets. **Budget monitoring** at airports takes place monthly, and even daily. An airport's finance department continually pays invoices and records revenues, and as part of that, tracks progress against the budget. A **variance report** shows actual expenditures as a percentage of the budgeted amount. This is useful, for example, so that if the year is half over and more than 50 percent of the budgeted amount for a particular area has been spent, changes in spending will likely need to be made to avoid either spending more than the budgeted amount or running out of money before the end of the year. Likewise, if an ARFF truck is budgeted for and is purchased in April, the variance report will show 100 percent of that budget amount spent before mid-year. The difference between the actual revenues and expenses and the budgeted revenues and expenses is the variance. Each area director needs to remain aware of the budget for their area and the progress made toward that budgeted amount—i.e., the variance.

BUDGET PREPARATION

Preparing an airport budget is a multi-step process that typically occurs over several months. If an airport's new fiscal year begins on October 1, for example, preparation of the coming year's budget may begin in the spring. The first step is for the airport to review its current financial picture, including revenues and expenses for the current year. Next, revenues are estimated for the coming year. Airports, specifically those served by air carriers, have very passenger-dependent revenues. A commercial-service airport can, for instance, consider current revenues based on a certain number of enplaned passengers. If the number of enplaned passengers increases by 3 percent in the coming year, revenues can also be projected to increase by a specific percentage.

Next, fixed and variable expenses must be projected for the coming year. **Fixed expenses** are those expenses that don't change (such as debt service), while **variable expenses** change from month to month (for example, utilities). As part of this, capital equipment requests are presented. Each department prepares requests (operating and capital) and then submits these requests to the finance department and/or airport director, who then reviews each department's requests. Requests are prioritized and they may not all be approved. Eventually, approved requests are incorporated into the airport's budget. This process may require some give-and-take, requiring patience, negotiating skills, and justification for any requested expenditures (especially for capital items). In the end, department directors must accept the budget as approved by the airport's governing body, even if they don't completely agree with it (see Figure 13-1).

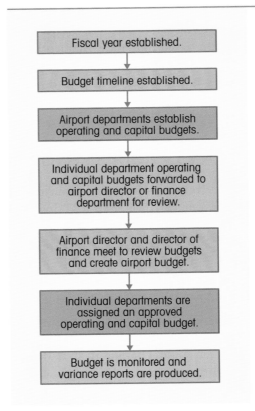

Figure 13-1. Airport budgeting process.

Fiscal year established.

Budget timeline established.

Airport departments establish operating and capital budgets.

Individual department operating and capital budgets forwarded to airport director or finance department for review.

Airport director and director of finance meet to review budgets and create airport budget.

Individual departments are assigned an approved operating and capital budget.

Budget is monitored and variance reports are produced.

BUDGET TECHNIQUES

Budgets can be prepared in a number of ways. The various techniques used are often dependent on management preference. This means that it's possible for a department director to be familiar with utilizing a certain technique to develop a department budget at one airport, only to accept a department director position at another airport and be required to use a different budget preparation technique. The various budgeting techniques include:

- **Traditional budgeting**—Based on a percentage increase or decrease of revenues and expenditures, which builds from the current year budget. This is also known as incremental budgeting, in reference to incremental increases or decreases from the current year budget. A 3–5 percent increase from year to year is common.

- **Lump sum budgeting**—More common at GA airports, this budgeting technique involves a lump sum of money that the airport then uses its judgment in expending throughout the year.

- **Activity-based budgeting**—Presents costs as a ratio of the number of full-time employees to the required action or work in a specific budget category. Allocates funds to specific activity areas.

- **Performance-based budgeting**—Based on the allocation of funds according to outcomes associated with specific goals. If performance goals are met or exceeded, funding at the highest levels will be made available.

- **Program plan budgeting**—Focuses on cost-benefit analyses. Takes a long-term view of projects and their associated costs, breaking them down into yearly operating budgets. It is centered on a functional or organizational area, identifying facilities, personnel, or equipment needed.

- **Zero-based budgeting**—Each budget is developed from zero, as if no current budget exists, which requires a careful analysis of all revenues and expenditures. Each department must prioritize, rank, and justify needs.

- **Target-based budgeting**—Similar to zero-based budgeting, but allows more flexibility. Revenues are estimated with an associated cap placed on expenditures based on the revenue estimate.

- **Revenue/cost-centered budgeting**—Focuses on break-even needs associated with revenue and cost centers. This requires care in developing cost and revenue centers, as well as allocating revenues and costs to these areas.

- **Line-item budgeting**—A very detailed form of budgeting in which all expenditures are broken down into cost centers, with a chart of accounts. A detailed numbering and coding system is developed for each line item.

(AAAE, 2010)

Revenues

In simple terms, **revenues** are the money earned or collected at or by the airport. Similar to the salary/wages that individuals earn, airports earn revenues for the services and facilities they provide. Airports are generally not in the business of selling products, but they are in the business of providing services (fueling, valet parking, police, ARFF, etc.) and facilities (parking structures, terminal buildings, runways, taxiways, ramps, etc.). These services and facilities are in demand and cost money to provide, and thus charges can be assessed on those using these services and facilities. Revenues can be in the form of aeronautical or non-aeronautical.

AERONAUTICAL REVENUES

To provide runways, taxiways, ramp areas, and safety areas, and maintain these areas, airports incur significant costs. It costs a considerable amount of money to design and construct large expanses of paved areas. It costs more money to install signage, markings, and lighting. The pavement, as well as signage, marking, and lighting, must then be maintained. Grass must be cut, pavement must be repaired, markings need to be repainted, lights burn out and require replacement, etc. Additionally, personnel must be hired and paid to carry out these maintenance tasks, as well as inspect the airfield. All told, an airport spends tens of thousands to millions of dollars annually to provide an airfield that allows safe and efficient use of the airport by various users. As expenses are incurred in this area, revenues must be earned to cover these costs. Since these are aeronautical expenses, **aeronautical revenues** are charged to cover these expenses. In essence, aeronautical revenues are those revenues earned from aeronautical users and aeronautical activity.

Landing Fees

At airports that serve air carriers, the most common aeronautical source of revenue is **landing fees**. In fact, landing fees typically account for almost one quarter of airport operating revenues. This is the most effective way to recover those expenses necessary to provide and maintain the airfield (see Figure 13-2).

Landing fees are assessed per 1,000 pounds of certificated maximum gross landing weight (CMGLW) of aircraft. This is important for two reasons. First, air carriers are charged based on their activity at the airport, as well as the size of the aircraft they fly. Admittedly, larger, heavier aircraft place higher levels of stress on airfield pavements. Therefore, they must pay more. Second, the landing fee is based on certificated landing weight, not actual landing weight. Thus, an aircraft could be full of passengers (100 percent load factor) or empty (0 percent load factor) and in both of these cases, the same landing fee would be assessed for the same aircraft. This is important because it means airports

Figure 13-2. The landing of an air carrier aircraft, generating landing fee revenues for the airport.

need not be concerned about airline load factors and actual passengers on board (at least concerning landing fees) when assessing landing fees.

Airports collect millions of dollars in landing fees annually. Landing fees may range from pennies to several dollars or more per thousand pounds CMGLW. As discussed in Chapter 12, landing fees for signatory airlines are generally somewhat less than landing fees for non-signatory airlines. At Orlando International Airport, for example, 2015 landing fees were assessed to airlines at the rate of $1.5901 per 1,000 pounds CMGLW (Greater Orlando Aviation Authority, 2014).

Fuel Fees

Airlines are required to pay the market rate for fuel at an airport. Airport fuel systems, although typically installed by the airport, are often managed and maintained by an airline or private operator, such as Aircraft Service International Group (ASIG). Some airports/airlines/operators also assess a **hydrant fuel system fee** (for those underground systems served by fuel hydrants at each gate). This fee is on a per-gallon basis, with a large portion of the fee designed to cover the rent, operations, and maintenance of the hydrant fuel system. At Orlando International Airport, for example, the hydrant fuel system fee was $0.0348 per gallon in 2015 (Figure 13-3).

Although landing fees are easily assessed on scheduled air carriers that have entered into an operating agreement with the airport, collecting landing fees from GA aircraft, especially transient users, is difficult if not impossible. Consider a GA aircraft that performs only one touch-and-go. How would a landing fee be collected from this pilot? To counteract this difficulty and yet also charge GA aircraft for their use of the airfield, **fuel flowage fees** may be charged. These fees are assessed on a per-gallon basis for each gallon of Avgas and Jet fuel

Figure 13-3.
Fueling of an air carrier aircraft.

(aberenyi/Bigstock.com)

that is pumped into GA aircraft at the airport. Since the airport has an agreement in place with the FBO (or owner of the self-service pump), fuel flowage fees can be collected and then submitted to the airport on a regular (typically monthly) basis. In this way, GA aircraft share in the cost burden of providing and maintaining the airfield. Although exact fuel flowage fees vary, $0.05 to $0.20 per gallon is common. Often lowest at commercial service airports that generate substantial landing fees from air carriers, the fuel flowage fee at Orlando International Airport in 2015, for example, was assessed at the rate of $0.025 per gallon. Just as with state and local fuel taxes, the fuel flowage fee is part of the per gallon advertised price. Therefore, users generally have little idea as to how much fuel flowage fee they're paying as they fuel their aircraft. As long as the total price per gallon is acceptable, the user will purchase fuel (and pay fuel flowage fees in the process).

Land Lease and Terminal Rent

Discussed in Chapter 12, land and terminal rent could be characterized as either aeronautical or non-aeronautical. In the aeronautical sense, airlines pay a significant amount each month to airports for the use of space in terminals. This space includes ticket counter space, baggage claim space, ticket counter office space, operations office space, baggage claim office space, etc. Additionally, an airline or corporate operator will likely lease the land on which their hangar sits. These revenues factor into the airport revenue equation and typically account for one quarter of airport operating revenues.

The trend at airports has been to incorporate not only national brands (such as Subway, Burger King, McDonald's, Starbucks, and Chili's), but also local and regional brands (such as Whitt's Barbeque, Rhythms Café, and Grandaddy's Bar). The most important concept is to provide choices for patrons, and ensure that the concessions are well-located so that regardless of the gate or terminal, passengers have convenient access to food and beverage concessions. This is even more important post-9/11, as only ticketed passengers and employees can access the terminal past the security screening checkpoint. Another important component is to offer pricing as close to "street-pricing" as possible. In other words, prices should not be excessive, and should be similar to prices at the same establishments off airport property. In 2014, Orlando International Airport earned $18.1 million in food and beverage concession revenues (Figure 13-7).

Figure 13-7. Airport food and beverage concessions.

Services

In addition to the typical food and beverage and retail concessions at airports, there has been a transition in recent years toward offering more personal services at airports. These services may include shoe shine, hair salon, nail salon, massage spa, business center, airline clubs/lounge, credit union/bank, currency exchange, yoga studio/gym, traveler's insurance, etc. (Figure 13-8). These services are greatly appreciated by passengers who often do not have ready access to off-airport services. Adding services concessions within an airport terminal can create a more welcoming environment and enhance traveler productivity, while reducing stress. In 2014, Orlando International Airport earned $11.6 million in services concession revenues.

Figure 13-8.
Airport shoe shine,
a common airport
services concession.

Advertising

Airports often have advertising present within the passenger terminal buildings (see Figure 13-9). This advertising serves three purposes. First, it provides an interesting graphical aesthetic within the terminal building providing passengers and meeters and greeters (as well as employees) something visually appealing to look at. Second, due to the significant number of passengers and others that serve as a captive audience within a terminal building, the advertiser often receives significant "bang for the buck" with their advertising dollar. Third, advertisers pay for the space they utilize and as a result, the airport earns advertising revenues.

Figure 13-9. In-airport
advertising.

STATEMENTS OF CASH FLOWS
YEARS ENDED SEPTEMBER 30, 2011 AND 2010

	2011	2010
CASH FLOWS FROM OPERATING ACTIVITIES		
Operating Cash Receipts from Customers	$ 170,691,406	$ 155,738,871
Cash Payments to Suppliers for Goods and Services	(64,906,326)	(64,919,225)
Cash Payments to Employees for Services	(32,019,139)	(32,806,551)
Cash Receipts from Federal Reimbursements	1,230,326	1,230,326
Net Cash Provided by Operating Activities	74,996,267	59,243,421
CASH FLOWS FROM CAPITAL AND RELATED FINANCING ACTIVITIES		
Proceeds from Issuance of 2011 Suntrust Notes	88,053,335	-
Proceeds from Issuance of Commercial Paper Notes	-	6,180,000
Redemption of Commercial Paper Notes	(85,180,000)	-
Payments of Suntrust Notes and Commercial Paper Issuance Costs	(133,086)	(7,424)
Principal and Interest Paid on Revenue Bond Refunding	-	(5,655,776)
Principal Paid on Revenue Bond Maturities and Commercial Paper Notes	(47,290,000)	(40,225,000)
Interest Paid on Revenue Bonds and Commercial Paper Notes	(36,702,872)	(38,669,533)
Acquisition and Construction of Capital Assets	(40,845,067)	(96,235,516)
Net Proceeds from Direct Financing Lease and Other Assets	8,387	17,328
Federal and State Grants	8,207,381	18,466,297
Passenger Facility Charges	33,369,461	32,479,400
Net Cash Used by Capital and Related Financing Activities	(80,512,461)	(123,650,224)
CASH FLOWS FROM INVESTING ACTIVITIES		
Purchases of Investment Securities	(85,020,369)	(98,667,663)
Proceeds from Maturities of Investment Securities	85,418,857	101,397,696
Income Received on Investments	2,839,223	2,861,522
Net Cash Provided by Investing Activities	3,237,711	5,591,555
NET CHANGE IN CASH AND CASH EQUIVALENTS	(2,278,483)	(58,815,248)
Cash and Cash Equivalents - Beginning of Year	115,009,479	173,824,727
CASH AND CASH EQUIVALENTS - END OF YEAR	$ 112,730,996	$ 115,009,479
RECONCILIATION OF OPERATING LOSS TO NET CASH PROVIDED BY OPERATING ACTIVITIES		
Operating Loss	$ (11,106,784)	$ (15,982,749)
Adjustments to Reconcile Operating Loss to Net Cash Provided by Operating Activities:		
Depreciation and Amortization	81,962,284	81,714,186
(Increase) Decrease in Accounts Receivable	1,648,443	(1,939,855)
(Increase) Decrease in Prepaid Insurance and Other Assets	89,203	(223,910)
Increase (Decrease) in Accounts Payable - Trade	1,181,098	(1,315,094)
Increase (Decrease) in Accrued Expenses, Deferred Revenue, and Other Liabilities	1,222,023	(3,009,157)
Net Cash Provided by Operating Activities	$ 74,996,267	$ 59,243,421
NONCASH ACTIVITIES		
Unrealized Gain on Investments	$ 798,985	$ 4,426,138
Amortization of Bond Premium - Net	$ (3,348,672)	$ (3,687,400)
Amortization of Deferred Loss on Bond Refundings	$ 1,207,094	$ 1,385,606
Other Capital Contributions	$ -	$ 1,066,903

to $112,730,996. This statement also takes the operating loss of $11,106,784 from the Statement of Revenues, Expenses, and Changes in Net Assets and provides a reconciliation of operating loss to net cash provided by operating activities.

STATEMENT OF CHANGES IN EQUITY

The fourth financial statement is known as the **statement of changes in equity**, or the statement of retained earnings. This statement details the change in owners' equity or retained earnings over an accounting period by detailing the changes or movement in reserves which make up the shareholders' or owners' equity. Since most public-use airports in the United States do not have shareholders, the statement of changes in equity is not often seen in an airport's annual report. The statement of retained earnings, while not as common as the previous financial statements discussed, may be seen as it relates simply to changes in the airport's retained earnings.

RELATIONSHIP AMONG FINANCIAL STATEMENTS

Although it is tempting to consider each financial statement in isolation, in reality, they are closely related to each other. The balance sheet begins the period and once profits and losses are calculated, these are fed into the income statement and cash flow statement. Next, as capital is raised and dividends paid (for those firms with shares of issued stock), this affects the statement of changes in equity and the cash flow statement. Finally, gains and losses recognized directly in equity affect the statement of changes in equity, while cash flow used in investing activities and cash flow from financing debt affect the cash flow statement. Lastly, the balance sheet at the end of the period is impacted from these activities (see Figure 13-13).

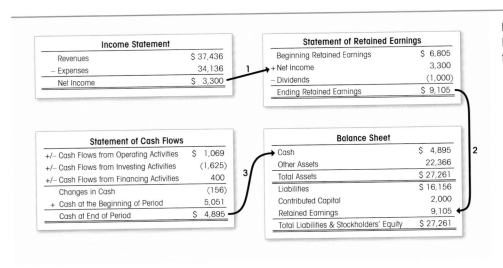

Figure 13-13.
Relationships among financial statements.

ANNUAL REPORT

The U.S. Securities and Exchange Commission (SEC) requires companies with more than $10 million in assets and a class of equity securities that is held by more than 500 owners to file Form 10-K (**Annual Report**) each year. This report provides a comprehensive summary of the company's performance. When discussions center around an annual report, however, they are usually referring to the very glossy and image-rich document that presents the year's highlights and financial statements to shareholders, stakeholders, the media, and others interested in the company. Publicly owned and operated airports prepare an annual report for the benefit of citizens, business leaders, and others interested in the financial health of the airport, as well as the airport's accomplishments during the past year. The annual report will also provide a glimpse into the future of the airport.

Although airport annual reports vary in length and information provided, and may be so unique that they are unlike any other, the following elements are rather common:

- *Letter from the chairman or executive director:* This letter is a general letter from top management that highlights successes from the past year, possibly presents some challenges faced, and closes on a positive note and maybe even includes a thank you to the airport's team of employees for their hard work during the year.

- *Sales and marketing:* This section contains detailed information about the airport's facilities and services, accomplishments, airlines, destinations, and a description of major divisions and groups and their areas of responsibility.

- *Ten-year summary of financial results:* Rather than present only one year of financial data, an airport may include a presentation of financial results over a ten-year period. Trends can be uncovered by reviewing financial results over this longer horizon.

- *Management discussion and analysis:* Management often discusses significant financial trends during the past few years and may offer explanations for any poor performance.

- *Letter of CPA opinion:* Financial statements must be audited by an independent qualified Certified Public Accountant (CPA). There will generally be a letter from the CPA certifying the review/audit and expressing any qualifications with the financial statements or the manner by which they were prepared. These letters are almost always positive. Any concerns or issues should be worked through with the CPA before the annual report is produced.

- *Financial statements:* The "meat" of the annual report is the financial statements. At minimum, the income statement, balance sheet, and cash flow statement should be included. Almost as important as the statements are the footnotes, which often contain extremely important information that cannot be included in the statements.

- *Footnotes:* Provides more detailed information about the financial statements.
- *List of directors and officers:* Although this list may appear at the front of the report, listing directors and officers of the airport provides insight into the management structure. Officers may include the president, chief executive officer, vice presidents, senior directors, etc.

FINANCIAL RATIOS

To make sense among all the financial numbers and to allow for comparisons between airports, various **financial ratios** have been developed. By using financial ratios, the financial strength of small airports can be compared to large airports, or to the entire industry. Breaking down all the dollars and cents to a ratio can be very helpful in conducting such comparisons. Without these, it could be argued that larger airports have more assets and make more money than smaller airports. Yet comparing airports using the various financial ratios allows equal comparisons to easily be made. Although a number of ratios can be developed and utilized, the following are the most common ratios used in the airport industry.

Return on Assets Ratio

$$\text{Return on Assets} = \frac{\text{Net Profits}}{\text{Total Assets}}$$

The **return on assets ratio** provides insight into the productivity of the airport's assets. The greater the net profits, the greater the ratio. Thus, higher ratios are preferred, with ratios closer to 1.0 desired. A ratio above 1.0 means the airport is earning more in net profits than they own in assets, which is indicative of a high level of productivity.

Using the sample financial statements (Figures 13-10, 13-11), the return on assets ratio is -0.007. This extremely low ratio is the result of an operating loss of over $11 million. In essence, this airport not only has no return on assets, but has a negative return. The ratio below zero should raise a red flag.

$$-0.007 = \frac{(\$11,106,784)}{\$1,474,938,103}$$

Current Ratio

$$\text{Current Ratio} = \frac{\text{Current Assets}}{\text{Current Liabilities}}$$

The **current ratio** is used to measure the difference between the amount of current assets and current liabilities. This ratio provides an indication as to the ability of the airport to pay current liabilities with current assets. Higher current ratios are preferred. With twice as many current assets as current liabilities, for example, a ratio of 2.0 would result. A ratio of 0.5 would result if an airport owes twice as much as it owns (in the form of current assets).

Using the sample financial statements (Figure 13-10), the current ratio is 2.81. In essence, this airport has almost three times as many current assets as it has current liabilities. So although it had an operating loss for the year (and a very low return on assets ratio), it has more than sufficient assets (mostly consisting of cash and investments) to cover current liabilities.

$$2.81 = \frac{\$214,553,525}{\$76,386,249}$$

Operating Ratio

$$\text{Operating Ratio} = \frac{\text{Operating Expenses} + \text{Maintenance Expenses}}{\text{Operating Revenue}}$$

The **operating ratio** measures the share of revenues absorbed by operating and maintenance costs. A low ratio is preferred. A higher ratio (close to 1.0) indicates that little additional revenue is available for capital expenditures. Depending on the financial statements, maintenance expenses may be incorporated into total operating expenses.

Using the sample financial statements (Figure 13-11), the operating ratio is 0.55. In essence, a little more than half of operating revenues are absorbed by operating expenses. Although this ratio could be lower (and thus, stronger), it shows that there are operating revenues remaining after covering operating expenses.

$$0.55 = \frac{\$92,496,355 + 0}{\$169,515,761}$$

Net Take-Down Ratio

$$\text{Net Take-Down Ratio} = \frac{\left[\text{Total Revenue} - \left(\begin{array}{c}\text{Operating} \\ \text{Expenses}\end{array} + \begin{array}{c}\text{Maintenance} \\ \text{Expenses}\end{array}\right)\right]}{\text{Total Revenue}}$$

Although similar to the operating ratio, the **net take-down ratio** also takes into account non-operating revenues (interest income, for example). It is, as a result, a broader measure of airport revenues remaining after payment of operating expenses.

Using the sample financial statements (Figure 13-11), the net take-down ratio is 0.47. This ratio is similar to the operating ratio for this airport because non-operating revenues were only $3,611,822, which is only 2 percent of the total revenues.

$$0.47 = \frac{[(\$169,515,761 + \$3,611,822) - (\$92,496,355 + 0)]}{(\$169,515,761 + \$3,611,822)}$$

$$0.47 = \frac{\$173,127,583 - \$92,496,355}{\$173,127,583}$$

Debt-to-Asset Ratio

$$\text{Debt-to-Asset Ratio} = \frac{\text{Gross Debt} - \text{Bond Principal Reserves}}{\text{Net Fixed Assets} + \text{Working Capital}}$$

The **debt-to-asset ratio** measures the total assets provided by creditors. In this formula, gross debt = total debt = total liability. Bond principal reserves will often be presented within the notes to financial statements. Net fixed assets is calculated by deducting accumulated depreciation from fixed assets (or noncurrent assets), shown on the sample statement as "total capital assets, net." Working capital is current assets minus current liabilities. A low ratio indicates each dollar of debt is secured with more dollars of assets. A high ratio would indicate a highly leveraged airport, which is not preferred. This is important in case assets have to be sold to pay off bondholders.

To obtain bond principal reserves, see Notes to Financial Statements Excerpt in Figure 13-14. Using this and the sample financial statements (Figure 13-10), the debt-to-asset ratio is 0.49. Rather than being too low or high, this ratio indicates this airport has about twice as much in assets as in debt.

$$\frac{\$770,781,283 - (\$46,203 + \$89,107,264)}{\$1,253,954,644 + (\$214,553,525 - \$76,386,249)}$$

$$= \frac{\$681,627,816}{\$1,253,954,644 + \$138,167,276}$$

$$= \frac{\$681,627,816}{\$1,392,121,920}$$

$$= 0.49$$

Debt Service Safety Margin

$$\text{Debt Service Safety Margin} = \frac{\text{Gross Revenues} - \left(\text{Operating Expenses} + \text{Maintenance Expenses} + \text{Annual Debt Service}\right)}{\text{Gross Revenues}}$$

The **debt service safety margin** measures the percentage of revenues available to service new debt, as well as the financial reserves available in the event of the airport experiencing unexpectedly low revenues. Debt must be "serviced" by paying interest and eventually paying off the bonds. The margin refers to a "safety net" to service the debt, which includes paying interest on the outstanding bonds. A high ratio indicates a larger safety net. Annual debt service is found in the notes to financial statements.

To obtain annual debt service, see Notes to Financial Statements Excerpt in Figure 13-14. Using this and the sample financial statements (Figure 13-11), the debt service safety margin is -0.02. With a negative debt service safety margin, this airport is paying more in operating expenses and annual debt service than it makes in gross revenues. In fact, for this airport, the annual debt service of

RESTRICTED ASSETS

The Trust Agreement, among other things, requires all airport revenues, excluding PFCs, grants, bond proceeds and their earnings, and revenues from certain nontrust funded projects, be deposited in the Revenue Fund, the establishment of certain trust accounts, and defines the priority and flow of cash receipts. Certain of these trust accounts require specified balances and are restricted as to use. Bond proceeds issued for construction are held by a trustee appointed by the Authority per the bond agreement. Debt Service and Debt Reserve accounts are held by a trustee designated by the Trust Agreement and are pledged as collateral for debt service. A summary of the balances in these accounts as of September 30, 2011 and 2010 is as follows:

	2011	2010
Restricted for Debt Service:		
Bond Prinicipal, Interest, and Redemption Sinking Fund	$ 46,203	$ 57,641
Bond Reserve Fund	89,107,264	88,489,083

DEBT AND OTHER NON-CURRENT LIABILITIES

Revenue Bonds

The total principal maturities and debt service requirements for all revenue bonds through the year 2038, as of September 30, 2011 are as follows:

Year Ending September 30	Principal	Interest	Total Debt Service
2012	$ 50,720,000	$ 33,674,481	$ 84,394,481
2013	53,205,000	31,109,119	84,314,119
2014	56,055,000	28,402,094	84,457,094
2015	58,985,000	25,464,006	84,449,006
2016	54,560,000	22,418,631	76,978,631
2017–2021	186,465,000	71,765,950	258,230,950
2022–2026	56,685,000	43,406,763	100,091,763
2027–2031	43,950,000	30,181,650	74,131,650
2032–2036	57,070,000	17,071,050	74,141,050
2037–2038	27,395,000	2,257,375	29,652,375
Total	$ 645,090,000	$ 305,751,119	$ 950,841,119

$84,394,481 almost equals operating expenses of $92,496,355. This ratio is particularly insightful for potential investors as they examine the likelihood the airport will be able to pay interest on bonds. In this case, this airport is not a particularly strong investment.

$$\frac{\$169,515,761 + \$3,611,822 - (\$92,496,355 + 0 + \$84,394,481)}{\$169,515,761 + \$3,611,822}$$

$$= \frac{\$173,127,583 - (\$176,890,836)}{\$173,127,583}$$

$$= \frac{(\$3,763,253)}{\$173,127,583}$$

$$= -0.02$$

Establishing Fees, Rates and Charges

In order to cover the costs associated with operating and maintaining an airport, airports implement various fees, rates, and charges. The term "**fees, rates, and charges**" refers to numerous items, depending upon the activity and the agreement. Some airports have established hundreds of unique fees, rates and charges. At Dallas/Fort Worth International Airport, for example, the FY2015 schedule of charges includes:

- Aircraft Operations
  - › Landing fee rates
  - › Common-use gate turn times
  - › Terminal aircraft parking fees
  - › Penalty for failure to move aircraft from a common-use gate
  - › Exemption to airfield charges
  - › Corporate aviation charges
- Terminal Rental Rates
  - › Airline terminal rates
  - › Terminals B/E & D, Common gate use charges
  - › Terminal hardstand operations
  - › Common-use charges for preferential leaseholders
  - › Federal Inspection Service (FIS) Fees
- Ground Rental and Foreign Trade Zone
  - › Ground rental
  - › Foreign Tradezone
- Parking Charges
  - › Public parking charges
  - › Off-airport charges
  - › Exemptions from parking charges
  - › Vehicular access charges
  - › Other parking charges
- Ground Transportation
  - › Operating authority fees
  - › Access fees
  - › Meet and greet service fees
  - › Central queue service fees
  - › Mystery shop reimbursement
- Public Safety Medical and Service
  - › Aircraft rescue and firefighting (ARFF) and structural fire training
  - › Emergency medical service (EMS)

Chapter Summary

- The operating budget focuses on expenses and revenues associated with ongoing operations of the airport.
- The capital budget focuses only on capital projects, such as terminals, parking garages, new runways/taxiways, ARFF trucks, etc.
- Preparing an airport budget is a multi-step process that occurs over several months.
- Fixed expenses are those expenses that don't change (such as debt service), while variable expenses change from month to month (for example, utilities).
- Traditional budgeting is commonly based on a percentage increase or decrease of revenues and expenditures, which builds from the current year budget.
- Lump sum budgeting involves a lump sum of money that the airport then uses its judgment in expending throughout the year.
- Activity-based budgeting presents costs as a ratio of the number of full-time employees to the required action or work in a specific budget category and allocates funds to specific activity areas.
- Performance-based budgeting allocates funds according to outcomes associated with specific goals.
- Program plan budgeting focuses on cost-benefit analyses and takes a long-term view of projects and their associated costs, breaking them down into yearly operating budgets.
- Zero-based budgeting is developed from zero, as if no current budget exists, which requires a careful analysis of all revenues and expenditures.
- Target-based budgeting is similar to zero-based budgeting, but allows for more flexibility.
- Revenue/cost-centered budgeting focuses on break-even needs associated with revenue and cost centers.
- Line-item budgeting is a very detailed form of budgeting in which all expenditures are broken down into cost centers, with a chart of accounts.
- Financial statements are used by airports to convey financial information about the airport to stakeholders, shareholders, citizens, business leaders and others who may desire such information.
- The income statement reveals how much money was earned and spent during a given time period (typically one year).
- The balance sheet reveals the assets, liabilities, and owner's equity of the airport.
- The statement of cash flows reveals the money that was exchanged between the airport and other organizations, entities, and individuals.

- The annual report provides a comprehensive summary of the company's performance.
- Financial ratios are used to gauge the financial performance of an airport and allow for easy comparison among airports, regardless of size.
- Revenues are either aeronautical (e.g., landing fees, fuel fees, and land lease and terminal rent) or non-aeronautical (e.g., parking, rental cars, retail concessions, food and beverage concessions, and advertising).
- Airports adopt innovative revenue-generating techniques to enhance revenues and capitalize on the land and facilities that are available.
- There are two types of airport expenditures: (1) operations and maintenance (O&M) and (2) capital.
- Airports establish fees, rates, and charges to earn revenues from tenants and airport users.
- Risk management requires airports to mitigate liability and obtain appropriate insurance.

Review Questions ⬊

1. What is the purpose of a budget?

2. Define fiscal year.

3. Explain the operating budget.

4. Explain the capital budget.

5. What is the capital improvement plan (CIP)?

6. What is the purpose of budget monitoring?

7. Explain the budget preparation process.

8. What is the purpose of financial statements?

9. Explain the income statement.

10. Explain the balance sheet.

11. Explain the statement of cash flows.

12. What is the purpose of the annual report?

13. What is the purpose of financial ratios?

14. Define aeronautical revenues, including the various types.

15. Define non-aeronautical revenues, including the various types.

16. Define non-operating revenues.

17. Explain operations and maintenance (O&M) expenditures.

18. Explain capital expenditures.

19. Explain risk management.

20. What insurance policies are available for airports and tenants?

Scenarios ↘

1. As the director of finance at a large-hub airport, you are tasked with developing the airport's budget each year. The fiscal year is from July 1 to June 30. As you get back to work after the first of the year, you know a new budget needs to be developed for next fiscal year. What steps will you take? What timeline will you develop for this process? How will you ensure the timeline is adhered to and a cost-effective budget is developed for the new fiscal year? Which budgeting technique would you prefer?

2. As the airport manager of a small hub airport, you are faced with declining revenues and reduced air service. It is imperative that you do whatever is necessary to reduce expenditures and increase revenues. What are some considerations for you in this regard?

3. As airport manager of a small airport with significant flight training activity (two on-airport flight schools) and aeronautical events (monthly fly-ins), you are concerned whether or not you are doing enough to manage risk. What insurance policies would be necessary? What are some other thoughts to manage risk?

4. Calculate the Return on Assets Ratio, Current Ratio, Operating Ratio, Net Take-Down Ratio, Debt-to-Asset Ratio, and Debt Service Safety Margin using the following data. Once calculated, interpret these ratios to gauge the financial strength of this hypothetical airport.

Current Assets	$300,526,887
Fixed Assets	$1,537,558,689
Accumulated Depreciation	$399,987
Current Liabilities	$289,668,983
Noncurrent Liabilities	$1,210,558,325
Operating Expenses	$1,800,669
Maintenance Expenses	$431,698
Operating Revenue	$32,558,559
Nonoperating Revenue	$5,000,689
Bond Principal Reserves	$2,589,332
Annual Debt Service	$358,611

5. As director of finance at a medium hub airport served by three air carriers, your director has asked you to develop a fair, but financially sustainable schedule of fees, rates, and charges. Your medium hub airport is typical of many medium hub airports with regard to services and facilities provided. Considering the financial information provided in scenario 4, the list of fees, rates, and charges categories at DFW within this chapter, and internet resources, what will your schedule look like? What will your approach be to setting fees, rates, and charges? What other data might you need to fully meet your director's request?

References and Resources for Further Study

American Association of Airport Executives. 2010. "Body of Knowledge Module 1. Finance and Administration." Washington, DC: AAAE.

Boise Airport. n.d. "Budget." Retrieved from http://www.iflyboise.com/airport-guide/about-the-airport/budget/

Dallas Fort Worth International Airport. 2007. "Chesapeake Energy Corporation Taps First Natural Gas Well at DFW International Airport." News release, May 22. Retrieved from https://www.dfwairport.com/pressroom/Chesapeake_Energy_Corporation_Taps_First_Natural_Gas_Well_Airport.pdf

Greater Orlando Aviation Authority. 2014. Air Carrier Guide. Retrieved from http://orlandoairports.net/aviation/docs/aircarrierguide.pdf#page=9

Greater Orlando Aviation Authority. 2015. *Comprehensive Annual Financial Report for the years ended September 30, 2014 and 2013*. Retrieved from http://orlandoairports.net/finance/cafr/CAFR_2014.pdf

Kemp, S. and Dunbar, E. 2003. *Budgeting for Managers*. McGraw Hill.

Merrill Lynch. 2000. *How to Read a Financial Report*. Retrieved from http://www.scribd.com/doc/11755202/Merrill-Lynch-How-to-Read-a-Financial-Report#scribd

Moore, C. and Ashford, N. 2013. *Airport Finance*. New York: Springer.

Morris, K. M. and Morris, V. B. 2004. *The Wall Street Journal Guide to Understanding Money and Investing*. 3rd ed. New York: Fireside.

Morris, K. M. and Morris, V. B. 2004. *The Wall Street Journal Guide to Understanding Personal Finance: Mortgages, Banking, Taxes, Investing, Financial Planning, Credit, Paying for Tuition*. 4th ed. New York: Fireside.

Orlando International Airport. n.d. "Parking." Retrieved from http://www.orlandoairports.net/ops/parking.htm

Chapter 14

Funding and Financial Impacts

Objectives ↘

Upon completion of this chapter, you should understand:

- the sources of capital development funding
- the need for matching funds
- the role of bonds in airport funding
- bond ratings
- the types of bonds
- the alternative minimum tax (AMT)
- PFCs
- the AIP
- the grant application process
- the role of grant assurances
- the role of internally-generated funds
- the role of state and local sources
- the method used to determine the economic impact of airports
- the impacts of airline bankruptcies on airports
- the role of performance management and benchmarking

Key Terms ↘

alternative minimum tax (AMT)
appropriation
authorization
benchmarking
bond indenture
bond rating (or grade)
bonds
capital development funding
Chapter 7 bankruptcy
Chapter 11 bankruptcy
direct economic impacts
discretionary
economic impact analysis/study
entitlement
general obligation (GO) bond

grant assurances
indirect economic impacts
induced economic impacts
interest
letter of intent (LOI)
matching funds
other transaction agreements (OTAs)
peer benchmarking
performance management
PFC-backed bond
principal
revenue bond
self-benchmarking
underwriter

In Chapter 14

FEATURES

Impact of Delta/Northwest Merger on Memphis International Airport 550

Once a thriving Northwest Airlines hub airport, Memphis International has experienced significant negative impacts from the Delta/Northwest merger.

Introduction

For airports to carry-out capital improvement in the form of new runways, new taxiways, new terminals, ground run-up enclosures, etc., funding must be secured. Depending on the extent of the project, costs can total tens of millions of dollars to one billion dollars or more. Adequate capital development funding is integral to enabling an airport to expand, improve facilities, and better develop infrastructure. This chapter focuses on sources of funding, as well as issues such as grant assurances, revenue diversion, and the economic impacts of airports.

Sources of Capital Development Funding

Funds for airport development are derived from a variety of sources, and include federal, state, and local grants; bond proceeds; passenger facility charges; airport-generated funds (from landing and terminal fees, parking, and concessions revenue); and tenant and third-party financing. During the early 2000s, **capital development funding** at airports was financed 50% via bonds, 29% via AIP, 17% via PFCs, 4% via state and local contributions, and 4% via airport revenue (see Figure 14.1).

With these many sources of capital development funding, airports often mix and match funds. Indeed, it is rare for an airport to receive 100% of the funding needed for a capital development project from a single source. **Matching funds** is the term used to refer to the act of securing multiple sources of funds for a capital development project. Vision 100 (the FAA Reauthorization Act signed on December 12, 2003) raised the federal share for capital projects from 90% to 95% for airports smaller than large-hub and medium-hub, and for airports in states participating in the State Block Grant Program (Georgia, Illinois, Michigan, Missouri, New Hampshire, North Carolina, Pennsylvania, Tennessee, Texas, and Wisconsin). The federal share for most projects at large and medium hub airports is 75% (80% for noise compatibility projects). Airports are responsible for securing additional funds to finance a project to total 100% (Kirk, 2010).

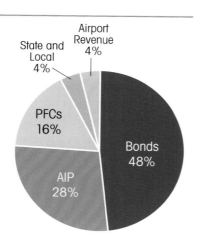

Figure 14-1. Sources of capital development funding (early 2000s).

PROCEEDS OF BONDS AND OTHER FORMS OF DEBT

Bonds, in the simplest form, represent IOUs. An investor loans money to an airport and in return gets an IOU in the form of a bond. A bond is nothing more than a piece of paper that specifies the principal amount, the interest rate, duration, and repayment terms. The **principal** is the amount the investor loaned. If the bonds are issued at $5,000 face value, an investor loaning $10,000 to the airport would receive two $5,000 bonds in return. The investor is investing money to earn a return, which is tied to the **interest** rate or coupon rate. For example, a $5,000 bond paying 5% would result in a payment of $250 annually to the investor for each $5,000 bond owed. Although this example uses an annual payment as an example, the airport may pay interest monthly, quarterly, semi-annually, or annually. The duration of the bond specifies the number of years until the bond matures. Upon maturity, the investor is repaid the full amount of the face value of the bond. This means, of course, that the investor gets 100% of their money back. At this point, the airport satisfies the IOU.

Bonds are a very common form of capital funding, and airport bond issues are often in the amount of hundreds of millions of dollars. Airports have authorization to issue bonds through the **bond indenture** (also known as the bond resolution or bond ordinance). The bond indenture defines the definition and computation of airport revenues and expenses, as well as the funds and accounts set aside for the payment of interest and principal on the bonds (debt service), and the covenants between the issuing entity and the bondholders, including a rate covenant that requires the airport operator to set rates and charges at sufficient levels to produce enough revenues to service the debt (Nichol, 2007).

Generally, institutional investors purchase airport bonds. They may be mutual funds, investment banks, or wealthy investors, but the average individual investor would likely not own any airport bonds. Bond issues are handled by an **underwriter** or several underwriters, generally in the form of large investment banks. The airport has no preference for the investors that purchase the bonds, as all will be treated the same, according to the terms of the bond issue.

Although the terms of the bond issue will be developed by the airport in consultation with the underwriter(s) based on current market conditions, it should be noted that bonds behave in certain ways. To investors, two items are important. First, the interest rate being paid is foundational. All investors desire their money to work for them and create more money, and as interest is paid by the airport, the investor makes money for their "loan" to the airport. During the recession of 2009–2011, banks were paying 1% or less on savings accounts, and certificates of deposit were not earning much more. However, in these circumstances, a bond paying 3% may be more attractive to an investor compared to lower-yielding investments.

The next item that is important, however, is the grade of bond. In other words, to what degree can the investor be assured that the airport issuing the bonds will not go bankrupt and will indeed satisfy the IOU according to the terms of the bond issue? Several agencies grade or rank bonds, and this is useful to investors in judging the financial strength of the airport issuing the bonds and the likelihood that the bonds will be satisfied according to the terms of the bond issue. Not all airports are financially strong, and ratings assigned to a bond issue should reveal this.

The three major credit rating agencies (Moody's Investors Service, Fitch Ratings, and Standard & Poor's) evaluate bonds and assign a **rating (or grade)** based on several fundamental factors relevant to the issuer's long-term and short-term risk profile (see Table 14-1).

Table 14-1. Investment grade bond ratings.

Moody's		S&P		Fitch		rating description
Long-term	Short-term	Long-term	Short-term	Long-term	Short-term	
Aaa	P-1	AAA	A-1+	AAA	F1+	Prime
Aa1		AA+		AA+		High grade
Aa2		AA		AA		
Aa3		AA-		AA-		
A1		A+	A-1	A+	F1	Upper medium grade
A2		A		A		
A3	P-2	A-	A-2	A-	F2	
Baa1		BBB+		BBB+		Lower medium grade
Baa2	P-3	BBB	A-3	BBB	F3	
Baa3		BBB-		BBB-		
Ba1	Not prime	BB+	B	BB+	B	Non-investment grade speculative
Ba2		BB		BB		
Ba3		BB-		BB-		
B1		B+		B+		Highly speculative
B2		B		B		
B3		B-		B-		
Caa1		CCC+	C	CCC	C	Substantial risks
Caa2		CCC				Extremely speculative
Caa3		CCC-				Default imminent with little prospect for recovery
Ca		CC				
		C				
C		D	/	DDD	/	In default
/				DD		
/				D		

Ratings are developed by asking the following two questions:

1. What is the risk to the debt/bondholder of not receiving timely payment of principal and interest?
2. How does the level of risk compare with that of all other debt securities?

Answering these two questions requires certain steps. First, the rating agency has a meeting with airport management to ascertain the history of the airport, airport mission and vision, management structure, management quality and experience, debt structure, and financial strength. This meeting often lasts from several hours to a full day. A tour of the airport and surrounding area may also occur. Next, the rating committee meets to consider the findings from the meeting with management and introduce the relevant risk factors and other issues that should be considered. According to Moody's, "the role of the lead analyst at the rating committee meeting is to present the rating recommendation and rationale, and to ensure that all relevant issues related to the credit are presented and discussed." (Moody's, n.d.). After 60–90 days of analysis, discussions, and evaluation, the rating will be publicly released, and subsequently an interest rate and other terms of the bond issue will be established.

General Obligation Bonds

A common form of bond for municipalities nationwide, including many airports, is the **general obligation (GO) bond**. The GO bond is supported by the overall tax base of the issuing entity. For airports owned and operated by cities, counties, or states, the state or municipality pledges general revenues (from the tax base) to back the bonds and service the debt (pay interest and ultimately repay the face value of the bonds). Taxpayer approval is required. Many airports, however, are owned and operated by an authority or other entity without the ability to levy taxes. In that case, GO bonds could still be issued, although airports that do not have tax revenue would back the bonds with airport sources of revenue (Nichol, 2007).

GO bonds are an important form of financing, especially for smaller airports. Some reasons for this include:

- Stronger credit with lower interest rates—Generally, a bond backed by the full faith and credit of a municipality is stronger than a bond backed solely by revenues, which may be uncertain. As a result, the GO bond issue will generally have a stronger rating, which then requires the airport to pay lower interest rates to attract investors. A bond rated AAA can be issued for 3%, for example, while a C-rated bond may need to pay 12% to attract investors to such a risky investment.

- Lower issuance costs

- No coverage requirement

Economic Impact of Airports

Airports are often tremendous economic engines for the communities in which they operate. This is obvious with extremely busy airports, such as Los Angeles International Airport, Hartsfield-Jackson Atlanta International Airport, Chicago O'Hare International Airport, and Dallas/Fort Worth International Airport. However, even smaller airports (with or without commercial-service) generate positive economic impacts. It's important for airports to conduct **economic impact analysis** so that these economic impacts are quantitatively determined and can be shared with municipal officials and the local community. This is especially important for smaller airports that often face opposition in the community. Sharing the good news of the positive economic impacts of the airport is a worthwhile endeavor.

Economic impact studies determine direct economic impact, as well as indirect and induced economic impact. Easiest to determine, **direct economic impacts** consist of the amount of spending that will remain within the local economy. Although some mistake direct economic impacts as the total dollars initially spent on a purchase, if a portion of these revenues is being sent to company headquarters in another state, that portion should not be included in an estimate of direct economic impacts. Thus, direct economic impacts may be less than actual revenues.

Indirect economic impacts are those impacts that result when a business makes purchases from other businesses. For example, as patrons purchase goods from airport vendors, those vendors will then make more purchases from suppliers to replenish inventory. The financial benefit to the suppliers comprises the indirect impacts.

Finally, **induced economic impacts** result from the expenditures of employee wages. For example, the employees working at an airport food and beverage concession are paid a wage and these employees in turn use these wages to purchase products and services in the local community. With an understanding of these three types of economic impacts, one can see the importance of "buying locally."

Impacts of Airline Bankruptcies on Airports

The instability of the airline industry has had substantial impacts on airports. For instance, in the months following September 11, 2001, and during the economic recession which began in 2007, many airlines completely eliminated service in smaller communities and cut back capacity at larger airports, through the use of smaller aircraft or a loss of routes or frequency of service.

Additionally, airlines with serious financial difficulty may declare bankruptcy. According to U.S. bankruptcy laws, a company may declare either Chapter 7 or Chapter 11 bankruptcy (in reference to the specific chapter of bankruptcy law). **Chapter 7 bankruptcy** is also known as liquidation or straight bankruptcy. With Chapter 7, the airline is planning to go out of business. Assets are sold, creditors are paid, and the airline then ceases to exist. This is usually a last-ditch effort after other attempts have been made at financially "repairing" the business.

The bankruptcy process which aims to allow the airline to continue operating is known as **Chapter 11 bankruptcy**. In this case, a bankruptcy judge is appointed and the airline is given time to reorganize its finances into a more stable position. Often, employee labor agreements are renegotiated, airport leases are renegotiated (with facilities possibly given up), retirement plans are altered, etc. If all goes well, the airline emerges from Chapter 11 bankruptcy in a stronger position to compete effectively. Occasionally, another airline or investor purchases the airline during the bankruptcy process. The bankrupt airline may think it is better to stay afloat, even if it means being absorbed by another airline, than to cease operations indefinitely.

Although Chapter 7 bankruptcy has a detrimental impact to airports that completely lose service by the bankrupt airline, an airline declaring bankruptcy under either Chapter 7 or 11 can create serious concern for airport management, especially if that airline serves their airport and leases facilities and space. To better cope with future airline bankruptcies, many airports have adopted

▼ Impact of Delta/Northwest Merger on Memphis International Airport

Memphis International Airport (MEM) was once the home of a Northwest Airlines hub. However, Delta Airlines and Northwest Airlines merged in 2008. With Atlanta, the site of Delta's major hub, only 370 miles to the east of Memphis, Delta announced that effective September 2013, MEM would no longer be a hub for the combined airline. This move resulted in the loss of about three-dozen flights and about 230 jobs. The reduction marked the first time in nearly 30 years that MEM would find itself without a major passenger airline hub. As a result of the merger and Delta's decision to drop MEM as a hub, passenger enplanements declined 29.4 percent between 2008 and 2012. International enplanements declined 75.7 percent. Adjusted for inflation, the total direct economic impact of MEM in FY2012 was approximately 15.5 percent less than it was in FY2007.

In reality, it made little sense for Delta to maintain two hubs in such close proximity to each other. Even so, the loss of the Northwest hub has been a significant setback for the Memphis International Airport, which now has lower passenger enplanements than it did in 2008. Fortunately, cargo is growing and the airport ranks number one in the country for total cargo handled. Mainly thanks to FedEx, cargo was up 3.8 percent from just over 4.3 billion pounds in 2008 to nearly 4.5 billion pounds in 2012. With revenue per pound averaging $2.66, this equates to more than $11.9 billion in revenue associated with cargo enplaned in Memphis.

("An Economic Assessment," n.d.; Mutzabaugh, 2013)

shorter lease terms and shorter-term use agreements. In this way, the airport is afforded more flexibility in addressing airline bankruptcies.

With possible effects similar to airline bankruptcy, a merger of two airlines may result in reduced airline service at an airport. For instance, the two merged airlines will likely consolidate operations and routes, which may negatively impact an airport. Consider an airport served by only two airlines. If these two airlines merge, the airport is now served by only one airline. With no competition, airfares may increase, and the space needed by the one airline will likely be less than the space previously needed by the two airlines combined. Thus, lease revenues would be reduced.

Performance Management and Benchmarking

To assist with determining the strength of performance (financial or otherwise) of the airport, airports often integrate **performance management** and **benchmarking**. Indeed, it can be quite helpful to airport management to know how the competition is performing and what they are doing to acquire new air service, increase parking revenues, etc. According to the Infrastructure Management Group (2010, p.10):

> Measuring and managing performance is crucial to airport success. Performance measurement is not just about identifying and tracking some numbers; it is ultimately about managing to achieve results. Performance measurement is a cyclical process that starts with identifying the ultimate outcomes an airport wants to achieve, such as safety, customer service, and financial success.

Airports use airport performance indicators (API) to judge their performance among peer airports. Although airports may be interested in different metrics or measurements, the following are common APIs (by category) in use among airports today:
- Airfield operations
  › Aircraft operations
- Air service
  › Cargo tons—Change over prior period
  › Enplanements—Change over prior period
  › Nonstop destinations—Change in number of domestic and international
  › Passenger flights—Change in number of domestic and international
- Concessions
  › Concession revenue to the airport as percent of total operating revenue
  › Concession revenue to the airport per enplaned passenger
  › Rental car revenue to the airport per destination passenger

- Financial
  - › Airline cost per enplaned passenger
  - › Airport cost per enplaned passenger
  - › Bond rating
  - › Days unrestricted cash on hand
  - › Debt per enplanement
  - › Debt service coverage ratio
  - › Non-aeronautical operating revenue as percent of total operating revenue
  - › Non-aeronautical operating revenue per enplanement
  - › Operating cost per enplanement
- General aviation
  - › Based aircraft
  - › Fuel use/sales—Change over prior period
  - › Hangar rental and ground lease income
- Human resources
  - › Minority/Women/DBE participation rate; actual versus cost
  - › Salary + Wages + Benefits cost as a percent of total operating cost
  - › Salary + wages + Benefits cost per airport employee
  - › Employee turnover
- Parking
  - › Parking revenue to the airport per originating passenger
- Planning/construction
  - › Construction projects—Actual versus budgeted costs of significant projects
- Properties/contracts
  - › Landing fee rate
- Safety risk management
  - › Employee accidents and injuries—Lost work days
- Service quality
  - › Customer satisfaction with airport

(Hazel, Blais, Browne, & Benzon, 2011).

As airports attempt to measure their performance among their peers, benchmarking is crucial. In practice, this can include both self-benchmarking and peer benchmarking. **Self-benchmarking** allows an airport to determine how well it is doing internally, compared perhaps to prior years or quarters. **Peer benchmarking**, on the other hand, requires the airport to compare its performance with peer airports. The APIs listed above are used in both techniques, with most APIs suited to self-benchmarking, some suited to peer benchmarking, and some suited to both (Hazel, et al., 2011).

Concluding Thoughts

Airports typically have capital development needs that amount of millions of dollars. Fortunately, an airport may obtain funding for these projects from a variety of sources. However, the airport director must be proactive and diligent in pursuing funding from these sources. Additionally, although AIP funding is "free" funding, it does come with strings attached in the form of grant assurances. It is imperative for the airport to comply with these numerous assurances to avoid jeopardizing future AIP funds.

Chapter Summary

- Funds for airport development are derived from a variety of sources and include federal, state, and local grants; bond proceeds; passenger facility charges; airport-generated funds (from landing and terminal fees, parking, and concessions revenue); and tenant and third-party financing.

- Bonds represent an IOU, and require the bond issuer to pay regular interest and eventually pay off the bond principal.

- A bond issue is assigned a rating or grade by one or more of the bond rating agencies to enable potential investors to determine the strength of the firm issuing the bonds.

- The general obligation (GO) bond is a common form of bond for municipalities nationwide, including many airports, and is supported by the overall tax base of the issuing entity.

- The revenue bond is becoming more common among airports and is supported by revenues of the issuing entity.

- The PFC-backed bond is a form of revenue bond that is supported by PFCs assessed by the airport.

- Bonds issued on future grant funds require a letter of intent from the FAA.

- The alternative minimum tax was designed to ensure that all taxpayers pay at least a minimum amount of federal taxes on their income, preventing individual taxpayers from taking unfair advantage of the various federal tax preferences and incentives. Tax-exempt governmental bonds are not subject to the AMT.

- PFCs allow airports that support millions of passengers annually to tap into a significant revenue source authorized by the FAA by assessing a facility charge on each passenger.

- The Airport Improvement Program (AIP), funded by the Airport and Airway Trust Fund, generates funding for AIP-eligible capital development at airports.

- AIP entitlements are based on passenger enplanements, whereas AIP discretionary funds are at the discretion of Congress and include funds for noise programs, the military airport program, reliever airports, and projects that enhance capacity, safety, and security.
- The grant application process includes submitting a five-year CIP, developing a project schedule, developing a project scope, completing an environmental review, hiring a consultant and designing the project, advertising and awarding the contract, constructing the project, and submitting grant closeout documentation.
- Grant assurances are the "strings" attached to an AIP grant, requiring the airport to comply with numerous requirements.
- Internally generated funds can be set aside to provide some or all of the matching funds for a grant.
- State and local funding may also be available to airports for capital development.
- Economic impact studies determine direct economic impact, as well as indirect and induced economic impact.
- Chapter 7 bankruptcy is also known as liquidation or straight bankruptcy. With Chapter 7, the airline is planning to go out of business.
- Chapter 11 bankruptcy allows the airline to continue operating, and requires the airline to reorganize operations.
- Airports often integrate performance management and benchmarking to assist in determining the strength of their performance (financial or otherwise). Benchmarking is crucial in measuring performance against peer airports.
- Airports use airport performance indicators to judge their performance among peer airports.

Review Questions ↘

1. List the sources available to airports in securing funding for capital development.

2. Explain the typical breakdown of capital development funding sources.

3. Explain matching funds.

4. Define bond indenture.

5. Explain the role of the underwriter.

6. What two questions are first asked by the rating agencies when rating a bond issue?

7. Define general obligation (GO) bonds.

8. Why are GO bonds an important form of financing, especially for smaller airports?

9. Define revenue bonds.

10. Define PFC-backed bonds.

11. Define bonds to be backed by future grants.

12. Define alternative minimum tax.

13. Explain passenger facility charges.

14. Define AIP entitlements funds.

15. Define AIP discretionary funds.

16. Describe the grant application process.

17. Explain grant assurances.

18. What impact do airline bankruptcies have on airports?

19. Explain Chapter 7 and Chapter 11 bankruptcies.

20. Explain performance management and benchmarking.

Scenarios ↘

1. As airport manager of a nonhub airport with 23,000 enplanements annually, you are faced with a CIP that has over $6 million in capital improvements planned for the next five years. What options are available to secure funding? Based on the size of the airport, which options are most practical?

2. As the CFO of a large hub airport with 30 million enplanements, you are considering applying for authorization to collect a $4.50 PFC. Your airport is currently authorized to collect a $3.00 PFC. Would it be more advantageous to collect a $4.50 PFC, considering the AIP funding that would have to be foregone?

3. As the newly hired director of performance management at a large hub airport, you are considering how to best measure the performance of the airport. This will require benchmarking and comparison to peer airports. Which airport performance indicators (API) will you use and why?

4. The airport for which you serve as director of finance is preparing a $110 million bond issue. You are tasked with preparing for a visit by a bond rating agency. How do you prepare? Develop a schedule for their two-day visit.

5. The community has recently been vocal in their opposition of the airport for which you serve as airport director. They seem to think your airport does nothing for the local community. Although your airport is only a GA airport, it clearly plays an important role in the community. Conduct online research on airport economic impacts. Review some airport economic impact studies and begin preparing your response to the community. Your goal is to determine your airport's economic impacts and show how beneficial your airport is to the local economy.

References and Resources for Further Study

Bureau of Transportation Statistics (BTS). n.d. Airline Financial Data Press Releases. Retrieved from http://www.rita.dot.gov/bts/sites/rita.dot.gov.bts/files/press_releases/airline_financial_data.html

"An Economic Assessment of the Impact of the Memphis International Airport." n.d. Accessed May 2015 at http://memphis.edu/sbber/pdfs/impactstudies/mem_economic_impact_2012_executive_summary.pdf

Federal Aviation Administration (FAA). 2012a. "Overview: What is AIP?" Retrieved from http://www.faa.gov/airports/aip/overview/

————. 2012b. 2013–2017 National Plan of Integrated Airport Systems (NPIAS). Retrieved from http://www.faa.gov/airports/planning_capacity/npias/reports/

————. 2014a. "Current Aviation Excise Tax Structure." Retrieved from http://www.faa.gov/about/office_org/headquarters_offices/apl/aatf/media/14.1.17ExciseTaxStructureCalendar2014.pdf

————. 2014b. Grant Assurances Airport Sponsors. Retrieved from http://www.faa.gov/airports/aip/grant_assurances/media/airport-sponsor-assurances-aip.pdf

Hazel, R. A., J. D. Blais, T. J. Browne, and D. M. Benzon. 2011. "Resource Guide to Airport Performance Indicators." ACRP Report 19A. Washington, DC: Transportation Research Board.

Infrastructure Management Group. 2010. "Developing an Airport Performance-Measurement System." ACRP Report 19. Washington, DC: Transportation Research Board.

Kirk, R. 2010. "Airport Improvement Program: Reauthorization Issues for Congress." Congressional Research Service.

Moody's. n.d. "How to Get Rated." Retrieved from https://www.moodys.com/ratings-process/How-to-Get-Rated/002001

Mutzabaugh, B. 2013. "Delta to pull plug on Memphis hub after Labor Day." *USA Today*, June 4. Retrieved from http://www.usatoday.com/story/todayinthesky/2013/06/04/delta-air-lines-to-pull-plug-on-memphis-hub/2390515/

Nichol, C. 2007. "Innovative Finance and Alternative Sources of Revenue for Airports." ACRP Synthesis 1. Washington, DC: Transportation Research Board.

Future Challenges and Opportunities

Objectives ↘

Upon completion of this chapter, you should be able to explain the challenges and opportunities presented by:

- airline bankruptcies and mergers.
- new large aircraft.
- capital development funding.
- unfunded federal mandates.
- passenger leakage.
- customer service.
- sustainability.
- airside congestion.
- unmanned systems.

Key Terms ↘

costs per enplaned passenger (CPE)

unmanned aircraft system (UAS)

In Chapter 15

FEATURES

Introduction

One thing all airport leaders have in common is the need to meet future challenges they and their airports will face. The aviation industry is dynamic, requiring airport leaders to forecast, adjust plans as necessary, and proactively meet future challenges. To be successful, this requires an "outside-the-box" mindset. Airport leaders who adopt the attitude of "we've always done it that way" and who have an "old school" mentality will likely multiply the challenges they face. On the other hand, airport leaders who innovate, lead with an outstretched hand, and stay in touch with industry trends will be much better able to meet future challenges head on.

Airline Bankruptcies and Mergers

The airline industry is in an ever-evolving state. Especially since deregulation of the industry in 1978, we have witnessed numerous bankruptcies, mergers, and acquisitions. The airline industry of today is a far cry from that of 1978. As a result, airports have been forced to adjust to this dynamic industry. Although GA airports exist to serve the GA industry, commercial-service airports mainly serve air carriers. And even with a substantially larger revenue base than most GA airports, these commercial-service airports are at the mercy of the air carriers and the seemingly monthly announcements of bankruptcies, mergers, etc.

All of this activity in the industry does not lead to expansion. Rather, it leads to consolidation of the industry. And this consolidation greatly impacts airports. For instance, consider the commercial-service airport served by only one air carrier. What if that sole air carrier declares bankruptcy? That airport will suddenly be faced with no commercial service, which can be severely detrimental to a community. Or consider an airport that is served by two air carriers, each having about 50 percent of the market. What if these two carriers merge? Suddenly, this airport will be served by only one air carrier, and due to routes previously shared by the two carriers, the airport may see a reduction in service beyond the anticipated 50 percent previously had by the independent air carrier.

In essence, commercial-service airports have a vested interested in maintaining a healthy airline industry with numerous carriers. Competition is good for business, resulting in lower airfares for consumers and more of a cushion for an airport. Airports served by a dozen or so air carriers are in a much better position than airports served by a sole air carrier. Airports would like to avoid "putting all their eggs in one basket." This requires airports to cater to their air carriers, just as they cater to passengers and meeters and greeters.

Just how should an airport do this? First, airports should focus on minimizing costs for airlines, often measured in terms of **cost per enplaned passenger (CPE)**. This includes landing fees, terminal rent, baggage claim rent, and other fees charged to the airlines. Although airports are expected to charge airlines reasonable fees for the facilities they use, if an airport focuses on increasing non-aeronautical revenues, more reasonable fees can be charged to the airlines. Additionally, airports should practice excellent customer service to the airlines. On a practical level, this means possibly creating an airline station manager's committee or association. Additionally, any work requests or immediate repairs phoned in by an airline to the airport should be addressed in a timely manner. The airlines should feel they are well taken care of and appreciated by the airport. It is also helpful for senior airport personnel to visit with the airlines at their corporate headquarters at least annually. Proactively stressing the positive attributes of the airport and community to the airline's route planners and senior leadership can develop and continue a positive relationship that may serve the airport well into the future. For instance, if an airline begins to experience financial difficulty and consider service cutbacks, a supportive airport may receive a more favorable review than an airport that is not as supportive.

In sum, senior airport personnel should view airlines serving their airport as partners in the health of the airport. Having sufficient airline service for the community will actually make the airport director appear quite successful. Many airport boards and communities place sufficient airline service as a top priority, meaning they equate this airline service with success on the part of the airport director. The irony is that oftentimes the airport director has little to do with the airline service at an airport, although the success of this individual is judged in light of this service. True, the airport director can meet with airline route planners and senior leadership, but airlines are for-profit enterprises and if there is not enough demand in a community to ensure the airline will at least break even, the airline won't begin service regardless of the airport director's good intentions. Incentives (such as reduced or no landing fees for a short period time, such as six months) may entice a carrier to take a chance on a community, but if revenues don't materialize, the airline won't hesitate to pull out.

New Large Aircraft

In past years, airports were not too concerned with aircraft that might exceed the airport's limits. At least at most commercial-service airports, little thought generally was given to the load limits of runways, taxiways, and ramps; wingtip clearances for aircraft maneuvering the airfield; or passenger loads on terminal buildings. However, in today's world of larger aircraft able to accommodate up to almost 900 passengers, airport leaders must consider the impact of these new large aircraft on their airport—both airside and landside.

FAA Advisory Circular 150/5300-13A, *Airport Design* (introduced in Chapter 5), clearly spells out the aircraft approach category, airplane design group, and visibility minimums that make up the runway design code. The Airbus A380 is the first civilian aircraft that falls into Airplane Design Group VI (Figure 15-1). Prior to the A380 entering service, Group V was the largest category of civilian aircraft that would be expected to serve an airport. What

Figure 15-1.
Airbus A380.

(Nan Phanitsuda
Sophonpanasak, Denver
International Airport)

challenges do this new Group VI aircraft bring to an airport? Design criteria will be impacted, as adequate wingtip clearance, for example, is provided for this and other large aircraft.

Although an airport may request a modification to standards (as discussed in Chapter 7), an airport desiring to meet the design requirements of a Group VI aircraft will be required to alter various components of the airfield. For instance, an existing E-V airport will need to expand the runway from 150 feet in width to 200 feet in width to become an E-VI airport. Additionally, taxiways will need to be widened from 70 feet to 100 feet in width. Bringing an entire airfield up to these standards requires a substantial investment. And if the Group VI aircraft will only service the airport several times per week, an airport may decide to petition the FAA for a modification to standards.

Also consider the impacts on the landside of the new large aircraft. Traditionally, when a Boeing 737 parks at a gate, only about 130 passengers unload. However, if an A380 parks at the gate, more than 500 (and up to 853) may unload. This large number of passengers will impact the restrooms, food and beverage, retail, people movers, baggage claim, rental cars, taxis, hotel shuttles, etc. In essence, a fully loaded A380 will have the same impact on the landside as more than six arriving 737s. On the airfield, however, the A380 represents one operation, just as a 737 does.

Capital Development Funding

Airports are always planning 10–20 years into the future to meet projected demand, which is why an airport master plan commonly has a 20-year planning horizon. If an airport were to wait until projected demand is realized before breaking ground on a new terminal or parking garage, for instance, it would be too late. From planning to completion, large capital development projects take years to complete, so planning ahead is imperative. Due to this, it seems that many airports (especially commercial-service) always have a construction project underway. This capital development can be expensive and capital development funding must be in place for such projects.

As explained in Chapter 14, capital development funding can come from many different sources, including bonds, PFCs, AIP, internally generated, and state and local sources. Possibly the most challenging of these for airports is AIP funding. This is true even today. For the 2013–2017 timeframe, for example, $42.5 billion in AIP-eligible capital development projects were identified in the NPIAS, which amounts to $8.5 billion annually. However, AIP grants rarely total much more than $3 billion annually. This amounts to more than $5.5 billion in annual airport capital development needs that are not met by AIP grants. Clearly, this is a huge shortfall. Although it would not be feasible for the FAA to grant more AIP funds to airports than the Airport and Airway Trust Fund can generate, it is important for airport leadership to convey the importance of capital development funding to elected representatives who may have an impact on securing more funding for airports in the future.

Airports have been forced to either obtain funding from other sources (such as bonds, PFCs, and retained earnings) or forgo planned improvements. In particular, PFCs have been helpful, with collections typically exceeding $2 billion annually. However, this challenge is not likely to go away; as construction costs increase and airport capital development needs grow, funding for capital development will become increasingly needed.

Unfunded Federal Mandates

Unfunded federal mandates refers to regulatory requirements that are mandatory, cost money to meet, and yet don't have any funding tied to them. In essence, airports are asked by the FAA or TSA to adopt a certain measure, which may cost hundreds of thousands of dollars or more to implement, and then are required to find the money to implement the measure. Although certain airports may have sufficient revenues to meet these mandates, others may have difficulty in securing the financing needed to comply.

The challenge for airports is that they are tasked with a new regulation or requirement, and yet are forced to find their own source of funds to pay for the projects, personnel, or other expenses associated with meeting the new regulation or requirement. A simple example was the requirement for airports in the FAA southeast region to mark runway closures with a raised, lighted "X." Prior to this requirement, there were inexpensive ways to mark closed runways, such as with yellow-painted plywood secured with sandbags. With the new requirement, airports were forced to purchase lighted Xs at a cost of about $50,000 each. Where did this money come from? True, an airport could obtain funding through various sources, but the FAA didn't send a $100,000 check to each of the certificated airports in the southern region to purchase the required lighted Xs.

Unfunded federal mandates will require airport leadership to be more innovative in securing funds to comply with these mandates. Proactive airport leaders have found that it is wise to develop a contingency fund for unplanned expenses, including unfunded mandates.

Passenger Leakage

Commercial-service airports must always remain aware of their passenger enplanements. This number changes regularly and can impact the categorization of the airport (such as large hub) as well as funding. In essence, passenger leakage refers to individuals living in the local area or metropolitan statistical area (MSA) that, rather than take a flight out of their local airport, choose instead to drive an hour or several hours away to take a flight out of another airport. By driving out of the local area and taking a flight out of a competing airport, the local airport experiences leakage because the airport "lost" a potential passenger.

Airport leaders agree that passenger leakage such as this cannot be completely eliminated. Individuals have freedom of choice. They can choose to fly out of Airport A or Airport B. They can also choose to drive, take the bus, or choose not to go. Another factor involves the motivation for choosing to fly out of another airport. Airfares greatly affect this decision. Non-stop flights also have an impact on this decision.

Passenger Retention Analysis at Gillette–Campbell County Airport

Located in Gillette, Wyoming, Gillette–Campbell County Airport, through their consultant, performed a passenger retention analysis in March 2013. This airport, a nonhub airport, enjoyed 32,714 enplaned passengers in 2014 and was served by two air carriers—Delta and United. With a catchment area of 40,433, Gillette had nonstop service to two major hubs, Denver and Salt Lake City. According to the study, Gillette–Campbell County Airport retained 59 percent of all passengers over the survey period. However, the study found that passengers leaked to Rapid City, South Dakota, a two-hour drive, as well as Denver, Colorado, a nearly six-hour drive. Passengers leaking to Rapid City most often chose United, Delta, or American. Passengers leaking to Denver most often chose air carriers that do not serve Gillette, often low-cost carriers like Frontier and Southwest. The study found that leakage of passengers from Gillette is decreasing overall, likely due to the finding that average airfares in Gillette are falling, with the price gap between Gillette and nearby airports shrinking. Generally, passengers drive to another airport outside their local area for either lower airfares or more direct and better service. Airports that address these issues, in coordination with air carriers, can minimize leakage.

(Gillette Campbell County Airport, 2013)

Consider these factors that may affect an individual's decision on which flight to take:

- Airline (frequent flyer miles, safety record, baggage fees, etc.)
- Number of intermediate stops (non-stops are usually much preferred)
- Time of departure (convenient departure times are much preferred)
- Airfare (lower cost a priority)
- Airport parking and services (pricing, convenience, etc.)
- Distance from competing airport (number of miles the individual must drive, with cost of fuel part of the decision)

Even with these variables, airport leaders agree that airports can make a concerted effort to minimize leakage. Advertising campaigns can be initiated to encourage individuals in the local area to choose their local airport. Any new airline service (including seasonal, new airlines, or increased frequency) should be advertised heavily in the local community. An airline may pay for this, but the airport can also play a part in "selling" the airport to the local community. In other words, it is important to make it a difficult decision for an individual considering driving to an airport outside the local area. The easy decision should be to utilize the local airport (see Figure 15-2).

Figure 15-2.
Advertising air service: Emphasizing low fares may help reduce passenger leakage.

(Wikimedia Commons; see credit on page 624)

Customer Service

On all levels, airport employees' priority must be to provide exceptional customer service. Especially today, with the extensive use of technology (including automated phone systems) and numerous charges for what was free in the past (such as airline baggage fees), customer service in some areas of the aviation industry is almost nonexistent. With this realization, airports can step up and provide a positive customer experience, even for passengers who have had a poor experience with an airline in the past.

Providing exceptional customer service requires a daily focus on the customer (both internal and external) and this begins with the commitment of senior airport leadership. It requires employees to anticipate customer needs and work to satisfy those needs before the customer even asks. There are FBOs in this country that are well-known for providing exceptional customer service and it often means that their personnel anticipate customer needs, strive to meet

AIRPORT MANAGEMENT

those needs, and exceed customer expectations—treating everyone as if they are the CEO of a company arriving onto the ramp (flight crew included). To encourage exceptional customer service, the airport director could, for example, begin a new customer service initiative with customer service training for employees, and an award program for employees going above and beyond.

Customer service will remain a future challenge for airports because as new employees are hired and others resign or retire, the culture of the organization may change, requiring a constant reprioritizing of airport values, including customer service. Additionally, customer service can begin to suffer as employees become comfortable and somewhat uninvolved over the years. If the airport director initiates a new customer service initiative with training provided to employees, but then does nothing else, it will be only a matter of years (if not months) before customer service will suffer once again. And especially if the airport has a negative culture, it will take time to change the culture and obtain buy-in from employees regarding the benefits of providing exceptional customer service. It does, after all, require additional effort on the part of employees. But this is effort well expended.

Sustainability Initiatives

Airports also must remain aware of public perception. This often revolves around the impact airports have on the environment. Proactive airport leaders are aware of this and remain committed to reducing their airport's carbon footprint. Fortunately, airports have various options for accomplishing this.

A common sustainability initiative involves the use of renewable sources of energy. This may include the use of solar, wind, water, geothermal, and biomass. Of these renewable sources, airports have most commonly capitalized on solar energy, for several reasons. Airports often occupy hundreds if not thousands of acres with ready access to the sun (Figure 15-3). Also, photovoltaic panels can

Figure 15-3.
Use of solar power as a source of renewable energy at an airport.

(bspguy/Bigstock.com)

be installed close to the ground, minimizing any concerns with height restrictions (unlike with wind turbines). Of course, a solar power installation can be expensive, requiring the airport leader to be innovative in securing funds for such a worthwhile project.

In addition to capitalizing on renewable sources of energy, airports proactive in this area have developed environmentally friendly buildings, such as LEED-certified terminal buildings. These may include air filtration systems, low flow or waterless toilets, natural light via skylights, low energy consumption lighting, sustainable building materials, etc. To achieve this, airport leaders must specify the need for an environmentally friendly building in the initial planning stages as architects and engineers are developing the plans for the building.

Aircraft noise is always a challenge for airports and airport leaders must remain aware of the impacts of negative publicity associated with aircraft noise. Initiatives can be undertaken to minimize aircraft noise, including noise abatement programs, hiring a noise officer, installing a noise monitoring system, and building a ground run-up enclosure to allow aircraft to be powered above idle while on the ground, with much of the resulting noise absorbed and deflected upward.

In sum, environmental challenges will never cease, requiring airport leaders to be proactive in this area. Likely, this will become even more important in the future, especially as discussions of global warming continue.

Airside Congestion

Some airports, especially commercial-service airports located in major metropolitan areas, experience times when demand exceeds capacity, resulting in delays and even congestion on the airfield (Figure 15-4). With AIP funding levels below what would be required at many airports to increase capacity with airfield improvements, airports may not be increasing capacity at the rate needed by the airlines. Generally, airports only have so much land and room to expand. For example, San Diego International Airport has only one runway and doesn't have land for another. Thus, the airport's available land constrains its

Figure 15-4.
Airfield congestion.

capacity today and in the future. Other airports, like Hartsfield-Jackson Atlanta International Airport, have created more capacity by building new runways and airfield features such as end-around taxiways and high-speed exits, but the sheer number of operations and enplanements (along with airlines' tightly bunched schedules) ensure that airfield demand exceeds capacity at certain times.

As such, congestion on the airfield will continue to challenge airport leaders in the future. It will be important for airport leaders to not only adopt efforts to increase capacity and better utilize existing capacity, but also petition the airlines to de-peak their flight schedules so that arrivals and departures are not so bunched. Clearly, if airlines schedule ten arrivals at 8:30, delays will result. However, if those ten arrivals are spread out over even a ten-minute period, the airfield could possibly accommodate the demand with minimal or no delay.

Unmanned Aircraft Systems

An **unmanned aircraft system (UAS)** includes the unmanned aircraft (UA) and all of the associated support equipment, such as control station, data links, telemetry, communications and navigation equipment, required to operate the unmanned aircraft. The UA is the flying portion of the system, flown by a pilot via a ground control system, or autonomously through use of an on-board computer, communication links, and any additional equipment that is necessary for the UA to operate safely. Although the military has been using UAS dating back to WWI, commercial use of UAS is a much more recent phenomenon (FAA, 2015).

According to the FAA, "Unmanned aircraft systems (UAS) are inherently different from manned aircraft. Introducing UAS into the nation's airspace is challenging for both the FAA and aviation community, because the U.S. has the busiest, most complex airspace in the world" (FAA, 2015). However, after approving six UAS test sites in 2014/2015, the FAA issued an NPRM, Operation and Certification of Small Unmanned Aircraft Systems, on February 23, 2015. This NPRM presents proposed guidelines for commercial use of UAS that weigh less than 55 pounds. According to this proposed rule, among other requirements, the operation of small UAS must remain within visual line of sight by the operator or visual observer, operation will be restricted to daylight only, UAS may operate at a maximum altitude of 500 feet AGL, and operators will be required to obtain an unmanned aircraft operator certificate with a small UAS rating.

Clearly, the UAS landscape is continuing to evolve, with many significant changes expected in the near future. There is great demand by firms of all types to operate UAS in the national airspace system for profit-driven purposes. Airports leaders must remain current on this continually changing landscape and determine what impact, if any, UAS will have on their airport and aircraft operations. Although UAS are being integrated into the national airspace system, albeit cautiously by the FAA, airport leaders will need to stand up to protect their airports and ensure the safety of aircraft operating into and out of their facility. That being said, an airport leader should not simply avoid this reality. For the innovative airport leader, the increasing popularity of UAS may present significant opportunities for new and enhanced uses of the airport and airport property.

Concluding Thoughts

Airport leaders of the future will need to be innovative, proactive, and well-aware of current aviation trends affecting the airport industry. Although some of this can be learned, this textbook does not attempt to be the sole resource for the airport professional. For those students desiring to enter the airport industry, it is important to learn the history, the terms and concepts, and the practical application of this knowledge. The scenarios in this textbook were designed to allow the reader to apply knowledge gained toward solving real-world issues. Likewise, the case studies were designed to provide practical insight into real-world airport issues that were encountered and successfully resolved. In addition to this resource, it is important to learn from professionals active in the industry, whether through an internship or a less-formal shadowing arrangement. It is only through practical knowledge and actual airport experience that airport professionals will be prepared to meet the future challenges of the airport industry.

Chapter Summary

- The airline industry is dynamic and quite volatile, with mergers and acquisitions commonplace, especially in a post-deregulated environment.

- Airports serving air carriers should strive to minimize cost per enplaned passenger.

- The impacts of new large aircraft, such as the A380, must be considered in terminal design, airfield design, landside access, etc.

- The methods by which to fund capital development, and the amount of funding available for capital development, will remain a challenge for airports.

- Unfunded federal mandates are becoming the norm, and airports will be required to develop alternative financing strategies to fund compliance with these mandates.

- Air carrier airports are always concerned about passenger leakage, especially if an airport is located within driving distance to an alternative air carrier airport. Thus, creative strategies of minimizing passenger leakage must be considered to minimize this to the extent possible.

- In the service-oriented airline industry, airports must place an emphasis on meeting customer needs. Offering top-notch customer service requires consistently exceeding customer expectations.

- Environmental concerns are now a mainstream topic and airports that focus on implementing green initiatives will be welcomed by the community.

- As the industry grows, and few (if any) new air carrier airports are built, congestion will continue to increase. Airports must creatively adopt strategies to minimize congestion whenever possible, as this will provide benefits to airlines, passengers, air traffic control, other users, and the airport itself.

- Unmanned aircraft systems and their integration in the national airspace system continues to evolve, requiring airports to remain current on this topic.

Review Questions ↘

1. Considering the current industry climate, which airlines are likely to merge and why?

2. Explain the manner in which airline mergers are beneficial for consumers.

3. Explain the manner in which airline mergers are detrimental to consumers.

4. Should airlines that are on the verge of bankruptcy be allowed to go out of business?

5. In what ways do new large aircraft create better efficiencies for airports?

6. Explain the challenges for airports of new large aircraft.

7. Discuss the importance of adopting an innovative mindset in securing capital development funding.

8. Why is more than one source of capital development funding often necessary to fully fund a project?

9. If unfunded mandates are such a concern, what can airport professionals do to meet this challenge?

10. Why is customer service such a challenge for airports?

11. Describe a poor customer service experience you've had.

12. Explain passenger leakage.

13. How can an airport prevent leakage?

14. Explain why customer service is important.

15. Why are many airports adopting green initiatives?

16. What are the most common green initiatives adopted by airports?

17. How common is airside congestion at commercial-service airports?

18. What are some methods to ease airside congestion at airports?

19. What are some methods to ease landside congestion at airports?

20. What do you consider to be the most significant challenge confronting airports over the next ten years, and why?

Scenarios ↘

1. As executive director of a large hub airport, you are in the middle of a master plan update. As part of this process, you have asked the consultant responsible for the master plan update to consider future challenges that your airport may face. Why is this important? Are there any challenges not addressed in this chapter that you feel could affect your airport in the future? Why?

2. As the director of planning at a large hub, Group V airport, you are told by the executive director that Singapore Airlines may begin service with A380 aircraft in 6–9 months. What options are available to you in accommodating this aircraft?

3. As the director of marketing at a small hub airport, your job performance is judged in part by the number of passengers enplaned at the airport. Concern has been expressed by the amount of leakage, as many potential passengers in the local area drive two hours south to take flights that are oftentimes less expensive. Passenger enplanements at your airport have declined 9 percent from the previous year since low-fare service was introduced by Allegiant at this other airport. How do you counteract this leakage? Develop a plan to confront this challenge head on.

References and Resources for Further Study

Federal Aviation Administration. 2015. "Unmanned Aircraft Systems." Retrieved from https://www.faa.gov/uas/

Gillette Campbell County Airport. 2013. Passenger Retention Analysis. Retrieved at http://www.ccgov.net/ArchiveCenter/ViewFile/Item/129

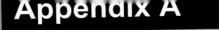

Airport Solar Farm

Developed by Gene Conrad, C.M. & Brett Fay, C.M.
Lakeland Linder Regional Airport

BACKGROUND

High operational costs continue to be a major issue for airports across the country and can create significant obstacles to achieving financial self-sufficiency. With energy rates continuing to rise, reducing the cost of electricity at airports has never been more important. In a continuing effort to lower energy costs and reduce environmental impacts, the Lakeland Linder Regional Airport began discussing the possibility of a large solar panel installation to be located on the airport in late 2007. The concept involved creating a 40-acre solar farm on the western edge of the airport property, outside of the Airport Operations Area. To ensure the realization of this new alternative energy source, the airport would need to secure funding and address a wide range of issues and challenges.

FUNDING

The first major step in building this solar farm was to secure funding for the project. The funding would be established through a unique public–private partnership between the City of Lakeland and Sun Edison. In the agreement, Sun Edison would pay for the construction of the solar farm and the City of Lakeland would purchase the electricity for a long term fixed rate over the next twenty five years. The airport would provide the land for the solar farm in exchange for energy credits at a rate of two cents per kilowatt-hour (kWh). This agreement would generate nearly $250,000 annually for the airport with no cost associated with planning or construction. With clear benefits to the airport and surrounding communities, a suitable location would need to be agreed upon.

LOCATION

It was decided that determining a suitable location for the airport solar farm would be critical to the overall success of the project. After conducting a site survey and review of the airport master plan, the airport determined that locating the solar field just outside of the existing runway protection zone (RPZ) for runway 9/27 would be the optimal location. This determination was based on several critical factors. First, the solar panels would require an east/west orientation to track the sun throughout the day and maximize efficiency. Next, all equipment would need to be located in an area that would not create any interference with navigational aids or air traffic operations. Finally, selecting a location that would not hinder the future development plans for the airport was critical. The final location resulted in a site that would meet all requirements for both the airport and the project. After determining a final location, several potential safety concerns were identified and would need to be thoroughly evaluated before the project could move forward.

Figure A-1.
Solar farm with airport in the background.

(Brett Fay, C.M.)

GLARE

Safety in and around the airport environment is paramount and remains at the forefront of any decision regarding site selection and location. The airport had been proactive in addressing any potential safety concerns early in the project development phase. However, due to the location of the solar panels, the Federal Aviation Administration was concerned that light reflecting from the solar panels had the potential to cause glare for pilots landing or departing Runway 9/27. Subsequently, the airport conducted a "glare analysis" to determine any potential negative effects on pilot visibility. The results of the analysis concluded that photovoltaic panels absorb nearly two-thirds of all light reaching the panels. In addition, new solar panels have an anti-reflective coating which further reduces the amount of sunlight reflected. The result is highly efficient solar panels that produce a glare potential similar to that of grassy vegetation (see Figure A-2).

ENVIRONMENTAL

In addition to safety issues, the airport made a concerted effort to identify any potential environmental hazards that might be associated with the project. Even when a project is inherently environmentally friendly, there can be unintended environmental impacts associated with the construction. The City of Lakeland conducted an environmental study that identified several issues requiring

Airport Operations Department Administrative Challenges

Developed by Richard Steele, C.M.
Los Angeles World Airports

AIRPORT OPERATIONS DEPARTMENT OVERVIEW

This airport is a medium hub, FAA Class I, TSA Category I airport. The FAA air traffic control tower (ATCT) is open 24 hours per day. The airfield includes two intersecting runways, and five parallel taxiways with appropriate intersecting taxiways. There are four fuel handling companies and one fuel farm on the property. The operations department includes an Airside Operations Section, Communications Center Section, and the Airport ID Badging Section. Airside Operations and the Communications Center must be staffed 24 hours per day. Airside Operations responsibilities include airfield operations and terminal operations. There is a separate Landside Operations Department during the regular work week, but the Airside Operations personnel cover the landside functions after-hours and on weekends and holidays. There is a $5,000 line item for training in the department operating and maintenance (O&M) budget. There are a total of 15 operations personnel with responsibilities divided as follows:

- *Airside Operations Section:* Five operations supervisors documented as being trained in compliance with 14 CFR Part 139 to conduct duties under the airport certification manual (ACM), which includes requirements of Subpart D—Operations of Part 139, as well as respond to all 49 CFR Part 1542—Airport Security related incidents.

- *Communications (Comm.) Center Section:* One communications center supervisor and seven operations coordinators/dispatchers who are responsible for monitoring the access control system, digital video surveillance system (DVSS), facility fire alarm system, crash phone ring down system, and other covert alarm systems. The Comm. Center dispatches airport operations, airport fire (ARFF), airport police, and airport maintenance to emergency and non-emergency events related to the airport emergency plan (AEP) and 49 CFR 1542—Airport Security. Eighty percent of the Comm. Center personnel's daily functions include operating the Justice Department Interface Controller (JDIC) to run driver's licenses, license plates, weapon serial numbers, VIN numbers, etc. for airport police.

- *Airport ID Badging Section:* Two badging administrative assistants who process all documentation related to 2,500 badge airport employees consisting of tenants, contractors, agencies, and airport authority employees.

IMMEDIATE TASKS

The Airside Operations Department had to successfully complete the following tasks within 12 months.

1. Executive management explained they were not pleased with how the Operations Department was previously being managed. There were continuous problems with the department identifying significant airfield discrepancies late in the year, just prior to the annual 14 CFR Part 139 inspection related to markings, signage, lighting, pavement, and safety areas. The Finance Department seemed to be continuously jumping through hoops to fund these last-minute repairs. Executive management did not feel that the Operations Department personnel knew what they were looking for during the daily inspections. Executive management also expected the department to focus on three cornerstones as it redirected down a new path:

   › Safety

   › Security

   › Financial Efficiency

2. Within the next two weeks, the NCAA BCS Championship Football game would be hosted in an adjoining city. The last time the BCS Championship game was hosted in this area, it brought in an additional 150 GA aircraft requiring ramp services and parking. Due to the teams in this year's game, the FBOs were expecting 250 aircraft, likely requiring the closure of multiple taxiways for aircraft parking.

3. The next phase of the airport's camera system upgrade project was due to be presented to the airport authority commission within two months. This long-term project started three years prior, and involved converting the system from analog to digital, adding additional cameras, and adding servers for video storage. The presentation required a written explanation of the next project phase, a PowerPoint presentation, and submission of the final bid with an itemized breakdown.

4. The annual 14 CFR Part 139 required tabletop exercise must be completed within three months in order to meet the 12 consecutive month requirement.

5. The next fiscal year budget proposal was due within the next three months.

6. During the recent 14 CFR Part 139 inspection, the airport received a total of four Part 139 discrepancies after several years of receiving zero discrepancies. All discrepancies must be corrected within the next six months.

7. The FAA has released a revised airport emergency plan advisory circular (AC). AC 150/5200-32C requires all Part 139 airports to update their AEP by the summer of the following year. Significant progress needs to be made by the end of this year to include the establishment of working groups.

8. The FAA Runway Safety Action Team (RSAT) has identified some action items that the airport needs to correct by the end of the current year.

ACTION PLAN AND INITIAL MEETINGS

Due to the limited resources available, these eight tasks were a significant challenge. First, it was important to prioritize projects for this year. It was also necessary to ensure that:

1. Everyone in the department understood the upcoming tasks for the department

2. Everyone understood executive management's expectations

3. Tasks were delegated while understanding each employee's needs and areas of strength

4. A preliminary plan was developed to navigate through this year with input from department personnel and guidance from fellow managers.

Within two weeks, an all-personnel department meeting, referred to as an "all-hands" meeting, was held and included all airside operations sections, the Landside Operations Department (three employees), and the Security Department (one employee). The only personnel not in attendance at the meeting were the three to four personnel that were either on graveyard shift or on their day off. These individuals were met with on an individual basis in the days following this meeting. The tasks and executive management's expectations were discussed in the meeting, as well as a preliminary plan and expectations to successfully complete the eight tasks.

During the meeting, everyone was asked, "What initially motivated you to work in airport operations." Ninety percent of them said it was either due to the "challenge" or because "no two days at the airport were alike." Personnel possessed a wide range of backgrounds, including former airline employees, TSA employees, police officers, paramedic dispatchers, prison security guards, parking cashiers, and airport operations. With such a well-rounded team, the manager decided to schedule individual meetings to learn about each person's interests; what motivated them to come to work every day; their experiences; educational background; and training received at the airport. The manager also expressed his support to the entire team.

After individual meetings with all of the airside operations personnel, the manager felt he had a good understanding of everyone's strengths, experiences, educational background, and interests. He matched up specific department responsibilities with the employee that had the most experience, education, and/or interest in each area—including airfield markings, signage, and lighting; AEP; ACM; camera systems; access control systems; airfield pavement; etc. Each person was established as a "champion" or "lead" for a certain area, and if something came up related to their responsibility, the manager and individual would discuss the task and together establish a plan and milestones. It should be noted that these assignments were in addition to the daily airfield/terminal inspections, emergency responses, dispatching, and documentation required of personnel as part of their regular responsibilities.

The manager held weekly, minimum 30-minute meetings with each person who directly reported to him to discuss how they were doing personally, discuss new and ongoing items, and update the tasks they were working on. In this way, the manager maintained a good idea of the department's week-to-week progress along the critical path to the task milestones and final goals. Of course, some meetings had to be rescheduled or canceled due to operational needs, but the team stayed on track.

During this process, the manager identified areas to focus on:

1. *Training*—The Department was not investing in department personnel. Some of the airside supervisors had gone to the American Association of Airport Executives (AAAE) Basic and Advanced Airport Safety and Operations Specialist (ASOS) courses, but that was the extent of the initial and recurring technical training related to 14 CFR Part 139. Most personnel in the Airside and Comm. Center sections had received their initial on-the-job training, but nothing since. There were no ongoing meetings, safety meetings, team meetings, etc. Training in the following areas was lacking:

   › Technical training—related to 14 CFR Part 139, 49 CFR Part 1542, systems functionality, Microsoft products, and department procedures.

   › Personal training and development—related to leadership, supervisory skills, workplace conduct, and industry qualifications/certifications.

2. *Documentation*—related to training, meeting notes, agendas, reports, and daily logs.

3. *Processes and Procedures*—some written policies and procedures were in place, but most were out of date.

TASK COMPLETION SUMMARY

1. **Executive Management's Concerns (due date = long-term):**
   Two key items were identified to address these concerns:

   a. Training:

      i. The department desperately needed resources for training other than on-the-job training (OJT). Prior to that year, the 12 consecutive month training requirements by 14 CFR §139.303 were being completed one to two weeks prior to the annual Part 139 inspection. It only took approximately 2 hours to cover all of the topics, and they would not be revisited in a formal setting until just prior to the subsequent year's inspection. Technical knowledge was being lost. The manager immediately established a monthly all-hands meeting to address this.

      ii. Each meeting discussed at least one 14 CFR Part 139 topic and one 49 CFR Part 1542 topic. The manager conducted the training for the first few months and then began assigning each supervisor a topic to present in the following months. This helped supervisors build their

**FAA
Airports**

March 2014

ASSURANCES

Airport Sponsors

A. General.

1. These assurances shall be complied with in the performance of grant agreements for airport development, airport planning, and noise compatibility program grants for airport sponsors.

2. These assurances are required to be submitted as part of the project application by sponsors requesting funds under the provisions of Title 49, U.S.C., subtitle VII, as amended. As used herein, the term "public agency sponsor" means a public agency with control of a public-use airport; the term "private sponsor" means a private owner of a public-use airport; and the term "sponsor" includes both public agency sponsors and private sponsors.

3. Upon acceptance of this grant offer by the sponsor, these assurances are incorporated in and become part of this grant agreement.

B. Duration and Applicability.

1. **Airport development or Noise Compatibility Program Projects Undertaken by a Public Agency Sponsor.**

   The terms, conditions and assurances of this grant agreement shall remain in full force and effect throughout the useful life of the facilities developed or equipment acquired for an airport development or noise compatibility program project, or throughout the useful life of the project items installed within a facility under a noise compatibility program project, but in any event not to exceed twenty (20) years from the date of acceptance of a grant offer of Federal funds for the project. However, there shall be no limit on the duration of the assurances regarding Exclusive Rights and Airport Revenue so long as the airport is used as an airport. There shall be no limit on the duration of the terms, conditions, and assurances with respect to real property acquired with federal funds. Furthermore, the duration of the Civil Rights assurance shall be specified in the assurances.

2. **Airport Development or Noise Compatibility Projects Undertaken by a Private Sponsor.**

   The preceding paragraph 1 also applies to a private sponsor except that the useful life of project items installed within a facility or the useful life of the facilities developed or equipment acquired under an airport development or noise compatibility program project shall be no less than ten (10) years from the date of acceptance of Federal aid for the project.

3. **Airport Planning Undertaken by a Sponsor.**

Unless otherwise specified in this grant agreement, only Assurances 1, 2, 3, 5, 6, 13, 18, 25, 30, 32, 33, and 34 in Section C apply to planning projects. The terms, conditions, and assurances of this grant agreement shall remain in full force and effect during the life of the project; there shall be no limit on the duration of the assurances regarding Airport Revenue so long as the airport is used as an airport.

C. Sponsor Certification.

The sponsor hereby assures and certifies, with respect to this grant that:

1. **General Federal Requirements.**

It will comply with all applicable Federal laws, regulations, executive orders, policies, guidelines, and requirements as they relate to the application, acceptance and use of Federal funds for this project including but not limited to the following:

Federal Legislation

a. Title 49, U.S.C., subtitle VII, as amended.

b. Davis-Bacon Act - 40 U.S.C. 276(a), <u>et seq.</u>[1]

c. Federal Fair Labor Standards Act - 29 U.S.C. 201, et seq.

d. Hatch Act – 5 U.S.C. 1501, <u>et seq.</u>[2]

e. Uniform Relocation Assistance and Real Property Acquisition Policies Act of 1970 Title 42 U.S.C. 4601, <u>et seq.</u>[1][2]

f. National Historic Preservation Act of 1966 - Section 106 - 16 U.S.C. 470(f).[1]

g. Archeological and Historic Preservation Act of 1974 - 16 U.S.C. 469 through 469c.[1]

h. Native Americans Grave Repatriation Act - 25 U.S.C. Section 3001, <u>et seq.</u>

i. Clean Air Act, P.L. 90-148, as amended.

j. Coastal Zone Management Act, P.L. 93-205, as amended.

k. Flood Disaster Protection Act of 1973 - Section 102(a) - 42 U.S.C. 4012a.[1]

l. Title 49, U.S.C., Section 303, (formerly known as Section 4(f))

m. Rehabilitation Act of 1973 - 29 U.S.C. 794.

n. Title VI of the Civil Rights Act of 1964 (42 U.S.C. § 2000d et seq., 78 stat. 252) (prohibits discrimination on the basis of race, color, national origin);

o. Americans with Disabilities Act of 1990, as amended, (42 U.S.C. § 12101 et seq.), prohibits discrimination on the basis of disability).

p. Age Discrimination Act of 1975 - 42 U.S.C. 6101, <u>et seq.</u>

q. American Indian Religious Freedom Act, P.L. 95-341, as amended.

r. Architectural Barriers Act of 1968 -42 U.S.C. 4151, <u>et seq.</u>[1]

s. Power plant and Industrial Fuel Use Act of 1978 - Section 403- 2 U.S.C. 8373.[1]

t. Contract Work Hours and Safety Standards Act - 40 U.S.C. 327, <u>et seq.</u>[1]

u. Copeland Anti-kickback Act - 18 U.S.C. 874.1

v. National Environmental Policy Act of 1969 - 42 U.S.C. 4321, <u>et seq.</u>[1]

w. Wild and Scenic Rivers Act, P.L. 90-542, as amended.

x. Single Audit Act of 1984 - 31 U.S.C. 7501, <u>et seq.</u>[2]

y. Drug-Free Workplace Act of 1988 - 41 U.S.C. 702 through 706.

6. **Consistency with Local Plans.**

The project is reasonably consistent with plans (existing at the time of submission of this application) of public agencies that are authorized by the State in which the project is located to plan for the development of the area surrounding the airport.

7. **Consideration of Local Interest.**

It has given fair consideration to the interest of communities in or near where the project may be located.

8. **Consultation with Users.**

In making a decision to undertake any airport development project under Title 49, United States Code, it has undertaken reasonable consultations with affected parties using the airport at which project is proposed.

9. **Public Hearings.**

In projects involving the location of an airport, an airport runway, or a major runway extension, it has afforded the opportunity for public hearings for the purpose of considering the economic, social, and environmental effects of the airport or runway location and its consistency with goals and objectives of such planning as has been carried out by the community and it shall, when requested by the Secretary, submit a copy of the transcript of such hearings to the Secretary. Further, for such projects, it has on its management board either voting representation from the communities where the project is located or has advised the communities that they have the right to petition the Secretary concerning a proposed project.

10. **Metropolitan Planning Organization.**

In projects involving the location of an airport, an airport runway, or a major runway extension at a medium or large hub airport, the sponsor has made available to and has provided upon request to the metropolitan planning organization in the area in which the airport is located, if any, a copy of the proposed amendment to the airport layout plan to depict the project and a copy of any airport master plan in which the project is described or depicted.

11. **Pavement Preventive Maintenance.**

With respect to a project approved after January 1, 1995, for the replacement or reconstruction of pavement at the airport, it assures or certifies that it has implemented an effective airport pavement maintenance-management program and it assures that it will use such program for the useful life of any pavement constructed, reconstructed or repaired with Federal financial assistance at the airport. It will provide such reports on pavement condition and pavement management programs as the Secretary determines may be useful.

12. **Terminal Development Prerequisites.**

For projects which include terminal development at a public use airport, as defined in Title 49, it has, on the date of submittal of the project grant application, all the safety equipment required for certification of such airport under section 44706 of Title 49, United States Code, and all the security equipment required by rule or regulation, and has provided for access to the passenger enplaning and deplaning area of such airport to passengers enplaning and deplaning from aircraft other than air carrier aircraft.

13. **Accounting System, Audit, and Record Keeping Requirements.**

   a. It shall keep all project accounts and records which fully disclose the amount and disposition by the recipient of the proceeds of this grant, the total cost of the project in connection with which this grant is given or used, and the amount or nature of that portion of the cost of the project supplied by other sources, and such other financial records pertinent to the project. The accounts and records shall be kept in accordance with an accounting system that will facilitate an effective audit in accordance with the Single Audit Act of 1984.

   b. It shall make available to the Secretary and the Comptroller General of the United States, or any of their duly authorized representatives, for the purpose of audit and examination, any books, documents, papers, and records of the recipient that are pertinent to this grant. The Secretary may require that an appropriate audit be conducted by a recipient. In any case in which an independent audit is made of the accounts of a sponsor relating to the disposition of the proceeds of a grant or relating to the project in connection with which this grant was given or used, it shall file a certified copy of such audit with the Comptroller General of the United States not later than six (6) months following the close of the fiscal year for which the audit was made.

14. **Minimum Wage Rates.**

   It shall include, in all contracts in excess of $2,000 for work on any projects funded under this grant agreement which involve labor, provisions establishing minimum rates of wages, to be predetermined by the Secretary of Labor, in accordance with the Davis-Bacon Act, as amended (40 U.S.C. 276a-276a-5), which contractors shall pay to skilled and unskilled labor, and such minimum rates shall be stated in the invitation for bids and shall be included in proposals or bids for the work.

15. **Veteran's Preference.**

   It shall include in all contracts for work on any project funded under this grant agreement which involve labor, such provisions as are necessary to insure that, in the employment of labor (except in executive, administrative, and supervisory positions), preference shall be given to Vietnam era veterans, Persian Gulf veterans, Afghanistan-Iraq war veterans, disabled veterans, and small business concerns owned and controlled by disabled veterans as defined in Section 47112 of Title 49, United States Code. However, this preference shall apply only where the individuals are available and qualified to perform the work to which the employment relates.

16. **Conformity to Plans and Specifications.**

   It will execute the project subject to plans, specifications, and schedules approved by the Secretary. Such plans, specifications, and schedules shall be submitted to the Secretary prior to commencement of site preparation, construction, or other performance under this grant agreement, and, upon approval of the Secretary, shall be incorporated into this grant agreement.

3) the location of all existing and proposed nonaviation areas and of all existing improvements thereon; and

4) all proposed and existing access points used to taxi aircraft across the airport's property boundary. Such airport layout plans and each amendment, revision, or modification thereof, shall be subject to the approval of the Secretary which approval shall be evidenced by the signature of a duly authorized representative of the Secretary on the face of the airport layout plan. The sponsor will not make or permit any changes or alterations in the airport or any of its facilities which are not in conformity with the airport layout plan as approved by the Secretary and which might, in the opinion of the Secretary, adversely affect the safety, utility or efficiency of the airport.

b. If a change or alteration in the airport or the facilities is made which the Secretary determines adversely affects the safety, utility, or efficiency of any federally owned, leased, or funded property on or off the airport and which is not in conformity with the airport layout plan as approved by the Secretary, the owner or operator will, if requested, by the Secretary (1) eliminate such adverse effect in a manner approved by the Secretary; or (2) bear all costs of relocating such property (or replacement thereof) to a site acceptable to the Secretary and all costs of restoring such property (or replacement thereof) to the level of safety, utility, efficiency, and cost of operation existing before the unapproved change in the airport or its facilities except in the case of a relocation or replacement of an existing airport facility due to a change in the Secretary's design standards beyond the control of the airport sponsor.

30. **Civil Rights.**

It will promptly take any measures necessary to ensure that no person in the United States shall, on the grounds of race, creed, color, national origin, sex, age, or disability be excluded from participation in, be denied the benefits of, or be otherwise subjected to discrimination in any activity conducted with, or benefiting from, funds received from this grant.

a. Using the definitions of activity, facility and program as found and defined in §§21.23 (b) and 21.23 (e) of 49 CFR § 21, the sponsor will facilitate all programs, operate all facilities, or conduct all programs in compliance with all non- discrimination requirements imposed by, or pursuant to these assurances.

b. Applicability

1) Programs and Activities. If the sponsor has received a grant (or other federal assistance) for any of the sponsor's program or activities, these requirements extend to all of the sponsor's programs and activities.

2) Facilities. Where it receives a grant or other federal financial assistance to construct, expand, renovate, remodel, alter or acquire a facility, or part of a facility, the assurance extends to the entire facility and facilities operated in connection therewith.

3) Real Property. Where the sponsor receives a grant or other Federal financial assistance in the form of, or for the acquisition of real property or an interest in real property, the assurance will extend to rights to space on, over, or under such property.

c. Duration.

The sponsor agrees that it is obligated to this assurance for the period during which Federal financial assistance is extended to the program, except where the Federal financial assistance is to provide, or is in the form of, personal property, or real property, or interest therein, or structures or improvements thereon, in which case the assurance obligates the sponsor, or any transferee for the longer of the following periods:

1) So long as the airport is used as an airport, or for another purpose involving the provision of similar services or benefits; or

2) So long as the sponsor retains ownership or possession of the property.

d. Required Solicitation Language. It will include the following notification in all solicitations for bids, Requests For Proposals for work, or material under this grant agreement and in all proposals for agreements, including airport concessions, regardless of funding source:

"The **(Name of Sponsor)**, in accordance with the provisions of Title VI of the Civil Rights Act of 1964 (78 Stat. 252, 42 U.S.C. §§ 2000d to 2000d-4) and the Regulations, hereby notifies all bidders that it will affirmatively ensure that any contract entered into pursuant to this advertisement, disadvantaged business enterprises and airport concession disadvantaged business enterprises will be afforded full and fair opportunity to submit bids in response to this invitation and will not be discriminated against on the grounds of race, color, or national origin in consideration for an award."

e. Required Contract Provisions.

1) It will insert the non-discrimination contract clauses requiring compliance with the acts and regulations relative to non-discrimination in Federally-assisted programs of the DOT, and incorporating the acts and regulations into the contracts by reference in every contract or agreement subject to the non-discrimination in Federally-assisted programs of the DOT acts and regulations.

2) It will include a list of the pertinent non-discrimination authorities in every contract that is subject to the non-discrimination acts and regulations.

3) It will insert non-discrimination contract clauses as a covenant running with the land, in any deed from the United States effecting or recording a transfer of real property, structures, use, or improvements thereon or interest therein to a sponsor.

4) It will insert non-discrimination contract clauses prohibiting discrimination on the basis of race, color, national origin, creed, sex, age, or handicap as a covenant running with the land, in any future deeds, leases, license, permits, or similar instruments entered into by the sponsor with other parties:

a) For the subsequent transfer of real property acquired or improved under the applicable activity, project, or program; and

b) For the construction or use of, or access to, space on, over, or under real property acquired or improved under the applicable activity, project, or program.

f. It will provide for such methods of administration for the program as are found by the Secretary to give reasonable guarantee that it, other recipients, sub-recipients, sub-grantees, contractors, subcontractors, consultants, transferees, successors in interest, and other participants of Federal financial assistance under such program will comply with all requirements imposed or pursuant to the acts, the regulations, and this assurance.

g. It agrees that the United States has a right to seek judicial enforcement with regard to any matter arising under the acts, the regulations, and this assurance.

31. **Disposal of Land.**

a. For land purchased under a grant for airport noise compatibility purposes, including land serving as a noise buffer, it will dispose of the land, when the land is no longer needed for such purposes, at fair market value, at the earliest practicable time. That portion of the proceeds of such disposition which is proportionate to the United States' share of acquisition of such land will be, at the discretion of the Secretary, (1) reinvested in another project at the airport, or (2) transferred to another eligible airport as prescribed by the Secretary. The Secretary shall give preference to the following, in descending order, (1) reinvestment in an approved noise compatibility project, (2) reinvestment in an approved project that is eligible for grant funding under Section 47117(e) of title 49 United States Code, (3) reinvestment in an approved airport development project that is eligible for grant funding under Sections 47114, 47115, or 47117 of title 49 United States Code, (4) transferred to an eligible sponsor of another public airport to be reinvested in an approved noise compatibility project at that airport, and (5) paid to the Secretary for deposit in the Airport and Airway Trust Fund. If land acquired under a grant for noise compatibility purposes is leased at fair market value and consistent with noise buffering purposes, the lease will not be considered a disposal of the land. Revenues derived from such a lease may be used for an approved airport development project that would otherwise be eligible for grant funding or any permitted use of airport revenue.

b. For land purchased under a grant for airport development purposes (other than noise compatibility), it will, when the land is no longer needed for airport purposes, dispose of such land at fair market value or make available to the Secretary an amount equal to the United States' proportionate share of the fair market value of the land. That portion of the proceeds of such disposition which is proportionate to the United States' share of the cost of acquisition of such land will, (1) upon application to the Secretary, be reinvested or transferred to another eligible airport as prescribed by the Secretary. The Secretary shall give preference to the following, in descending order: (1) reinvestment in an approved noise compatibility project, (2) reinvestment in an approved project that is eligible for grant funding under Section 47117(e) of title 49 United States Code, (3) reinvestment in an approved airport development project that is eligible for grant funding under Sections 47114, 47115, or 47117 of title 49 United States Code, (4) transferred to an eligible sponsor of another public airport to be reinvested in an approved noise compatibility project at that airport, and (5) paid to the Secretary for deposit in the Airport and Airway Trust Fund.

c.   Land shall be considered to be needed for airport purposes under this assurance if (1) it may be needed for aeronautical purposes (including runway protection zones) or serve as noise buffer land, and (2) the revenue from interim uses of such land contributes to the financial self-sufficiency of the airport. Further, land purchased with a grant received by an airport operator or owner before December 31, 1987, will be considered to be needed for airport purposes if the Secretary or Federal agency making such grant before December 31, 1987, was notified by the operator or owner of the uses of such land, did not object to such use, and the land continues to be used for that purpose, such use having commenced no later than December 15, 1989.

d.   Disposition of such land under (a) (b) or (c) will be subject to the retention or reservation of any interest or right therein necessary to ensure that such land will only be used for purposes which are compatible with noise levels associated with operation of the airport.

32. **Engineering and Design Services.**

It will award each contract, or sub-contract for program management, construction management, planning studies, feasibility studies, architectural services, preliminary engineering, design, engineering, surveying, mapping or related services with respect to the project in the same manner as a contract for architectural and engineering services is negotiated under Title IX of the Federal Property and Administrative Services Act of 1949 or an equivalent qualifications-based requirement prescribed for or by the sponsor of the airport.

33. **Foreign Market Restrictions.**

It will not allow funds provided under this grant to be used to fund any project which uses any product or service of a foreign country during the period in which such foreign country is listed by the United States Trade Representative as denying fair and equitable market opportunities for products and suppliers of the United States in procurement and construction.

34. **Policies, Standards, and Specifications.**

It will carry out the project in accordance with policies, standards, and specifications approved by the Secretary including but not limited to the advisory circulars listed in the Current FAA Advisory Circulars for AIP projects, dated _____ (the latest approved version as of this grant offer)